THE
EVERYTHING
WORLD'S RELIGIONS BOOK
2ND EDITION

Dear Reader,

Religion serves up a carnival of sights and sounds. It blares out its colors in the form of rituals and mythology. It invites us to wander down colorful corridors. Once inside the religious labyrinth, we hear, read, and experience centuries-old mysteries. Unwittingly, we add to our stock of ideas.

As a professor of philosophy, I have often found philosophy's pursuit of the truth and analytical ways to be opposed to the stress on belief found in religions. Philosophy takes less on trust and faith than religion does. For me, however, there are points at which the two meet. When I read of Buddha's Four Noble Truths and the Eightfold Path, I know I have located the essence of Buddhism's ethical philosophy. When I encounter the Jains—Jainism grew out of Hinduism more than 2,500 years ago—I am awed by their asceticism and philosophy of noninjury (ahimsa) toward all living things. In reading the arguments of countless medieval thinkers, such as Moses Maimonides and St. Thomas Aquinas, on the nature and existence of God, I know I have discovered yet another meeting point between theology and philosophy. The Ten Commandments are familiar to most, but how many are familiar with the 613 rules or mitzvot in the Pentateuch? And what of the mystics of most faiths, whose personal contact with divine realties changed them and provided the only "proof" they needed for the existence of God?

These are but a few of the moral and metaphysical notions that make an investigation of religions worthwhile.

Kenneth Shouler

Welcome to the EVERYTHING® Series!

These handy, accessible books give you all you need to tackle a difficult project, gain a new hobby, comprehend a fascinating topic, prepare for an exam, or even brush up on something you learned back in school but have since forgotten.

You can choose to read an *Everything*® book from cover to cover or just pick out the information you want from our four useful boxes: e-questions, e-facts, e-alerts, and e-ssentials.

We give you everything you need to know on the subject, but throw in a lot of fun stuff along the way, too.

We now have more than 400 *Everything*® books in print, spanning such wide-ranging categories as weddings, pregnancy, cooking, music instruction, foreign language, crafts, pets, New Age, and so much more. When you're done reading them all, you can finally say you know *Everything*®!

QUESTION

Answers to common questions

FACT

Important snippets of information

QUOTE

Words of wisdom from experts in the field

ESSENTIAL

Quick handy tips

PUBLISHER Karen Cooper

DIRECTOR OF ACQUISITIONS AND INNOVATION Paula Munier

MANAGING EDITOR, EVERYTHING® SERIES Lisa Laing

COPY CHIEF Casey Ebert

ACQUISITIONS EDITOR Lisa Laing

SENIOR DEVELOPMENT EDITOR Brett Palana-Shanahan

EDITORIAL ASSISTANT Hillary Thompson

EVERYTHING® SERIES COVER DESIGNER Erin Alexander

LAYOUT DESIGNERS Colleen Cunningham, Elisabeth Lariviere, Ashley Vierra, Denise Wallace

Visit the entire Everything® series at *www.everything.com*

THE
EVERYTHING®
WORLD'S RELIGIONS
BOOK
2ND EDITION

Discover the beliefs, traditions, and cultures
of ancient and modern religions

Kenneth Shouler, PhD

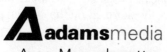

Aadamsmedia
Avon, Massachusetts

An Everything® Series Book.
Everything® and everything.com® are registered trademarks of F+W Media, Inc.

Published by Adams Media, a division of F+W Media, Inc.
57 Littlefield Street, Avon, MA 02322 U.S.A.
www.adamsmedia.com

ISBN 10: 1-4405-0036-3
ISBN 13: 978-1-4405-0036-7

Printed in the United States of America.

10 9 8 7 6 5 4 3 2 1

Library of Congress Cataloging-in-Publication Data
is available from the publisher.

This publication is designed to provide accurate and authoritative information with regard to the subject matter covered. It is sold with the understanding that the publisher is not engaged in rendering legal, accounting, or other professional advice. If legal advice or other expert assistance is required, the services of a competent professional person should be sought.

—From a *Declaration of Principles* jointly adopted by a Committee of the American Bar Association and a Committee of Publishers and Associations

Many of the designations used by manufacturers and sellers to distinguish their products are claimed as trademarks. Where those designations appear in this book and Adams Media was aware of a trademark claim, the designations have been printed with initial capital letters.

This book is available at quantity discounts for bulk purchases.
For information, please call 1-800-289-0963.

Contents

Dedication

To Father Paul John.

His delightful company and our many conversations have helped me to understand religions and their practices.

Top 10 Insights on
Understanding Religions

1. The intellectual is constantly betrayed by his vanity. Godlike he blandly assumes that he can express everything in words; whereas the thing one loves, lives, and dies for are not, in the last analysis, completely expressible in words.

   —*Anne Morrow Lindbergh*

2. We must respect the other fellow's religion, but only in the sense and to the extent that we respect his theory that his wife is beautiful and his children smart.

   —*H.L. Mencken*

3. I do not feel obliged to believe that the same God who has endowed us with sense, reason, and intellect has intended us to forgo their use.

   —*Galileo Galilei*

4. Question with boldness even the existence of a God; because, if there be one, he must more approve of the homage of reason, than that of blind-folded fear.

   —*Thomas Jefferson*

5. You don't have to be religious to have a soul; everybody has one. You don't have to be religious to perfect your soul; I have found saintliness in avowed atheists.

   —*Rabbi Harold Kushner*

6. The theologian considers sin mainly as an offence against God; the moral philosopher as contrary to reasonableness.

   —*St. Thomas Aquinas*

7. As a man can drink water from any side of a full tank, so the skilled theologian can wrest from any scripture that which will serve his purpose.

   —*Bhagavad Gita*

8. I still say a church steeple with a lightening rod on top shows a lack of confidence.
   —*Doug McLeod*

9. I love you when you bow in your mosque, kneel in your temple, pray in your church. For you and I are sons of one religion and that is the spirit.

   —*Kahlil Gibran*

10. Religion is the sigh of the oppressed creature, the sentiment of a heartless world, and the soul of soulless conditions. It is the opium of the people.

    —*Karl Marx*

Introduction

THIS BOOK EXPLAINS RELIGIONS; therefore, it is suited for inquirers who are religious, antireligious, or nonreligious. But it is also right for the undecided, agnostic explorer—whose intellectual curiosity has brought him to raise deeper questions about his place in the world. What questions? What do the religions say about the possibility of an afterlife? If there is an afterlife, will a person live on in a spiritual form or some other different bodily nature?

Religion can hold our interest in the manner that history or a study of cultures does. But it is also practical, since it offers the promise of bringing shape to our lives and laying out a path for living. Some of the ideas in religion are great and unblemished, even if people do not always live by them.

You don't have to embrace all the religions, any one specifically, or any combination of them in order to be curious about them. Even without participating in a religion, there are inherently interesting metaphysical and moral tenets for each of them. So, you don't need to be a Hindu at the end of your life to find the notion of spiritual liberation attractive. Then, too, you don't need to go to the extremes the Jains do in their asceticism or go as far in practicing *ahimsa* (or noninjury) toward all living things in order to respect their moral commitment. Likewise, you don't need to subscribe to each and every tenet of Lutheranism in order to understand—even feel—Martin Luther's furious objections to the corrupt practices of the church in the early sixteenth century.

Aside from the historical and intellectual curiosity that religion can arouse in us, who wouldn't find interest in the mystical explorations of the Carmelite nun St. Teresa of Avila, longing to make a personal contact with a god? And what of the peyotism of Native Americans who, after taking the hallucinogenic, found that it aided and abetted their own spiritual experience of nature? The aphoristic wisdom of Confucius, with his pith and counsels of humility and filial piety, rounds out our ethical understanding.

Finally, there are special passages revealing the uncanny moral insight of Christ. Perhaps the most revealing is the parable of the Good Samaritan (Luke, 10:25–37). The context of the parable is a man asking Jesus, "Teacher, what must I do to inherit eternal life?" Jesus asks him, "What is written in the Law?" The man replies, "Love the Lord your God with all your heart and with all your soul and with all your strength and with all your mind and love your neighbor as yourself." Jesus acknowledged his correct answer and said, "Do this and you will live." The man wanted further clarification: "and who is my neighbor teacher?' At this point Jesus related the story of a man robbed, beaten, and left for dead. A priest passed him by without tending to him. A Levite ignored him, too. But a Samaritan saw him and took pity. He bandaged his wounds, took him to an inn, and paid the innkeeper to look after him, promising to reimburse him for any extra expense. Jesus asked, "Which of these three do you think was a neighbor to the man who fell into the hands of robbers?" The man said, "The one who had mercy on him." Jesus instructed him, "Go and do likewise."

What makes the parable especially brilliant on a moral level is that it broadens the moral requirement. It expresses a positive command: "Do unto others as you would have others do unto you." In short, it is not enough to simply not do others harm, as the priest and Levite did. It is in the nature of love to do more, to better the condition of our neighbors.

CHAPTER 1

Religion Through the Ages

It can be asserted with confidence that no one knows exactly how many religions there are, although the best estimate is about 4,200. One religion is certainly not superior to another, and the longing for religion seems built into human nature. The words of Voltaire (1694–1778) still ring true: "If God did not exist, it would be necessary to invent him."

Defining Religion

The word "religion" derives from the Latin *religio,* meaning "to be bound to" or "to tie fast." Believers are bound to their faiths. You can say with a reasonable degree of assurance that a religion comprises a set of beliefs, values, and practices based on the teachings of a spiritual leader, though defining the term isn't always that simple.

Charles Dickens wrote to the Reverend Frederick Layton in 1847 in answer to a query regarding his religious beliefs: "As I really do not know what orthodoxy may be, or what it may be supposed to include—a point not exactly settled, I believe, as yet, in the learned or unlearned world—I am not in a condition to say whether I deserve my lax reputation in that wise . . . ."

Dickens wasn't, and isn't, alone in his skeptical opinion. No single definition has been offered on the subject of the varied sets of traditions, practices, ideas, and faiths that could constitute a religion. In addition, there is little agreement on the kinds of claims that religion makes. Whether a supreme being even exists, whether a soul exists and, if so, is it immortal—one can raise skeptical questions about these matters until the cows come home. There has rarely been unanimity about the nature of the subject among scholars, partly because believers see different things in religions and because the subject itself has been so involved in controversy throughout its history.

FACT

The Concise Oxford Dictionary defines religion as "the belief in a superhuman controlling power, especially in a personal God or gods entitled to obedience and worship." This is a broad and loose definition encompassing many beliefs and traditions.

Atheism and Theism: Are They Religions?

What constitutes a religion is a contentious matter. The question may come down to a choice of definitions. If your definition of religions involves a belief in a supreme and/or an afterlife, then nonbelief cannot be religion. But someone else might embrace a different definition of the word "religion," which derives from the etymological definition and references the

Latin *religio* (again, meaning "to be bound to" or "to tie fast"). In this sense of the word, nonbelief can be every bit as avid as belief.

Atheism is the view that there is no divine being, no God. This statement is the bone of contention between believers and nonbelievers. However, it is not just the existence or nonexistence of God that is disputed. For both sides of the issue know that the existence of God implies the existence of divine providence and the possibility of divine intervention in the world. Theists embrace a belief in this kind of active God. Such a God is a loving being and even answers prayers. When opponents voice an objection to this view of God, they aren't necessarily doubting the existence of God, but are disputing the being's caring nature. This opposing view isn't atheism, strictly speaking, but antitheism.

ESSENTIAL

A survey showed that 15 percent of Americans accept no religion. The decline in religions has occurred since the 1990s. Currently, only 76 percent of Americans are Christians as compared with a previous 90 percent. The decline has been in mainline denominations.

Atheism in this older sense is not just a negative answer to whether God exists. What is essential is the denial of the existence of a being who takes an interest in mankind, who intervenes in the world and is a positive force for mankind, at times changing the course of events. Antitheists deny that the world runs according to a wise and provident design. In addition, this older sense of atheism rejects the possibility that prayer makes a difference. Further, antitheists don't have the same faith that theists have in the assurance that evil doers will receive punishment in a future state.

This traditional atheism or antitheism, then, is less interested in the question of whether God exists. By contrast, it asserts that God's existence or nonexistence is secondary. Antitheists hold that there is no divine being whose existence would be relevant to a person's conduct.

Fundamentals of Religion

In any study of religion, students will come across a word that seems to be used in every religion: schism. *The Concise Oxford Dictionary* defines schism as "the division of a group into opposing sections or parties; the separation of a church into two churches or the secession of a group owing to doctrinal, disciplinary differences." People in a group will differ—not exactly spellbinding news. If they differ enough, however, they will pick up, go off, and start their own groups, creating different religions or variations of a religion.

Even in modern times, divisions arise when debating religion versus politics or religion versus science, even religious versus secular systems of government. Disagreement continues to foster religious belligerence throughout the world, often expressed through violence. We shouldn't hold our breath for common resolution to come about soon. What does seem certain is that many (though not all) people, regardless of caste, creed, or nationality, require and often seek out some kind of belief system to sustain themselves in their daily lives, giving them hope and comfort.

A Western Interpretation

This book provides an examination of the major religions of today—how they evolved and what they are about—from a Western perspective. Muslims contend that Islam is not a religion; it is a way of life. Similarly, Taoism is considered by many not to be a religion but "The Way." Buddhism, which does not serve a god, believes in "The Path." Nevertheless, it would seem that whatever name or designation given to a particular faith or belief, the needs of the adherents do not differ. In that, there is universal agreement.

FACT

In the religious calendar, the years prior to Jesus' birth were counted down from year one and designated "Before Christ," abbreviated B.C. The years following his birth were designated A.D. *(Anno Domini,* "The year of our Lord"). However, as non-Christian countries adopted the Gregorian calendar, the years were changed to "Common Era," abbreviated C.E., and "Before Common Era," abbreviated B.C.E.

For those readers stimulated by reading this book and seeking more information, I suggest consulting books that specialize in the religion you are interested in. It is not the intention of this book to provide extensive, scholarly data, but to provide accurate information to inform and whet the appetite of an inquiring mind. There is an extensive list of recommended readings in Appendix B.

In this book, the five major religions and their major offshoots (as Jainism is an offshoot of Hinduism) are in chronological order. Thereafter, the book takes up the less well-known religions also chronologically, beginning with Confucianism.

The Study of Religions

Most scholars agree that the nineteenth century was the formative period for the study of modern religions. Many disciplines were involved, including the philological sciences, literary criticism, psychology, anthropology, and sociology. Naturally, scholars brought their own academic biases into play. Their task was formidable because so many aspects of religion had to be evaluated—history, origins, development, philosophy, to name just a few.

It comes as no surprise to learn that unanimity among them was rare. The very nature of the subject was loaded with problems. Different scholars had differing views even about the nature of their subjects, be it Christian, Muslim, or Jewish. The subject is, after all, vast and must include not only getting the information together but interpreting it to understand its meaning. Questions immediately arise that go beyond the recorded facts. What, for example, is the religious experience and how is it exhibited? What are the principles at work in the various religions? Do these religions have laws, and if so how do they affect the adherents? In addition, there were questions of truth or falsity and the reliability of the recorded history of each religion. In short, it would be fair to say that the whole subject was fraught with controversy.

The analytic period of philosophy ushered in more skepticism about claims made by religions—claims about the afterlife, the nature of mystical and religious experiences, and even the perennial problem of evil, which pushes the believer to square God's nature as a perfect being with the fact of natural and moral evils in the world.

Classifying Religions

The whole issue of true and false religions and a classification that demonstrated the claims of each led to the necessity of defending one religion against another. Unfortunately, this type of classification, which is arbitrary and subjective, continues to exist. For example, in the sixteenth century, Martin Luther, the great Protestant reformer, went so far as to label Muslims, Jews, and Roman Catholic Christians as false. He held that the gospel of Christianity understood from the viewpoint of justification by grace through faith was the true standard. Another example would be Islam, which classifies religions into three groups: the wholly true, the partially true, and the wholly false. These classifications are based on the teachings of the Qur'an (Koran, the Islamic sacred scripture) and are an integral part of Islamic teaching. It also has legal implications for the Muslim treatment of followers of other religions.

QUOTE

"Since Luther's time there has been a conviction, more or less rooted, that a man may by an intellectual process think out a religion for himself, and that, as the highest of all duties, he ought to do so."—Walter Bagehot (1826–1877), *Physics and Politics, or Thoughts on the Application of the Principles of "Natural Science" and "Inheritance" to Political Society,* 5.1, 1872

Of course, such classifications express an implied judgment, not only on Protestants, Jews, Roman Catholics, and Muslims, but on all religions. This judgmental nature arises from the loyalties that exist in every society and religious culture. It is human nature for people to defend their own "tribe," and by association decry other tribes.

The field of psychology maintains that in the religious person, emotions such as wonder, awe, and reverence are exhibited. Religious people tend to show concern for values—moral and aesthetic—and to seek out actions that exhibit these values. They will likely characterize behavior not only as good or evil but also as holy or unholy, and people as virtuous or nonvirtuous, even godly or ungodly.

ESSENTIAL

The Greek philosopher Plato (428–348 B.C.E.) saw that in performing every good act, humans realize their link with eternity and the idea of goodness. He likened the human condition to the image of a man in a cave, chained by his earthly existence so that he cannot see the light outside, only the shadows on the wall. In order to see the light, man has to throw off his chains and leave the cave.

It is well known that in times of trouble—whether personal, national, or international—the number of people who embrace a religion increases. It could, therefore, be said that since trouble isn't going to go away, neither is religion. Both are here to stay.

CHAPTER 2

Hinduism

Hindus see their religion as a continuous, seemingly eternal, existence—not just a religion but a way of life. Its collection of customs, moral obligations—known as *dharma*—traditions, and ideals far exceed the recent Christian and Western secularist tendency to think of religion primarily as a system of beliefs. Hinduism has come to cover an incredibly wide range of concepts and concerns, including karma, methods for attaining salvation, and spiritual release from earthly existence.

Origins and Development

Although the English coined the word "Hinduism" around the beginning of the nineteenth century, the name "Hindu" has been in the language ever since Greek times. Some Hindus did not take to the word Hinduism, preferring the ancient name Vedic. The Vedic texts are known as the Vedas, and they provide the only textual source for understanding the religious life of ancient India. "Veda" means "sacred knowledge" or "learning" in Sanskrit, the oldest written language of India. In the beginning, the Vedas were comprised of 1,000 hymns, which served the priestly families. These were followed by the Veda of Chants, with musical notations for the performance of sacred songs. Prose works were added to explain the ceremonial aspects of the text.

Over the years, Vedic rites became so complicated and had so many rules that only highly trained priests could read the texts explaining them. It was from this background and legacy that the practice and belief in Hinduism evolved. The textbooks on Hinduism, composed in the early twentieth century, were written by Hindus to explain the faith so it could be taught to their young.

More than any other major religion, Hinduism celebrates the breadth and depth of its complex, multileveled spectrum of beliefs. Hinduism encompasses all forms of belief and worship. It has been said that no religious idea in India ever dies; it merely combines with the new ideas that arise in response to it.

Vedanta philosophy consists of three propositions. First, that real nature is divine; second, that the aim of human life is to realize this divine nature; and third, that all religions are essentially in agreement. Hinduism has neither a single prophet nor one god to worship; rather, it offers a plethora of ideas—a metaphor for the gods. It has been called a civilization and congregation of religions. Hinduism has no beginning, no founder, no central authority, no hierarchy, and no organization. Every attempt to classify or define Hinduism has proved to be unsatisfactory in one way or another. These efforts are confounded because the scholars of the faith have emphasized different aspects of the whole.

Hindu Deities

Though they do not worship one ultimate god, Hindus do believe in a supreme being who has unlimited forms. This is not a contradiction in terms because of the many forms these deities take. For instance, Vishnu and Lakshmi have the full powers of a god, but Brahm and Sarasvati have only partial godlike aspects. The Hindu approach to all this has their philosophy of nonspecific inclusion at its core.

The search for the worship of the "One that is All" is made through a favorite divinity, of which there are many. However, there is no exclusivity in the choice of the divinity to worship during the search. Imagine that the search for the "One that is All" is like a revolving mirrored ball in a dance hall. The observer meditates on the search and a beam of light goes on illuminating one side of the glass ball, which is slowly turning in the light. As it turns, mirrored facets are visible and the observer selects one on which to concentrate. The ball is the "One that is All"; its mirrored facets are its deities.

ESSENTIAL

The *avatara* is a Hindu concept, signifying the descent to earth of the deity. It has come to mean an incarnation or exemplar. Among the most popular and best-known avatars are some of the ten incarnations of Vishnu, which include Krishna and Rama. Krishna is probably number one in popularity.

Hindu teachings revolve around what, to Western eyes, might seem to be a vast series of interlocking narratives, rather like the actions in a play. In fact, that is exactly how some of them are presented. Their purpose is to draw the Hindu audience into a discourse. For several years, people have responded to prominent stories of a divine play and interactions between gods and humans. In watching the narratives played out, Hindus have often experienced themselves as members of a single imagined family. To play out the narratives, a deity enters this world as an *avatar*—a deity who descends and is manifest in a bodily form.

The plot of such a presentation follows. Women performers sometimes act out the story of a popular narrative called *ramayana*. The cast is comprised of Rama, Sita, and the wicked Havana. It is a tragic story, one of love, honor, and courage. Havana kidnaps Sita. Rama rescues Sita and kills Havana, but the lovers are forced to separate. The story represents the tragedy of life in the real world, where love of the soul for god is constantly tested.

Central Beliefs

In Hinduism, the law of *karma* states that all actions produce effects in the future. A concept that is linked to karma is that of *dharma,* one's duty or station in this life. The relationship between dharma and karma is discussed at length in the Bhagavad-Gita, a major text within the Hindu tradition. A rhyme is helpful: Doing one's dharma produces good karma.

Reincarnation

Essential to Hinduism is the idea of reincarnation. In more technical terms, Hindus accept the doctrine of transmigration and rebirth, and believe that previous acts are the factors that determine the condition into which a being is reborn in one form or another. The idea of reincarnation is virtually universal in India.

FACT

The idea of *samsara* (literally "wandering") refers to the endless cycle of birth and rebirth of souls. Samsara reminds us of the central problem that Hinduism poses to the individual: How do individuals escape from the endless cycle of rebirth and attain *moksha* or liberation?

According to a basic Hindu concept, people are born over and over again into a state of suffering. Deeply involved in this transformation is the *atman*—a Sanskrit word meaning "self," the eternal core of the personality that survives after death that is headed to a new life or is released from the bonds of existence. The atman is inextricably joined with *Brahman,* the Being itself, a concept that may also be thought of as high god. To be released from the cycle of rebirth, you must attain the atman/Brahman identity. That is, you must become one with Being.

One reason people are born over and over into suffering is that they do not understand this connection. As long as people think atman is separate from Brahman, or world soul, the cycle will continue forever.

Spiritual Goal

Another Sanskrit word, moksha, reflects the ultimate spiritual goal—the individual soul's release from the bonds of transmigration—to get out of the endless cycle of reincarnation. Now, if the individual is hampered by bad karma, moksha will not occur. But, if the individual has achieved moksha, then the atman is free to reunite with Brahman, thus concluding the cycle of suffering. Those who do not accept that their being is identical with Brahman are thought to be deluded—in such cases, you might say that the atman is clouded by *maya*, illusion. The only possible solution is to come to the realization that the core of human personality (atman) really is Brahman. The attachment to worldly goods blocks this understanding because it is an obsession that prevents people from reaching salvation and eternal peace.

To add to the difficulties in understanding this process, meanings and interpretations differ from one Hindu school to another. In spite of that, most of them agree that moksha is the highest purpose in life.

The Caste System

To some, Plato's *Republic* might bear relevance to the early Hindu doctrine of dividing society into groups, each of which had a role and a place. Brahmans were the priests; Kshatriyas were the warriors; Vaishyas were the merchants; and Shudras were the craftspeople.

This division was the beginning of the Indian caste system. As it progressed into Indian society, the castes multiplied, encompassing a vast range of occupations, rules, and traditions. The Laws of Manu (circa 100 c.e.) provide the text that explains all the complexities of this system. A person's caste and station in life determines their dharma. Members of one caste would not socialize or trade with another; certain professions were limited to certain castes; intermarriage between members of different castes was not permitted.

Eventually, a group (caste) who called themselves Dalit (downtrodden) formed. Members of this caste did what one might call the grunt work, menial work such as street cleaning and clearing away dead bodies, either human or animal. They became known as the "Untouchables."

In 1950, a law was passed outlawing the practice of "Untouchability"; nevertheless, this group remains socially and economically the dregs of the caste system. Some members of the caste deny they are Hindu in an effort to overcome the stigma of Dalit.

ESSENTIAL

The idea of caste refers to what in India is called *jati*, or social status, which is one's inheritance at birth. Caste is a religious idea, because the priesthood, the prerogative of the Brahman caste, and the superiority of the Brahmans is established in the authoritative Vedas.

Holy Writings

The sacred scriptures of the Hindus are the Vedas ("knowledge"). They were written in the ancient language of India, Sanskrit, and are considered to be the creation of neither human nor god. They are the eternal truth revealed or heard by gifted seers. Most of the Vedas have been superceded by other Hindu doctrines; nevertheless, their influence has been pervasive and long lasting.

In the western world, two publications stand out in the vast collection of Hindu scriptures and texts—The Upanishads and The Bhagavad-Gita. The name "Upanishads" means "sitting near," as in being near enough to listen to your sage or master. The conversations found in these writings took place between gurus and their students and concern the meanings of the Vedas.

The Upanishads

The Upanishads record the wisdom of Hindu teachers and sages who were active as far back as 1000 B.C.E. The texts form the basis of Indian philosophy. As they represent the final stage in the tradition of the Vedas, the teaching based on them is known as the Vedanta ("end of the Veda").

The philosophical thrust of the Upanishads is discerning the nature of reality. Other concepts dealt with include equating atman (the self) with Brahman (ultimate reality), which is fundamental to all Hindu thought; the nature of morality and eternal life; and the themes of transmigration of souls and causality in creation.

QUOTE

A verse in the Upanishads illustrates how the universe is pervaded by Brahman: "When a chunk of salt is thrown into the water, it dissolves into that very water, and it cannot be picked up in any way. Yet, from whatever place on may take a sip, the salt is there! In the same way, this Immense Being (Brahman) has no limit or boundary and is a single mass of perception."

Various translations of the Upanishads were published in Europe during the nineteenth century. Though they were not the best translations, they had a profound effect on many philosophical academics, including Arthur Schopenhauer.

The Bhagavad-Gita

The Bhagavad-Gita has been the exemplary text of Hindu culture for centuries. The Sanskrit title has been interpreted as "Song of the Lord," which is a philosophical poem in the form of a dialogue. Although it is an independent sacred text, it is also considered to be the sixth book in the Mahabharata.

The Mahabharata—the longest great Indian war epic poem—contains mythological stories and philosophical discussions. One of the main story lines is the conflict between Yudhishthira, the hero of the poem, and his duty or dharma. The Bhagavad-Gita's structure is in the form of a dialogue between two characters—Arjuna, the hero preparing to go into battle, and Krishna, his charioteer. But Krishna is not quite what he seems. Arjuna is characterized by not only his physical prowess but also his spiritual prowess, which involves a mystical friendship with Krishna. From the start,

Arjuna knows that his charioteer is no ordinary mortal. The power of Krishna's divinity gradually unfolds in all of its terrible glory, and Arjuna sees himself mirrored in the divine.

The Bhagavad-Gita offers a philosophy of karma when Krishna counsels Arjuna to do his duty as a warrior, as Arjuna hesitates at the thought of killing members of his own family on the battlefield.

Worship and Practices

Hindu worship is called *puja* and encompasses the ceremonial practices that take place in the home or in the temple. The majority of the worship is carried out in the home because Hinduism is part of life, so there are no special days for worship—any time is a time for worship. Puja is the daily expression of devotion. Virtually every home has a shrine with images of the gods and goddesses.

The ceremonial practices vary considerably according to sect, community, location, time of day, and requirements of the worshiper. An image of the worshiper's chosen deity is displayed in the home and accorded the honor that would be given to a royal guest. The worship can be modest or elaborate depending on the circumstances. A daily puja might involve offerings of flowers, fruit, rice, incense, sandalwood paste, and milk water. If a puja is performed at a mealtime, food will be placed at the shrine, blessing it before it is consumed. Also included might be a circumambulation of the shrine in the home. The temple would probably have a path circling the shrine. In either case, the worshipers chant their prayers as they walk.

Hindu temples range from buildings that can accommodate hundreds of worshipers to simple village shrines. However, the layout, both inside and out, is nearly universal. Most temples will have a ceremonial chariot called a *rath*, which is like a miniature temple on wheels. A small version of the main deity is placed on it. It is used in processions at festivals. The temple will have a shrine room for one or more deities in which only a Brahman priest may perform the puja.

The variations among temples will of course be considerable—ranging from the elaborate to the simple—but the mode and philosophy of worship will follow the same principles: Devotees will endeavor to create a constant exchange of love and commitment between themselves and the deities.

Rituals and Customs

Hindu domestic lifecycle rites are called *samskara*. The sacraments are designed to make a person fit for the next phase of his life by removing sins. Historically, there was a lengthy array of sacraments, which have been reduced to sixteen, many of which are bundled in the childhood phase.

Birth

Traditionally, birth rites included a prenatal rite for the prospective father to affect the child to be fair or dark, a learned son or daughter, and so on. This was called the impregnation rite. During pregnancy, there were other rites, but, of course, the most important one was at the birth.

Marriage

Marriage is the most important rite. Once a suitable spouse has been found for the son or daughter the match must be approved by both sets of parents. The approval process may include hiring the local astrologer to draw up the couple's horoscopes. Once mutual approval is achieved and the bride's family pays a dowry to the groom, the ceremony can proceed. As with most marriage ceremonies, the rite includes prayers and songs of blessing.

At the conclusion of the ceremony, the bride and groom offer their right hands, which are symbolically bound together with cotton thread that has been dyed with yellow turmeric. Water is then sprinkled over them. Then, they walk around a prepared sacred fire three times. The final ritual for the bride and groom is to take seven steps and make a vow at each step. The steps represent food, strength, prosperity, well-being, children, happy seasons, and harmony in their marriage. That's it; the couple is now married and after the typical prayers the wedding feast begins.

Death

When a Hindu dies, the body is usually cremated. Cremation is chosen because of the Hindu belief in reincarnation, thus the body is not required after death, only the atman (soul). The body is bathed, wrapped in a new cloth, and laid on a stretcher. Depending on whether the cremation is to take place on a river with the body laid on a pyre or put into a coffin and taken to the crematorium, appropriate scriptures are recited. After the cremation, and if practical, the ashes, flowers, and bones are collected and scattered on a body of water.

Calendar of Religious Festivals

The Republic of India uses the Gregorian calendar for its secular life. For its Hindu religious life, it uses the traditional Hindu calendar, which is based on a year of lunar months. The discrepancy between the years—365 days (solar) and 354 days (lunar)—is resolved by intercalation of an extra month every thirty months. Each month is divided into a bright fortnight (two weeks) when the moon is waxing and a dark fortnight when it is waning.

Hinduism has an extensive range of festivals both in India and throughout the rest of the world. Following are the nine major traditional religious festivals that are generally universally celebrated:

- **Mahashivaratri** celebrates the night of the new moon every month, honoring the image of Shiva.
- **Sarasvati Puja** honors the goddess Sarasvati, the patron of the arts and learning.
- **Holi** celebrates the grain harvest in India and recalls the pranks Krishna played as a young man.
- **Rama Naumi** celebrates the birthday of the god Rama.
- On **Rata Yatra**, a huge image of the god Vishnu is placed on an enormous chariot and pulled through the streets.
- The **Raksha Bandhan** is a ceremony of tying a *rakhi* (a thread or band, made of silk or decorated with flowers).
- **Janmashtami** celebrates the birth of Krishna and his delivery from the demon Kansa.
- **Navaratri** honors the most important female deity, Durga, consort of Shiva.
- **Divali**—the most widely celebrated festival—celebrates the return from exile of Rama and Sita.

The Four Stages of Life

The four ends of life or goals of humanity are called *purusharthas*. In Hindu tradition, these four comprise a scheme or set of goals that tell what life is for. The scheme has been maintained in its current form for over 2,000 years.

Artha

Artha is the first aim of life. It signifies material prosperity and achieving worldly well-being. The word literally means "thing, object, or substance," but signifies the whole range of tangible objects that can be possessed, enjoyed, and lost, and which you require in your life for the upkeep of a household, raising of a family, and discharge of religious duties. Wealth and material well-being is not its own end; rather, it is a means to an enriched life.

Successes in the stage of artha are means to ends, since they help you support a household and discharge your civic duties. But there are limitations even at this stage, since success can be very private—success here is private, not cooperative. There is another problem: Wealth, fame, and power do not survive death and are, therefore, ephemeral.

Kama

Kama, which is the second aim of life, has to do with fun, but more generally pleasure. In Indian mythology, Kama is the counterpart of cupid; he is the Hindu god of love. Kama refers to the emotional being, feelings and desires. According to Indian philosophy, people denied their emotional lives and fulfillment of pleasurable desires are repressed and live under a continual strain. All of this is ruinous to their sanity and well-being.

QUESTION

Who was the *Kama Sutra* written for?
There is little doubt that the *Kama Sutra* was written for a predominantly male audience, setting out to cater to their sexual desires. Some passages refer to how men might better satisfy women's sexual pleasure, but even these passages are male centered.

Kama teaching is exciting because it runs counter to frustrations resulting from arranged marriages of convenience. As time went on, marriages became more and more family managed affairs. There were no limits to how meddlesome the parents might be. Bargains struck by the heads of families, based on the horoscopes cast by astrologers and economic and social considerations, determined the fate of the young bride and groom.

Dharma

The third of the four aims includes, in essence, the sum and substance of your religious and moral duties comprising your righteousness. Indian literature contains rituals and numerous social regulations for the three upper castes. Brahman (priest), Ksatriya (noble), and Vaisya (merchant and agriculturalist) are meticulously formulated according to the teaching of the Creator himself (in the *Vedas*).

Dharma is the doctrine of the duties and rights of each group and person in the ideal society, and as such the law or mirror of all moral action. Ethical life is the means to spiritual freedom as well as its expression on earth. At this stage, the individual undertakes a kind of religion of duty. Here, energy is directed toward helping others, but this service is also finite and will come to an end.

Moksa

What people really want is found in the fourth aim, which is spiritual release. The chief end of man is the full development of the individual. The Upanishad tells us that there is nothing higher than people, but people are not mere assemblages of body, life, and mind born of and subject to physical nature. The natural half-animal being with which man confuses himself is not his whole or real being; it is the instrument for the use of spirit, which is the truth of his being. It is the ultimate aim, the final good, and as such is set over and above the other three. Artha, Kama, and Dharma, known as the *trivarga,* the "group of three," are the pursuits of the world; each implies its own orientation or "life philosophy," and to each a special literature is dedicated.

By far the greatest measure of Indian thought, research, teaching, and writing has been concerned with the supreme spiritual theme of liberation from ignorance and the passions of the world's general illusion. *Moksa,* from the root *muc,* ("to loose, set free, let go, release") means "liberation." These and other terms taken together suggest something of the highest end of man as conceived by the Indian sage.

CHAPTER 3

Judaism

Judaism is the oldest of the Abrahamic religions. The term "Abrahamic" describes three faiths: Judaism, Christianity, and Islam. All trace the origins of their traditions to Abraham, described in the Hebrew Bible used by both Christians and Jews. Accounts vary in the Qur'an, the holy book of Islam. There is some dispute about whether Abraham is a historical figure who lived in the nineteenth century B.C.E. This chapter will also explore the four main Judaic variations: Orthodox, Hasidic, Conservative, and Reform. Each has its own set of observations, many of which date back to ancient times.

A Belief in One God

What do the Abrahamic faiths have in common? They share a belief in a single, all-powerful God as the creator and sustainer of the universe. This view was not always the case; earlier Jewish texts maintain that the God of Abraham, Issac, and Jacob was just one among many gods and goddesses of the ancient Middle East. This changed about 700 B.C.E., however. By that time monotheism had become commonplace in Judaism. It also became true in Christianity and Islam.

In each of the Abrahamic faiths, God is the absolute power, and it is the believers' unwavering duty to follow God's ways in their daily lives. Islam puts special emphasis on such unquestioning obedience to God. By way of contrast, Christianity and Judaism have a scriptural tradition of questioning, arguing, and debating with God.

Origins and Development

The Covenant between God and Abraham that represents the start of Judaism appears in the Authorized King James Version of the Bible, Genesis 12:1–3:

Now the Lord had said unto Abram, Get thee out of thy country, and from thy kindred, and from thy father's house, unto a land that I will shew thee:

And I will make of thee a great nation, and I will bless thee, and make thy name great; and thou shalt be a blessing.

Abraham followed God's instructions in his search for the Promised Land, and after many years of wandering around ended up in a place called Canaan. Along the way, God tested his faith by asking him to sacrifice his son Isaac, but at the last minute, God intervened and stopped the sacrifice. He then repeated his promise to Abraham of becoming the father of a great nation. Abraham and his descendants settled in Canaan.

When the famine came, Abraham's son Jacob took his family to the land of Egypt. They settled in, and Jacob fathered many sons and the family prospered. The descendants of Jacob's sons would later become the twelve tribes of Israel. The new pharaoh of Egypt, worried that Jacob's family might become more powerful than the Egyptians, came up with an idea to restrict their proliferation: kill every newborn male child at birth. The account of this, recorded in the Bible in Exodus, has within its horror a wonderful story.

Moses

The midwives got around Pharaoh's edict with some success, so the Pharaoh stepped up the campaign and ordered that every newborn son be cast into the river. The Israelites' daughters were spared.

One Jewish mother decided to hide her newborn son. She made an ark from bulrushes, put the boy in it, and laid it by the riverbank. The daughter of Pharaoh came to the river to wash herself and when she walked along the bank, she saw the ark and told one of her maids to fetch it. The Pharaoh's daughter opened the ark and saw a baby boy; it was crying and she had compassion. The child became her son and she named him Moses.

When Moses was fully grown, he saw an Egyptian slave master beating an Israelite. Moses killed the slave master and had to flee Egypt. He settled in a rural farming area called Midian. Around the same time, Pharaoh died during a time of great suffering for the Israelites. God remembered his covenant with Abraham. He looked on the people and had respect for them.

Moses was tending to his work in the desert when he came to a mountain. An angel appeared to him in the form of a flame of fire on a bush. The flame burned intently but did not consume the bush. A voice then came from the bush and told Moses that he had been chosen to deliver the people from the Egyptians and take them to another land flowing with milk and honey. God commanded Moses to return to the new Pharaoh.

Pharaoh, as expected, refused the demands from Moses. As punishment, God sent ten plagues to the Egyptians, none of which had any effect. Finally, one did: it brought death in one night to the firstborn son of every Egyptian family.

After this final plague, Pharaoh let the Israelites go. Then, he had second thoughts and sent his army after them. They caught up with the Israelites at the banks of the Red Sea. The army prepared to destroy them, but God parted the Red Sea so the Israelites could get safely across. Once the

Israelites were safely on the other side, the Pharaoh's army gave pursuit. God made the Red Sea close again, drowning the entire army.

ESSENTIAL

God had warned Moses of the final plague and told him that all Israelite families should smear lamb's blood on their doorposts so their sons would not be killed on that night. The lamb's blood would be a token, and when God saw the blood, he would pass over the house. God told Moses that sacrifice should be observed forever, and it is still celebrated as the eighth day of the Jewish festival of Passover (Pesach).

The Ten Commandments

Moses was now the leader of a large number of contentious people on the move, and he had some problems. Being pursued was one of them; the others were hunger, thirst, and rebellion. Fortunately, God was still communicating with Moses and issuing instructions.

About three months after leaving Egypt, the Israelites were camping in the wilderness of Sinai. God told Moses to go up to the top of the mountain. There, God revealed to Moses the Ten Commandments, written on two tablets of stone. They dealt with the people's relationship with God and each other. God also gave Moses hundreds of more detailed rules and laws. The Ten Commandments form the basis of all the Jewish laws. They have had, and continue to have, immense influence on many other religions as well.

Pursuing the Promised Land

Deuteronomy 31 tells that when Moses was 120 years old, the Lord came to him and told him he was about to die and he would not reach the "Promised Land." God commanded Moses to write down the Law (or Torah) and give it to the Levites. Moses' brother Joshua was appointed by God to succeed as leader of the Israelites. Moses then climbed up Mount Pisgah, which overlooked Canaan, the Promised Land that he would never enter. Moses was never seen again, and how he died remains a mystery.

The two tablets containing the laws God gave to Moses were housed in a gold-plated chest called The Ark of the Covenant. The Israelites carried the Ark with them before they settled in the Promised Land, and from time to time took it into battle. It was taken to Jerusalem by King David, and was eventually placed in the Temple by King Solomon. Placed inside the Tabernacle within the Temple of Jerusalem, the Ark was seen only by the high priest of the Israelites on Yom Kippur, the Day of Atonement. The final fate of the Ark is unknown.

As time went on, the Israelites were ruled by a series of kings: Saul, David (who wrote many of the psalms in the Bible), and David's son, Solomon. After Solomon's death, the kingdom of Israel split in two and formed Judah and Israel. Throughout the centuries that followed, the Israelites were exiled to Babylon, although some came back. In 63 B.C.E., the Romans conquered the land and gave it a new name: Palestine. Three years later, the Jews revolted against Rome, but were defeated. The Temple in Jerusalem, which was rebuilt after the Israelites returned from exile in Babylon, was finally destroyed in 70 C.E.

FACT

All that remains of the Temple is the western wall, called the Wailing Wall. It is now a center of pilgrimage and prayer for Jews from all over the world. This site, Judaism's holiest place on earth, is used for private prayer (performed while facing the Wall) and for public services and bar mitzvahs.

Abraham, who may have lived about 3,000 years ago, is recognized as the father of the Jewish people. God made a covenant with Abraham that his descendants would be God's chosen people. For their part, believers must obey God's laws. The laws were given to Moses by God, on Mount Sinai. The Ten Commandments are but a fraction of the 613 *Mitzvot* or commandments. These statements and principles of laws and ethics are all contained in the Torah or Five Books of Moses. The Mitzvot are known as commandments of "Laws of Moses." They consist of a mixture of positive commandments to perform some act (to love God and to emulate His ways) and negative commandments to abstain from certain acts (not to profane His name or test Him unduly).

Although numerically a modest-sized religion (about 20 million adherents), Judaism has provided the historical foundation for two of the world's largest religions: Christianity and Islam.

Central Beliefs

Judaism is a religion of ethical monotheism. God is unique and the ultimate authority, but the utter and essential backbone of the entire religion is the Torah, comprised of the first five books of the Bible, attributed to Moses.

In addition to the Torah, the Hebrew canon includes the Nevi'im or the books of the prophets. Nevi'im are generally divided into two sections: the former prophets (comprised of twenty-two books) and the latter prophets, of which there are twelve. The writings of the twelve minor prophets are copied onto one scroll, so that they can be counted as one entry, so to speak. The total number of books in the Hebrew canon is thirty-nine, which was the number of scrolls on which they were originally written.

The Torah

The Torah, the most important section of the Jewish Bible, is a series of narratives and laws that chronicle the beginning of the world through the death of Moses. Jewish people and Christians agree that Moses was the author of the five books. The study of the Torah is considered an act of worship for the Jews; it is read religiously each Sabbath. Over the course of a year, the entire Torah will be read on Sabbath and festival days. There are daily and weekly classes and groups for those who wish to study the Torah.

The Talmud

The Talmud, which means study or learning, is a reference to the interpretations of the Torah. It is the supreme sourcebook of law, as it takes the rules listed in the Torah and describes how to apply them to different circumstances. It's not actually a legal code—there are other works for that—but it is the ultimate source material used to decide all matters of Jewish law. The Mishnah is the first part of the Talmud.

There is a confession of faith called a Shema, made up of three scriptural texts from Deuteronomy and Numbers, that demonstrates the power and demands emanating from the Jewish God. Because the original requirement to study the Torah night and day was understandably tough, the Shema became the substitute as a minimum requirement. It is said that pious Jews hope to die with the words of the Shema on their lips. Here is a short extract:

And ye shall teach them (these words) to your children, talking of them, when thou sittest in thy home, and when thou walkest by the way, and when thou liest down, and when thou risest up . . . remember and do all My commandments, and be holy unto your God. I am the Lord your God, who brought you out of the land of Egypt, to be your God: I am the Lord your God.

The fifth of the Ten Commandments says that nobody shall work on the Sabbath. The Jewish Sabbath, Shabbat, starts at dusk on Friday and ends at dusk on Saturday. The synagogue has services Friday night and Saturday morning. Jews start the Sabbath by dressing up for a good meal and maybe some singing and celebration. Saturdays they go visiting friends and family and sit around reading the Torah. A ceremony called Havdalah marks the end of the Sabbath on Saturday evening. The family gathers, a candle is lit, and a box of sweet-smelling spices is passed around. If dinner is served after Havdalah, it must have been prepared earlier because cooking is not permitted on the Sabbath.

Synagogues

The synagogue is the center of Jewish community life. It has three traditional functions: house of prayer where services are held on the Sabbaths and festival days; house of assembly where Jewish people can meet for any purpose; and house of study where the Torah and Talmud are studied. Children can also come to learn Hebrew and the Torah. Public congregational prayers are said at the synagogue every weekday. Prayers can only take place if there are at least ten men present in the synagogue. It is a Jewish man's duty to attend prayers as often as possible.

A rabbi has no more authority to perform rituals than any other member of the Jewish community; a synagogue can exist and operate quite well without one. However, a rabbi is usually employed by the congregation to run things and settle disputes regarding Jewish law. Generally, a rabbi has been formally educated in Halakhah (Jewish law). When a person has completed the necessary course of study, he or she is given a written document known as a *semikhah*, confirming his authority. A rabbi's status does not give him the authority to conduct religious services; any knowledgeable Jew can lead a religious service. However, rabbis are the spiritual leaders of the Jewish community. In many areas, particularly in the United States, rabbis carry out pastoral counseling, hospital and military chaplaincies, and teaching in Jewish schools.

A typical synagogue contains an ark—a special cupboard or alcove that faces Jerusalem—where the scrolls of the Law are kept; there will also be a perpetual lamp or "eternal light" before the ark. The synagogue will have a *bimah*, a raised platform near the center of the room used for reading the Torah and saying or singing prayers. Many Jewish prayers are sung; the singing may be led by a cantor or a choir or it can be congregational singing.

FACT

Men and women are still segregated in Orthodox synagogues. Historically, the women's section was located in the balcony, while men sat in the main part of the synagogue. Now, the men and women may sit side by side, separated by a border that bisects the synagogue. The practice of segregation has been abandoned in Reform and Conservative congregations.

The Torah scrolls, which are handwritten on parchment, are protected by being "dressed" in velvet coverings and silver ornaments. The scrolls are valuable; the handwriting on them is carried out by a skilled expert and can take a year to complete. In addition to the elaborate fastenings, there is a silver pointer used when reading the Torah, to avoid finger contact with the parchment. It is the duty of every adult male to take a turn reading the Torah, which requires special training. When a boy does this for the first time, it is considered an important occasion in his life.

The public readings and worship of the Scriptures can be a complicated and elaborate ceremony depending on the time and day of the week and which kind of festival is being observed.

Rituals and Customs

Virtually everything a devout Jewish person does from the beginning to the end of life is regulated by an adherence to Jewish law and obedience to the will of God. This is most evident in the various rites, rituals, and customs of the faith. Most Jews have a *mezuzah* on every doorpost in the home (excluding the bathroom and toilet) to remind everyone to keep God's laws.

ESSENTIAL

A mezuzah is a parchment inscribed with religious texts in a case attached to a doorpost in a Jewish home as a sign of faith. When it comes to prescribed ritual, rites, and customs, Jewish people generally happily conform to their religious heritage.

Birth

Birth, as far as Jewish boys are concerned, means circumcision on the eighth day. The Torah says it's the fulfillment of the covenant between God and Abraham (Genesis 17:10–14). This procedure is performed by a specially trained person called a mohel. The mohel recalls the Covenant and recites a blessing while cutting off the foreskin. The baby's name is said at the same time.

Bar Mitzvah and Bat Mitzvah

Bar mitzvah is a ceremony held when a Jewish boy is thirteen and considered old enough to take responsibility for himself and his obedience of the law. In Jewish religious terms, he is considered an adult. The boy will be able to wear phylacteries (religious symbols worn on the forehead and left arm) during weekday and morning prayers. He may also be counted as an adult when ten males are needed to make a quorum for public prayers.

The public act of acknowledging religious maturity requires the boy to be called upon during the religious service to read from the Torah. Bar mitzvah generally takes place on a Sabbath. After the ceremony, there is frequently a festive *Kiddush,* or prayer, over a cup of wine and a family social dinner or even a banquet.

In modern times, Reform and Conservative congregations introduced bat mitzvah ceremonies for girls, to parallel the bar mitzvah celebrations for boys. Thereafter, Modern Orthodox congregations also instituted ceremonies for groups of girls together, usually on a Sunday. More traditionalist Orthodox groups rejected the bat mitzvah altogether, seeing it as a modernist innovation imitating reform or Christian practice.

Marriage

Marriage and the raising of children is an important part of Jewish life, just as it is in other religions. The role of matchmaker is still an important one in Jewish communities. The wedding ceremony can be held in a synagogue or in the open air. In the Jewish faith, though, it cannot take place on the Sabbath or on a festival. The bridegroom places a gold ring on the bride's forefinger, then the *kethubah* or marriage contract is read and the rabbi recites the seven marriage blessings. At the end of the ceremony, the bridegroom traditionally breaks a wineglass under his foot.

QUESTION

What are the skull caps called that Jewish men wear?
They are called *yarmulkes* (Yiddish) or *kippahs* (Hebrew) and serve as physical symbols that demonstrate the wearer's submission to God. Most Jews, except the most liberal members of the Reform movement, wear yarmulkes during religious services. Some Jews wear yarmulkes any time they appear in public.

The Jewish marriage contract has, in some ways, similarities to a prenuptial agreement; it has conditions stipulated that guarantee the bride's right to property when her husband dies. In the Orthodox and Conservative congregations, it is a prerequisite for marriage. Originally, the contract was made to make divorce more costly for husbands as a deterrent against marriages that were made in a highly emotional state.

Death

Death in the Jewish faith goes along with the belief of other religions on the resurrection of the dead. Differences are evident when deciding on what happens to the body—burial or cremation—which depends on the sect to which the individual belonged. The body must be buried as soon as possible after death (within twenty-four hours is typical) and in Jewish consecrated ground. The body is washed, anointed with spices, and wrapped in a white sheet. For a week after the death, close relatives sit at home observing *shivah*, wearing a torn or cut upper garment and taking no part in everyday life. Friends and relatives have a duty to visit and bring food and succor. For eleven months after death, a prayer known as the *kaddish* is recited every day at the synagogue and the death is remembered every year thereafter.

Religious Festivals and Holy Holidays

Festivals are the backbone of the Jewish faith; they reflect Jewish history and its teaching. They fulfill the purpose of festival remembrance by maintaining and passing on, one generation to the next, the emotions of a heritage carried forward into the present and never lost. They nurture the sense of cohesiveness that has sustained the Jewish people throughout their long and often heartrending history.

In the Jewish calendar, festivals are divided into two segments: major and minor. The five major ones are as laid down in the Torah: Rosh Hashanah, Yom Kippur, Pesach (Passover), Shavuot, and Sukkot (Feast of Tabernacles).

- **Rosh Hashanah** or the Jewish New Year usually takes place sometime in September. This holiday is also known as the Day of Judgment or Day of Remembrance. Rosh Hashanah ushers in a ten-day period of self-examination and penitence.

- **The Day of Atonement**, known in Hebrew as Yom Kippur, arrives ten days after Rosh Hashanah. Yom Kippur is the most solemn Jewish religious holiday. On this day, Jews seek purification through the forgiveness of others and sincere repentance of their own sins. They abstain from food, drink, and sex.
- The days for the **Festival of Pesach** or **Passover** usually fall in March or April. Passover celebrates God's deliverance of the Israelites from captivity in Egypt. During this weeklong holiday, Jewish people eat unleavened bread known as *matzoh* in commemoration of the quickly made unleavened bread the Israelites had to subsist on during their escape from Egypt.
- **Shavuot**, translated into Greek as "Pentecost" by the early Christians, takes place seven weeks after Passover and was originally an agricultural festival that marked the beginning of the wheat harvest. Additionally, this holiday also commemorates the anniversary of Moses receiving the Law of God on Mount Sinai.
- **Sukkot** is also known as the Feast of Tabernacles. It is an autumn festival that celebrates the end of the harvest. During this holiday, which lasts a week, people build little huts, known as *sukkahs*, where they are required to spend some time in meditation.

All other festivals are considered minor, although Hanukkah, officially a minor festival, has become so popular that it is often celebrated more than some of the major festivals.

The Jewish calendar is a lunar calendar. This produces the need to add a thirteenth month every now and then so that the major festivals fall in their proper season. It takes a Jewish mathematician to track what is called the lunisolar structure.

Orthodox Judaism

Orthodoxy in Judaism came into existence around 1795 and supported a belief in the dual Torah. The dual Torah was revealed at Sinai and is concerned with oral and written versions of the law. The argument was that the written law could never have stood alone and must have been accompanied by an oral tradition. For example, Exodus 12:15 says that the number of days during which unleavened bread must be eaten amounts to seven, whereas in Deuteronomy 16:8, it is six. Orthodox Jews rely on the oral Torah to account for the discrepancy.

Orthodox Judaism is not a unified movement; it is many different movements adhering to a common principle. They believe the Torah—both written and oral—to be of divine origin and the exact work of God; the human element was not involved in its creation, so the words are immutably fixed and remain the sole norm of religious observance. Most of the movements have similar observances and beliefs; it's the details that vary.

Beliefs and Practices

While Orthodox Judaism adheres to the common Jewish principles, the following are some of the ways in which they are uncommon. In addition to the Sabbath, religious holidays include the three biblical pilgrimage festivals, Passover, Pentecost, Tabernacles, the New Year (Rosh Hashanah), and the Day of Atonement (Yom Kippur). All holidays except the Day of Atonement are observed for two days. The first two days of Passover and last two days of Tabernacles are days on which work is forbidden, as it is on the Sabbath and other holidays. The preparation of food is prohibited only on the Sabbath and the Day of Atonement. Hanukkah and Purim are post-Biblical holidays and do not include a prohibition against work.

Orthodox households have strict rules regarding the way foods and their utensils are used. Meat and dairy products may not be eaten together or at the same meal. A completely different set of utensils is used for the two types of food; there are different storage areas and the utensils should be washed separately. The law so affects Orthodox Jews that some find it virtually impossible to eat out, except in strict Kosher restaurants.

There are no restrictions about medical treatment. Orthodox Jews consider physicians instruments through which God can effect a cure. When it comes to death, funeral, and burial requirements, the form is to follow the established way, but it prohibits cremation. Apart from very unusual circumstances, such as promoting justice, autopsies are not permitted because they break the prohibition against mutilation of the body and show disrespect for the dead. A rabbi should be consulted before an autopsy is considered.

Contraception is limited to women. A vasectomy or use of a condom by males is not permitted. Abortion is permitted if the continuation of the pregnancy presents grave physical or psychiatric dangers.

The Essential Element

The essential element of Orthodox Judaism is the complete and utter adherence to the established laws. Everything in the life of an Orthodox Jew is directly related to the affirmation of that ethic. There are even some communities that maintain holy Israel should live wholly apart from gentiles. Other, more moderate, members agree that integration with Western culture while maintaining the law of the Torah together with secular politics and general social affairs is preferable.

It is estimated that only about 10 percent of the total Jewish population in America is Orthodox. The Union of Orthodox Jewish Congregations, which represents about 1,000 congregations, was founded in New York City in 1898.

Hasidic Judaism

Hasidic Jews are the most orthodox of the Orthodox movement, even though, strictly speaking, both are distinct branches of Judaism. Hasidic Jews adhere absolutely to the teachings of the written law (the Torah) and the oral law (the Talmud). The sect began in Poland in 1760, led by a revivalist named Eliezer Ba'al Shem Tov (Master of the Good Name), who stressed the study of Jewish literature. In the Hasidic tradition, a Master is also known as a Zaddik or righteous man.

The Master is has a direct line to God. After the founder's death, Hasidism spread throughout Europe and diversified. The main body of the sect remained in Europe until the Holocaust, when tremendous numbers of Hasidic Jews were slaughtered by the Nazis. Some escaped to the United States. In New York, they settled predominantly in Brooklyn, where today around 100,000 followers live.

Customs

Hasidic Jews often get attention on the street because of their appearance. The men are usually dressed completely in black with wide-brimmed hats, long coats, beards, and extended, rope-like sideburns. Originally, their dress was the local custom in Poland; today, it symbolizes their religious fervor.

ESSENTIAL

Jewish law says there should be a separation between the top and bottom halves of the body when praying. Most Hasidic men wear a *gartel*; others wear a regular belt.

Often, a Hasidic man will be seen with a black box (*tefillin*) on his head or arm to follow the Torah commandant to have a box containing parchment verses from the Torah. During morning services the box is worn on the head ("between your eyes") or on the arm ("upon your hand"). In some congregations, women also wear tefillin.

Another custom regards the hair, both on the head and on the face. As always, the law is open to interpretation. The most orthodox men who follow the law to the letter will not deviate from the commandment that a straight razor should not be used on one's temple or to shave one's beard. The sidelocks are also an answer to an interpretation of the law against shaving the temples. The long sideburns are called *peyot*.

Beliefs and Practices

Hasidic religious duties are carried out in a spirit of devotion. Prayer serves not to petition or supplicate God but as the way to ascend to a relationship of union with God.

While the Hasidic way of life may seem very restricted or even morose, it was the source of some profound music. In the 1700s, the Hasidic movement exerted a significant influence on what is called *klezmer* in Yiddish. The word is used to denote professional eastern European Jewish dance musicians. The term is a combination of two Hebrew words: *kle*, which means "vessel" or "instrument," and *zemer*, which means "song." In recent times, klezmer music has gained prominence. The Hasidic sect made religion more accessible to the masses by emphasizing dancing and singing with intense urgency to "ascend" to higher realms through their music.

Conservative Judaism

Conservative Judaism is predominantly centered in the United States. Inspired by Zacharias Frankel in the 1800s, it was expanded in 1902 in New York by a Jewish Talmudic scholar, Solomon Schecter. In 1913, Schecter founded the United Synagogue of America, which eventually grew to over 800 Conservative congregations.

Central Beliefs

Conservative Judaism believes in observing traditional Jewish laws, sacred texts, and beliefs and being open to modern culture and critical secular scholarship, which allows for changes in practices.

The theology of the Conservative movement is midway between Orthodox Judaism and Reform Judaism, with Orthodox being the strict element and Reform the more liberal. For instance, in 1985 the Rabbinical Assembly, an organization of Conservative rabbis in the United States, Canada, Europe, and Israel, founded in 1900, voted to allow the admittance of women as rabbis for the first time, something Orthodox Judaism has yet to do.

Many Conservatives stress Jewish nationalism, encourage the study of Hebrew, and support the secular Zionist movement, which emphasizes the importance of the Jewish national homeland and supports the development of Israel. In spite of the differences among the affiliations, the Conservatives have maintained continuity with tradition, which often makes it difficult to differentiate one theology from another. The Conservatives like diversity, which is why their views and practices range from Orthodoxy to Reform.

A Forward Movement

In 1960, the leadership of Conservative Jews agreed to allow the use of electricity on the Sabbath and a car to travel to the synagogue. This decision was a major step forward in the direction of modern thought for Conservative Jews.

Conservative Jews maintain their links with the past by insisting on the sacredness of the Sabbath and respecting some dietary laws, like the prohibition against eating pork. However, they do not require a strict kosher kitchen. The rabbinical assembly, Conservative Judaism's official body, is located in New York City at the Jewish theological seminary, which educates future rabbis for the movement.

Reform Judaism

Reform Judaism is a movement that modified or abandoned many of the traditional Jewish beliefs, laws, and practices in order to bring Judaism into the modern world in all aspects of social, political, and cultural conditions. The movement began in Germany in the nineteenth century in response to appeals to update the Jewish liturgy and other rituals. The Jews were being liberated from the ghettos, and many began to question Jewish tradition and its dietary laws, prayers said in Hebrew, and even the wearing of special outfits that set them apart as Jews.

The First Reform Services

A Jewish layman, Israel Jacobson, began a school in Seesen, Brunswick, Germany in 1801. In 1809, he held the first Reform services. The liturgy was in German, not Hebrew; men and women were allowed to sit together; organ and choir music were added to the service; and Jacobson instituted confirmation for boys and girls to replace the traditional bar mitzvah. The services also left out all references to a personal messiah who would restore Israel as a nation. The questions being asked were: "Who is Israel? What is its way of life? How does it account for its existence as a distinct and distinctive group?"

The Spreading Movement

The Reform movement was not a success in Europe. Many European governments that regulated religious communities didn't countenance more than one form of Judaism in any particular locale. It was in the United States, to which the movement was imported by the mass German-Jewish immigration in the 1840s, that it flourished. By 1880, almost all the 200 synagogues in the United States had become Reform.

In 1885, the Pittsburgh Platform, put together by Reform rabbis, declared that Judaism was an evolutionary faith and should be deorientalized. One conclusion was that the Talmud should be looked at as religious literature, not as legislation.

QUESTION

What do Reform Jews believe?
One of the guiding principles of Reform Judaism is the autonomy of the individual. A Reform Jew has the right to decide whether to subscribe to each particular belief or practice. As Rabbi W. Gunther Plaut wrote, "Reform Judaism affirms the fundamental principle of liberalism: that the individual will approach this body of mitzvot (commandments) of freedom and choice."

Current movements advocate a return to more traditional mores. In 1999, Leaders of Reform Judaism embraced rituals associated more with Conservative and Orthodox Judaism than with the Reform movement, wearing yarmulkes and prayer shawls, observing dietary laws, and conducting prayer services in Hebrew.

CHAPTER 4

Jainism

In the sixth century B.C.E., two exciting new schools of thought emerged. Jainism practiced reverence for life, celibacy, and moral conduct. It stressed a life of the mind and turning away from a life of bodily pleasures. The other school of thought was Buddhism, which taught that enlightenment came from the monkish existence of renouncing the world. This chapter will expound the philosophy of Jainism.

The Development of Jainism

Jainism is a religion and philosophy of India that, along with Hinduism and Buddhism, is one of the three most ancient religions still in existence in that country. It dates to 3,000 B.C.E. The three religions have common beliefs; for instance, all share the idea of karma, where the actions of an individual in successive lives affects and determines a future life. Each also has a historical literary heritage and a tradition of asceticism. Many Jains and Hindus worship images, and there are even places outside India where Hindus and Jains have joined to build a single temple and share worship space.

The name Jainism comes from the Sanskrit meaning "to conquer." Conquer in this context means conquering inner feelings of hate, greed, and selfishness. For Jains, the objective in life is to renounce materialistic needs in order to achieve bliss or moksha.

In Jainism, twenty-four significant perfected historical figures act as teachers in the search for perfection. These teachers operate in cycles of history. Jains look at time as eternal and formless, so the teachers, called Tirthankaras, appear from time to time to preach the Jain religious way. Each of the Tirthankaras has attained absolute freedom because they have broken away from the cycle of rebirths. Another sixty-four gods and goddesses, great souls, luminaries, and others are involved in the teaching as well.

ESSENTIAL

Jainism's influence on Indian philosophy, logic, art, architecture, grammar, mathematics, astronomy, and astrology has, in many ways, been greater than Hinduism and Buddhism, which have far more adherents. However, unlike those two, Jainism hasn't spread as far; the bulk of the adherents are in India, although there are a few small communities in the United States.

The Tirthanakas offer human beings a means to cross the ocean of samsara—the cycle of existence. Chief among these Tirthanakas was the Jain leader Mahavira (599–527 B.C.E.) An ascetic, Mahavira was esteemed among his followers as one whose life and example could release them from the wheel of rebirth. If the animal drives of the body could be left behind and the higher intellectual and spiritual potentialities of human beings were unlocked, a path of release was possible for the soul in this life.

Jainism Carves Its Own Path

According to Jainism, spiritual progress is made through accomplishments in one's own life. Jains reject the idea of a caste; in addition, like Buddhism, Jainism emphasizes that no matter what a person's station in life—no matter what level of the caste he occupies—that living properly provides release.

Jainism's views on the Vedas differ from that of Hindus and should be viewed as a separate religion unto itself. At the same time, its views of karma and samsara give its doctrine more than a little in common with the Indian thought that preceded it. Jainism rejects the idea that a person achieves release from life by offering sacrifices to the gods or other forms of worship.

FACT

Ahimsa means "nonkilling" and is primarily associated with the Jains. The notion of ahimsa is applied toward animal life primarily, but in Jain philosophy is recognized in the case of plants as well. Mohandas Gandhi admitted that his regard for all life was inspired by the Jains's practice of ahimsa toward all things.

Jainism redirects the focus from attention to the gods to a personal philosophy. One such philosophy is asceticism. Asceticism is the belief that one should deny and even conquer desires. The strong version of this belief is that one should deny all desires without exception. The weaker version is that one denies only the base desires of the body, like extreme lust, lasciviousness, and sensuousness of the world, such as the desire for material possessions, fame, and achievement.

According to Jainism, the more one denies pleasures and satisfactions of the body, the more one is able to achieve freedom from the endless cycle of birth and rebirth. The founders of Jainism went beyond the traditional Indian moral concern for cattle to teach that all forms of life are sacred and should be loved and preserved wherever possible. This doctrine of love and nonviolence toward all things is known as *ahimsa*.

Jainism split into two factions in the fourth or third century B.C.E.: the Digambaras (sky clad) and the Svetambaras (white-robed). The major difference between the two was the degree of asceticism. The Digambaras believed complete nudity was necessary to signify detachment from material things. The Svetambaras held that three simple white robes were acceptable. Both groups believed that before Mahavira there had been twenty-three Tirthankaras or spiritual leaders. While they agreed that Mahavira had renounced the world at the age of thirty, they disagreed on another matter, which divided them for all times.

Legend says that Mahavira meditated for twelve years before achieving the ultimate enlightenment. He then tore out five handfuls of his own hair instead of shaving his head, because he had become impervious to pain. The Digambaras believe that the gods took his clothes away, which would make him a naked wanderer. The Svetambaras disagreed; they believed his garment had been torn away by a thorn bush thirteen months after his wanderings began.

Why is the issue of clothing so important? The Digambaras say that although the absence of clothing doesn't signify a true monk, the presence of clothing indicates some residual shame, a deficit of character that wouldn't be found in a true monk. They believed that only previous Tirthankaras were nude and only Digambaras could attain moksha or freedom from bondage to the world.

The Amazing Mahavira

His real name was Nataputta Vardhamana, but he was better known to his followers as Mahavira or "Great Hero." He is traditionally identified as the founder of Jainism. As stated, Mahavira and the twenty-three prior to him who established Jainism are Tirthankaras, or "crossing builders," so called because they forged a bridge between this life and Nirvana or release from this world.

Beginnings

Mahavira's birth and death dates of 599–527 B.C.E. make him a contemporary of Siddhartha Guatama, Confucius, Lao-Tzu, and the great Hebrew prophets of the sixth century B.C.E., including Jeremiah, Ezekiel, and the anonymous author or authors of Isaiah 40–60. Like Buddha, Mahavira was born to parents of the Kshatriya or priestly caste and the family possessed great wealth. He married and had a daughter, but his social standing and wealth still left him unhappy and he sought a spiritual answer to that unhappiness.

For a time, Mahavira joined an order of wandering ascetics. First, however, he waited until his parents had died and the business affairs of his family had been taken over successfully by his older brother. Then he bade farewell to his family, turned his back upon his wealth and luxury, tore out his hair and beard by the handfuls, and went off to join the ascetics.

However, Mahavira concluded that their asceticism was not extreme enough. For the soul to find release from this life, the asceticism must be more extreme. Extreme asceticism was necessary but not sufficient. Mahavira eventually thought that one must practice ahimsa (noninjury). So Mahavira carved his own path to find release. This combination of ahimsa and extreme renunciation gave rise to practices that form the legend of Mahavira's life. In an effort to stay detached from things and people, he never stayed more than one night in any place when he traveled.

ESSENTIAL

Mahavira wandered naked, detached from the world, not answering questions put to him as he walked through villages. In return people turned their dogs on him. He was attacked by animals and humans. On some occasions, they drove nails into him to test the depths of his meditation and detachment.

As with many ascetics, he begged for his food. He preferred leftover food from people's meals rather than raw food so he didn't consume food that might cause his death. To heighten his self-torment, he sought out the coldest locations in the winter months and the most sweltering environments in the summer—always while naked.

He took his self-denial and seeking out of pain even further. If people were angry with him or just mean spirited, they would send dogs after him. Rather than resist, he allowed himself to be bitten. Following twelve years of the strictest asceticism, he achieved release (moksha), freeing himself from the bonds that tied his soul to the endless cycle of birth, death, and rebirth.

The Conqueror Develops a Following

Mahavira earned title of *jina* or "conqueror," denoting a person who had heroically conquered himself and faced the harshest inconveniences of life. He was a renunciant, able to ignore the inconveniences of body longing and pain in order to achieve spiritual realization. Though he achieved moksha at age forty-two, he lived until seventy-two.

Once he had attained enlightenment, he had conquered his weaknesses, escaping the cycle of human biological and psychological needs. The story goes that he now sat in a lotus posture, was in a steady omniscient trance, and sent forth only a divine sound. Above his head at all times was a white umbrella, symbolizing that no mortal was higher or holier. His nature as a Tirthankara or spiritual leader attracted all of the Jain community around him, including monks, nuns, laymen, and laywomen.

ESSENTIAL

A peerless ascetic, the Jain leader Mahavira lived most of his life without clothes, the most visible symbol of a renounced life. After some twelve years as an ascetic, he managed to overcome worldly desires and passions and become the "victor" or jina. Jains describe this state of mind as *kevalajnana* or perfect perception, knowledge, power, and bliss.

A Brahmin, Indrabhuti Gautama, came to Mahavira seeking an interpretation of a revelation of Jain teachings sent by the king of gods, Indra. All the teachings became clear to Gautama in the presence of Mahavira. Eleven Brahmins converted to become his followers. He continued teaching for thirty years. After his renunciation and detachment from the world, Mahavira attracted a very large congregation of devotees; the Svetambaras claim there were 14,000 monks, 36,000 nuns, 159,000 laymen, and 318,000 laywomen.

The Problem and Solution of Living

Jains agree with the Hindu idea that you must learn how to shake off the repetition of reincarnation: You are born, live your life, die, and then are born again. But how does one get away from this endless wheel of life (samsara)?

Jainism provided a different answer than Buddhism and, later, Sikhism. Jainism says if people are stuck in the wheel of birth and rebirth, it is because of the karma they possess as a result of their past actions.

Karma in an individual is not only created by actions so good they were saintly or so bad they were monstrous. Mahavira taught that karma was a result of even seemingly trivial actions or even inaction. The ideal existence was to live detached from life, thereby freeing oneself, as far as one could, from karma.

Despite rebelling against Hinduism, Jainism, like Hinduism, embraces the law of karma. The Jains also accept the omnipresence of the soul. Soul inhabits even the lowest forms of life, no matter how weighed down by karma. As such, the soul can descend from the weight of karma and can rise from the release of karma. Salvation can only come about through individual effort. One who follows the example of Mahavira and performs good works will achieve final liberation. In order to achieve liberation, Jain monks typically take five vows.

The Five Vows of Jainism

In the earliest Sanskrit, the term *vrata* meant not just a "temporary vow," but a dedication on a permanent basis to a single purpose. The adoption of the five *mahavratas* or "Great Vows" was the defining set of characteristics of monks and nuns after their ascetic initiation. The vows were to govern their behavior and provide a structure for their spiritual guidance.

The Jain custom was for an ascetic at a ceremony of initiation to read out the scriptural story of Rohini, the girl distinguished from her unwise sisters because she planted and reaped the rewards of five rice grains given to her by her father to demonstrate how the five Great Vows could be put to good use.

The traditional description of the Great Vows can be found in the second book of the Acaranga (or scriptures). Each of the five vows or renunciations is first stated then followed by realizations, which describe the further implications of the vow, ensuring that the vow will be correctly executed.

The Vow of the Noninjury of Life (Ahimsa)

Ahimsa is sometimes interpreted as "nonviolence," especially by Mohandas K. Gandhi, who credited the Jains with influencing his own practice of nonviolence. But this way of putting the matter is inaccurate, for the term "nonviolence" in ordinary usage involves only human beings. The Sanskrit term ahimsa appeared in the Upanishads in about 500 B.C.E., when many people among the Brahmins, Buddhists, and Jains emphasized reverence for all life, rather than the sacrifice of animals.

ESSENTIAL

When it comes to nonviolence, the Jains taught that it was wrong to kill any life form, and a Jain follower undertakes this vow for the rest of his life. Mahavira taught that it is "sinful" to act badly toward animals. A "wise man" should not act sinfully toward animals, nor even cause or allow others to do so.

The realizations then describes ways in which the ascetic must take care. First, he must observe how and where he walks lest he injure life forms on the way. This is especially relevant during the four-month rain retreat, for it is during the monsoon season that there is a great burgeoning of plant and insect life that might otherwise be injured by wandering ascetics.

The ascetic must also get hold of his own mind and speech, for these may be agents of violence. Further directions concern how an ascetic is to put down his alms bowl and how he must inspect all food and drink to ensure there are no life forms in it.

The noninjury of other life forms is perhaps best known among all Jain traits. Jains are vegetarians and will not own leather goods, since these require the killing of animals. They go to such extremes with vegetarianism that they will not even eat from pans in which meat has been cooked. They follow Mahavira's example of sweeping a path before them to avoid stepping on insects. Jains routinely shun occupations that might bring harm or death to another living thing. For this reason, they even avoid agricultural professions.

The following passage from the Akaranga Sutra, I.1 serves to illustrate the Jain respect for all life.

Earth is afflicted and wretched, it is hard to teach, it has no discrimination. Unenlightened men, who suffer from the effect of past deeds, cause great pain in a world full of pain already, for in earth souls are individually embodied. If, thinking to gain praise, honor, or respect . . . or to achieve a good rebirth . . . or to win salvation, or to escape pain, a man sins against earth or causes or permits others to do so, . . . he will not gain joy or wisdom . . . . Injury to the earth is like striking, cutting, maiming, or killing a blind man. . . . Knowing this, man should not sin against earth or cause or permit others to do so. He who understands the nature of sin against earth is called a true sage who understands karma.

The Akaranga Sutra goes on to say there are many living souls in water, plants, and even the wind, and man should not sin against these.

The Vow Not to Speak Untruth

Jains are widely respected for their truthfulness; the second Great Vow says an ascetic must abstain from lying. The realization here is that he must be deliberate in his speech and not given to anger, greed, fear, or mirth.

Philosophically, the Jains are relativists—they allow that there are truths in the doctrines of other philosophies. There is a well-known story of a blind man and an elephant that is said to illustrate this point. In this tale, several blind men are asked to describe an elephant. Each touches a different part of the elephant's body, and thus each describes it in a different way. To one man, the elephant is like a stone wall because he has touched the side. Another thinks the elephant is like a fan since he has touched its wide ear. Each man truthfully described what he felt, but since each had touched a different part, their descriptions varied. Truth here is relative to their perspectives and positions. Human knowledge, then, is likely to be misleading. Speaking what one knows to be false breaks the vow of the Jains.

The Vow Not to Steal

The third of the great vows says that an ascetic should not take what has not been given. Jain monks are forbidden from taking anything that doesn't belong to them. Like their observance of the second vow, this one aids and abets their reputation for honesty.

The Vow to Renounce Sexual Pleasures

This Great Vow states that an ascetic must renounce all sexual activity. Since asceticism has always viewed the pleasures of the flesh as evil, and since sex is one of the greatest pleasures of the flesh, it must be forsaken.

FACT

The vow to renounce sexual pleasures denounced any contact, mental or physical, with women or eating or drinking anything likely to stimulate the sexual drive. Mahavira did not only renounce sexual pleasures, he renounced women for good. The renunciation of all external pleasures and things owed to the fact that "Women are the greatest temptation in the world."

The Vow to Renounce all Attachments

The fifth Great Vow counsels the renunciation of any attachment to objects of the senses. This refers to possessions in general. To all the things that bind human beings to this life, the love for other persons and things are among the strongest bonds. Thus, Mahavira left behind his family and possessions and habitually didn't remain in one place for more than a day, lest he form attachments to people and things.

No Eating After Dark

A sixth vow was later added. The first appearance of this sixth vow describes it as a supplement to the Great Vows. In reality, it is but a subdivision of the first Great Vow of nonviolence. The reason for prohibiting eating at night is that ascetics cannot go out and seek alms at night, since this activity would involve trampling upon small life forms. In addition, cooking of food by the laity would attract insects that would be drawn into the flames. According to popular belief, the proper digestion of food can only take place in sunlight.

The Importance of the Great Vows

Do all Jains renounce all five vows? Here is where the matter becomes philosophically interesting. If an individual becomes a monk, he holds to all five. On the other hand, a Jain layperson integrates this philosophy with marriage, family, and the material well-being that accompanies such a life. But this sort of life will not lead to spiritual release.

The purpose of the Great Vows, and indeed of the other ancillary vows a Jain ascetic undertakes, is to bring about a state of internal purification. The first of the five—the renunciation of violence—is fundamental according to the Jains. For instance, not speaking falsely (the second vow) is important because of the connection between truth and violence. While lying should be avoided, truths that harm others should not be spoken. Also, the third Great Vow of not taking what has not been given concerns the ascetic's honesty in dealing with all people, but also includes not taking the lives of other beings. Likewise, the attachment to possessions and sense objects rejected by the fourth Great Vow stirs the passions in people, one of the primary causes of violence. In addition, sexual activity is prohibited not only because of the distraction and passion it causes, but because innumerable life forms are destroyed in each ejaculation of semen.

The Jains Today

While Jainism emerged as a protest against the Hindu caste system, Hinduism came to accept Jain asceticism and ahimsa. Still, Jainism doesn't claim many adherents, with slightly less than 4 million followers in the world today. Perhaps the strict requirements of Jainism keep it a minority religion.

No Jain can belong to any profession that takes a life or profits from slaughter. The off-limits professions include soldiers and butchers, leather workers and exterminators, and even farmers. Farming is forbidden because the profession involves plowing and tilling soil, which kills insects and worms that live in the soil. Since professions that involve killing are prohibited, Jains have entered less morally objectionable commercial professions.

Jains acknowledge no transcendent beings. In fact, they have no need for gods, since they embrace a secular ethic. They worship the twenty-four spiritual leaders or Tirthankaras who embody their philosophy. Some 40,000 temples in India worship these figures. One of the temples—erected on Mount Abu—is considered one of the seven wonders of India. In addition to temple worship, Jain worship extends to rituals in the home. This includes a broad variety of activities, including reciting the names of the first jinas (or saints), bathing their idols, and making offerings of flowers and perfume to these idols. Home ceremonies typically include meditation and the observance of vows, too.

The Jain's only religion is a kind of ethic, a way of life. The Jains might fall into two camps: a majority, who are immersed in their material lives and cannot give up their homes and accept the rigors of an ascetic life; and a minority, who become monks. They are quintessential Jains; their lives are guided by the five vows.

Rituals and Customs of Jainism

The lifecycle rites of the Jains differ slightly from those of the Hindus. One significant difference is that Jains object to some postfuneral rites that the Hindus observe concerning the transition of the deceased's soul from one existence to the next.

Weddings

There are similarities with the Hindu tradition in marriage, but a Jain wedding ceremony is far from a quick trip to a registry office. It actually begins seven days before the wedding, with the prewedding ritual involving invoking the heavenly goddesses. Another ceremony is held seven days after the wedding; its purpose is to thank and dismiss the deities. In the days before the marriage, the skin of the bride and groom is regularly massaged with perfumed oil, turmeric, and other substances to beautify them for the occasion.

The wedding ceremony is performed under a *mandap* or canopy. The four main posts that hold it up must be erected at an auspicious time of day. Since the mandap is usually rather large, the construction is done at the bride's home and often moved to a hired place for the ceremony. In the United States, it is possible to rent a mandap and have it professionally erected and taken down.

An elaborate series of rituals takes place, including the washing of the groom's feet by the bride's parents prior to the beginning of the actual service. At the conclusion of the ceremony, the priest congratulates the couple on their marriage and gives a final blessing. Their parents send the couple to the temple then to the bride's home.

Festivals

Jains celebrate their religious holidays by fasting, worshiping, reciting sacred texts, holding religious discourses, giving alms, taking certain vows, and other such acts of piety. Annual holidays are observed based on the lunar calendar. The most important celebrations are the birth of Mahavira in Caitra (March/April), his death in Kartik (October/November), and the holiday period Paryushana, which is held for eight or ten days in the months of Shravana and Bhadrapada (August and September). During Paryushana confessions are offered, visits are made for the purpose of asking and extending forgiveness, and fasting is held.

Festivals are also celebrated on pilgrimages, which can last for several days. There are many Jain holy places, temples, and shrines. Not surprisingly, many of the pilgrimages and festivals revolve around significant events in the lives of the Tirthankaras.

CHAPTER 5

Buddhism

The teachings of dharma and the Four Noble Truths were to become the essence of Buddhism. Buddha taught that the supreme good of life is nirvana, "the extinction" or "blowing out" of suffering and desire and awakening to what is most real. A Sanskrit term, "Buddha" means "awakened" or "enlightened one." Buddhism also teaches pacifism and nonviolence.

Origins and Development

Hinduism gave birth to Jainism and Buddhism, and the three religions have much in common. Jainism emphasized that spiritual release or salvation was possible, no matter what caste you occupied. The teachings of the Buddha consisted of the Four Noble Truths and the belief that the supreme goal of life is nirvana.

Buddhism and Hinduism share some core beliefs while rejecting others. For instance, Buddhism does not accept the Vedic literature and rites or the caste system, though it does retain the concept of reincarnation. They also use many of the same words: atman (self or soul), yoga (union), karma (deed or task), and dharma (rule or law), to name a few.

Buddhism grew up in the sixth century B.C.E. Like Jainism, it was an alternative to Hinduism and resembled Jainism in several respects. Buddhism rejected the authority of the Vedas and the caste system and offered a vision of salvation based on the actions of the individual and fueled by effort. Whereas Jainism was extreme in its ascetic precepts, Buddhism prescribed a more moderate path or "middle way" between the desire for worldly indulgence and the extreme asceticism of Mahavira. Due to this middle path, Buddhism drew more followers and held great appeal in India for several centuries. It would also hold great appeal in China, Japan, Korea, and Southeast Asia when Buddhist missionaries began traveling there.

In fact, three major traditions dominated Chinese culture up until the twentieth century: Confucianism, Daoism (Taoism), and Buddhism, and they coexisted—and often shared moral and social ideas—for about 2,500 years. But when Mao Zedong, better known as Chairman Mao, established China as a communist state, the regime destroyed long-established values. Traditional institutions, religions included, were closed and their adherents persecuted.

This trend of Buddhists residing mainly in Asia and Southeast Asia continues today. While Buddhism was spreading into foreign lands, it was losing ground to a resurgence in Hinduism in India, where Muslim conquest had also diminished the number of Buddhists.

Buddha

Buddha was the title given to Siddhartha Gautama, the founder of Buddhism. The majority of Buddhists believe that there have been, and will be in the future, many other Buddhas. Some even claim that Jesus Christ was a Buddha.

The absolute aim of Buddhist worship and its practice is following and preserving the teaching of the Buddha, Siddartha Guatama. This doesn't mean just following his teachings, but also manifesting their beliefs in every-day life.

The Life of Siddhartha

Guatama's mother, Mahamaya, queen of the kingdom of Sakyas, had a dream. In it, a beautiful silver elephant entered her womb through her side. Priests interpreted the dream and predicted the birth of a son who would be a Buddha. Ten lunar months later, the queen had to take a journey and gave birth in an enclosed park.

A haunting prediction at the time of his birth said that her son would become a king, but the same prediction said that he would give up his kingdom if he came face to face with human misery. To lessen the possibility of his son witnessing suffering, the father shielded him from sickness and death. Whenever Guatama left the palace in his chariot, his aids were instructed to clear the roads of four sights: dead people, aged people, diseased people, and ascetic monks. Siddhartha lived with his family in the seclusion and luxury of the palace and was provided with riches and comfort. His father had his son's life mapped out for him: he'd become a warrior and a great king. But Siddhartha had thoughts of his own.

The turning point came when Siddhartha went outside the palace with his charioteer. On the first trip, he saw an elderly, ill man tottering along. The next day he repeated the trip; this time saw a sick man on the ground, suffering and obviously very ill. When he went out on the third day, he saw a corpse. He was shocked by what he saw and asked his charioteer to explain what had he had seen. The charioteer told him the meaning of the sights. After the trip, Guatama returned to the palace and meditated about what he had seen.

He continued to search for some kind of meaning. On the fourth trip with his charioteer, he saw an old man with a shaven head wearing a yellow robe. The man possessed a calm, serene appearance. Siddhartha asked the charioteer who he was. The charioteer told him he was a holy man, an ascetic who had attained complete enlightenment and thus freedom from care. In the placid image of this mendicant Guatama saw his own destiny. He was so impressed that he started a pattern of fasting and self-mortification, as if such activities would show him the way to enlightenment. It was at this time that his son was born. He named him Rahula, which means "fetter" or "bond."

FACT

The story goes that Guatama felt no pleasure when his child was born. Indeed, the name of his son, Rahula, means "fetter." The name implies that even the joy of giving birth to a healthy child could bind one to his material existence and hinder the quest for spiritual liberation.

The Great Renunciation

Siddhartha then made what is known as the Great Renunciation, a journey every bit as momentous as it sounds. He decided to give up being a prince to become a wandering ascetic. He was twenty-nine years old when he saddled his horse and left in the middle of the night; he didn't want to wake his wife or son. He figured he would return to them one day. He rode south to Gotama, where there were centers of spiritual learning.

Siddhartha arrived at a wooded area near a village called Uruvela. A river was at hand to provide water and he could beg for food in the village. He tried a familiar spiritual discipline known as mortification of the body. He began by eating less food. His fasting became so extreme that he once subsisted on six grains of rice per day, becoming so thin that he could hold his stomach in and touch his backbone.

In the final analysis, asceticism as a philosophy, as a way of life, did not provide Siddhartha with the enlightenment he sought. He had taken renunciation of pleasure to such an extreme that he pursued anything and everything that was unpleasant. In addition, the fasting debilitated him, making him unfit for his pursuit of spiritual progress.

Central Beliefs

Siddhartha did not attain wisdom right away. He had tried asceticism with other monks and found that extreme self-denial did not contribute to spiritual growth. One day he mediated beneath a fig tree and was enlightened. Henceforth, he was Buddha, "the enlightened one."

FACT

Buddha is not a proper noun but a title. In Buddhist tradition, there have been many Buddhas in the past, as there will be many in the future. When the term "the Buddha" is used today, it's assumed to mean Buddha Gautama, the Buddha of the present era.

The content of his meditation that day became the very essence of his doctrine. He mediated on the endless cycle of birth and death mankind is subject to. People are trapped in this cycle because they have desires (*tanha*). Desire is manifest in thirst or craving which, since it is unfulfilled, always results in suffering. It was true in his own life that he only found enlightenment when he ceased to desire it.

In the city of Benares, he gave his first sermon. Five friends who had deserted him when he rejected their ascetic life now listened to him. He preached about how two opposite extremes—self-mortification and indulgence—were both unacceptable ways of life. The middle way (*madhyamika*) was the proper path to enlightenment. The friends embraced his teaching and together they formed the first sangha or order of monks.

ESSENTIAL

Monks who followed the Buddha were known by their yellow robes and shaved heads. Their only possession was a bowl, which they used for begging food. They embraced a three-part creed: "I take refuge in the Buddha; I take refuge in the dharma (law); and I take refuge in the sangha" (the community of Buddhist monks).

Having achieved his enlightenment or, the same, Buddhahood, at the age of thirty-five, the rest of his life was now clearly laid out before him. His band of disciples evolved in numbers and included women who formed an order of nuns. This was a major difference: Contrary to the orthodoxies of Jainism and Hinduism, Buddhism taught that women, too, could experience enlightenment.

The Buddhist Moral Code

There are moral precepts for the Buddhist code of living. Vegetarianism is not one of them; monks are permitted to eat meat. Lay Buddhists are expected to support the monks with food, clothing, and other necessities. Moreover, it is imperative that they obey a moral code consisting of five negative rules. The prohibitions include no killing, stealing, lying, engaging in improper sexual conduct, and partaking of intoxicants.

The Pali Sermons describe the conduct monks are to follow:

And How, O king, is a monk accomplished in morality?

Herein a monk abandons the killing of living things and refrains from killing; laying aside the use of a stick or a knife he dwells modestly, full of kindness, and compassionate for the welfare of all living things. This is his behavior in morality.

Abandoning the taking of what is not given he refrains from the taking of what is not given, he takes and expects only what is given, he dwells purely and without stealing.

Abandoning incontinence he practices continence and lives apart, avoiding the village practice of sexual intercourse. Abandoning falsehood he refrains from falsehood, he speaks truth, he is truthful, trustworthy, and reliable, not deceiving people.

Abandoning slanderous speech he refrains from slanderous speech; what he has heard from one place he does not tell in another to cause dissension. He is even a healer of dissensions and a producer of union, delighting and rejoicing in concord, eager for concord, and an utterer of speech that produces concord.

Abandoning harsh speech he refrains from harsh speech; the speech that is harmless, pleasant to the ear, kind, reaching the heart, urbane, amiable, and attractive to the multitude, that kind of speech does he utter.

Abandoning frivolous speech he refrains from frivolous speech; he speaks of the good, the real, the profitable, of the doctrine and the discipline; he is an utterer of speech worth hoarding, with timely speech and purpose and meaning.

He refrains from injuring seeds and plants.

He eats only within one meal time, abstaining from food at night and avoiding untimely food.

He refrains from seeing, dancing, singing, music, and shows.

He refrains from the use of garlands, scents, unguents, and objects of adornment; from a high or large bed; from accepting gold and silver; from accepting raw grain and raw meat.

He refrains from accepting women, girls, male and female slaves, goats and rams, fowls and pigs, elephants, oxen, horses, mares and farm-lands.

He refrains from going on messages and errands; from buying and selling; from cheating in weighing, false metal in measuring; from practices or cheating, trickery, deception, fraud, from cutting, killing, binding, robbery, pillage, and violence.

Buddha died at the age of eighty. Legend says that his final words were, "Subject to decay are all component things. Strive earnestly to work out your own salvation."

The Four Noble Truths: Buddha's Moral Doctrine

The core of Buddhist doctrine is the Four Noble Truths and the Eightfold Path. Buddha's view of the human condition and the solution to the spiritual ills of that condition can be found by living according to these truths. The first three of the Four Noble Truths are stages of a logical argument representing Buddha's evolution from a comfortable life as a prince to his search for enlightenment. Coupled with the Eightfold Path to those truths, this is Buddha's philosophy for finding salvation.

Buddha's Four Noble Truths are as follows:

The Noble Truth of Suffering

Life is suffering (or *dukkha*), a "vale of tears." Dissatisfaction is everywhere, as are unfulfilled desires, and the separation from what one wants. Sadness and sorrow are a constant on the landscape of existence. Even when we experience ecstasy, it lasts only a little while. For every joy there is a sorrow, but for every sorrow there may not be joy. Suffering can be found in three different categories:

1. Physical suffering—including pain, sickness, distress, and death—endured by all.
2. Suffering produced by change, such as when a joyful state of mind passes and depression, longing, or boredom results.
3. Suffering produced by conditioned states of consciousness (i.e., for every stage of existence there is a corresponding karmic effect). This is the deepest form of suffering.

The notion of self is the source of suffering. Remove the self and you will remove the suffering. Here Buddhism differs from Hinduism and Western philosophies, which assert the existence of the self. Finally, it is not merely illness and ageing, but the discontent and awareness of these developments that makes the suffering sharper.

The Noble Truth of the Cause of Suffering

The cause of this suffering is desire or attachment to the world in a way that makes you liable to suffering. The longing for desire is threefold: There is a desire for sensual pleasure and prosperity; a desire to see the end of unpleasantness; and a desire to go on living. Seeking pleasure is imprudent and futile—pleasure is elusive or, when it is achieved, turns to displeasure. Since people wish to continue in their existence, they end up clinging to life, which leads to despair. Seeking prosperity, too, ends in its own kind of despair, for an appetite for success is insatiable and thus never ending. Hankering for more pleasure and wealth may lead to the conclusion that your well-being depends on these things. A desire for increased status will always lead to bad karma.

The Noble Truth of the Cessation of Suffering

Since life is full of suffering, and the cause of suffering is unceasing desire, the way to eliminate suffering is to eliminate desire. This third truth concerns the cure for the abiding suffering of life. If you can destroy desire, suffering ends.

This is also called the Middle Path. The Buddha told his five disciples: "There are two extremes which should be avoided by a man who renounces the world. One of these is the practice of those things related to the passions, and particularly sensuality; this is low, uncivilized, unworthy and unprofitable, and is fit only for the worldly minded. The other extreme is the practice of self-mortification, which is painful, undignified, and equally unprofitable."

Both extremes were familiar to Buddha. As a young prince, he had followed a sensual life. He had also rejected the life of asceticism. Sensuality slowed his spiritual progress and asceticism weakened his intellect.

The middle-ground alternative was the Eightfold Path, which was neither self-mortification nor self-indulgence. Rather, the way to achieve enlightenment is through a path of spiritual, moral, and mental exercise. The path includes eight parts:

1. **Right Views (understanding):** This means seeing life as it is; realizing the nature of existence as summed up in the Four Noble Truths.
2. **Right Aspirations (thoughts):** This involves keeping a pure mind and avoiding those feelings that obstruct progress to perfection. Such feelings include lust, malice, and cruelty.
3. **Right Speech:** Your speech should bring out your correct thoughts. You should refrain from telling lies and idle lies and back-biting and address people in a tolerant manner. Correct speech should not be loud, excited, or opinionated.
4. **Right Conduct of Action:** Right action can be broken down into five precepts, each covering negative and positive behavior. The first of the five

commandments prohibit killing and prescribe charity and kindness to all living things. The other four precepts deal with theft and generosity; sensuality, sincerity, and honesty; and the use of intoxicating drink or drugs. Two tend to be stressed above the others: abstaining from taking life and sensual indulgence.

5. **Right Livelihood:** This urges people to steer clear of businesses or activities that compromise the conduct of life according to the Buddha, so any livelihoods that cause harm or injustice to others should be shunned. Five forms of trade in particular are to be avoided: trade in arms, living beings, flesh, intoxicating drinks, and poison. But the occupations of soldier, hunter, and fisherman are also to be avoided, as are usury and soothsaying.

6. **Right Endeavor or Effort:** Fostering noble qualities and rejecting ignoble vices.

7. **Right Mindfulness:** The development of intellectual awareness in order to make spiritual progress. This opens a new layer of Buddhist philosophy, since it urges you to train your mind in such a manner as to recognize what is important and not be led astray. Four areas of experience should be examined: your body, feelings, mind, and the ideas that arise in your mind. With attention to these four fundamentals, you perfect the seven factors of Enlightenment: mindfulness, investigation of the *Dhamma* (the teachings of Buddha), energy, rapture, tranquility, meditative concentration, and equanimity.

8. **Right Meditation or Concentration:** Emphasizes meditation, which leads to a full understanding of the impermanence of things and eventually to nirvana. Steady, easy breathing is ideal, while the mind tries to concentrate on tranquility. Early on, meditating should involve devices to assist memory, such as counting or repeating formulas in order to assist concentration. There are five mental hindrances that need to be conquered, or at least muted, before meditation can really begin: sensuality, ill will, laziness, worry, and skepticism.

These eight aspects of the path fit three attributes:

1. **Ethical conduct (sila)** includes universal love and compassion and tolerance. This especially includes parts three, four, and five on the path.

Right speech involves truth telling and refraining from malicious words. Right conduct includes peacemaking and refraining from violence, cheating, and illicit sexual liaisons. Right livelihood also refers to earning your living through honorable employment.

2. **Mental discipline (samadhi, for Hindus "holy vision"):** You must be disciplined, exercise self-control, and concentrate your mind on the noble truths (parts six, seven, and eight). To achieve this end concentration, you might practice breathing and other modes of yoga or meditation.

3. **Wisdom:** If you live in universal love and discipline, you will attain wisdom and enlightenment. Parts one and two especially serve this end.

All in all, Buddha's core philosophy is a practical and spiritual approach to living. The philosophy has led many to live peaceful, fulfilled lives.

Nirvana and Karma

As the Buddhists use it, the term karma applies to the many worlds that have passed away and the many more that are yet to come. They believe in the law of cause and effect: Positive actions build up merit; negative ones detract. Buddhists try to live the good life and believe that good karma causes a person to be reborn in a form that is more enlightened and, therefore, allows for greater progress toward the ultimate goal. According to Buddhism, the ultimate goal is to be released from the law of karma altogether—to attain nirvana.

There is considerable confusion over what "nirvana" means. Nirvana means "to extinguish." It represents perfect bliss. Followers of Buddha who achieve nirvana are said to have extinguished or conquered their desires. This means that they can avoid the cycle of rebirth.

Nirvana, or ridding yourself of the delusion of ego or freeing yourself the claims of the mundane world is the aim of a Buddhist's religious practice. Compare this to the approach of Hinduism, where the goal is to achieve the atman/Brahman identity. Buddhists teach the concept of anatman, no self.

For them, all that exists is the Brahman, the universal soul, and understanding the Brahman brings enlightenment. Those who successfully achieve enlightenment overcome the round of rebirths, thus achieving the final goal.

Literature

The teachings of the Buddha were first transmitted orally from one monk or nun to another. They were eventually written down on palm leaf manuscripts in Sri Lanka to create the Dhammapada. Written in Pali, the Indian dialect that the Buddha spoke, and known as the Pali canon, it records the conversations of the Buddha. The book is a wonderful spiritual testimony, one of the very few religious masterpieces in the world. It has been used in Sri Lanka for centuries as a manual for novices; it is said that every monk can recite it from memory. It is also popular in both Theravada and Mahayana traditions, which will be discussed later.

Other written works also contain records of conversations the Buddha had when he was teaching. Three such works were gathered into a Tripitaka or "Three Baskets," so called because the palm-leaf manuscripts were kept in three woven baskets. The Three Baskets are: Sutta Pitaka, the basket of discourse, attributed to the Buddha; Vinaya Pitaka, the basket of discipline, containing the regulations for monastic life; and Abhidhamma Pitaka, the basket of special doctrine, containing what might be called further knowledge (not entirely attributed to the Buddha, but highly venerated).

Worship and Practices

In countries where Buddhism is the majority religion, devotion to the Buddhist life is a natural part of it: diet; the job, trade, or profession chosen; daily meditation; and giving offerings at shrines, temples, and/or monasteries.

Like other religions, Buddhism has a collection of its own practices; two of these are deeply rooted in the Buddhist history. The first one is the veneration of the Buddha. Most Buddhists recognize the existence of many Buddhas, depending upon which Buddhist sect they belong to, the part of the country they live in, and maybe even how their family was brought up. When they go to the temple, they will make their devotions to any number of Buddhas. The devotions will be carried out in the shrine room; many adherents also have a shrine room in their homes. In carrying out a devotion, the person stands before a holy image—art that shows, perhaps, the Buddha sitting in the lotus position (a yoga meditation position with the legs crossed) with his outstretched arm touching the earth, signifying his enlightenment—then the adherent would recite the three refuges:

I take refuge in the Buddha.

I take refuge in the dharma.

I take refuge in the sangha.

After saying the devotions, the adherent usually bows three times before the holy image in respect to the three refuges, which are also known as the Three Jewels. Chanting may be done and offerings made.

The second basic practice is the exchange that takes place between monks and the laity. Buddhists have always stressed involvement in the community, and an understanding of the relationship between the monks and nuns and the lay segments of the community has developed.

Sangha

An assembly of monks, for instance in a monastery, is called by a generic name, sangha, which dates to the origins of Buddhism. Ordination as a Buddhist monk requires accepting and keeping certain monastic rules, including the Three Jewels and the Five Precepts that prohibit drinking, lying, stealing, harming a living being, and what some call misuse of the senses.

Most people know the common image of a Buddhist monk—the shaven head, robe, and look of serenity and pleasure. A monk will own nothing except the robe on his back and his alms bowl. Originally, the life of a monk was one of poverty and begging; today, most of these practices have become symbolic. Nevertheless, the life of a monk is still one of strict adherence to the monastic rules.

A new monk has to accept the Five Precepts as absolute rules. Other rules are contained in the Vinaya Texts, and depending on the school, number between 227 and 253 rules. The first part of the texts has the four gravest rules—the prohibition of sexual intercourse, theft, murder, and exaggeration of one's miraculous powers. A monk who breaks one of these rules may be expelled from the monastery.

Every two weeks the monks assemble and recite all the rules. They pause after each one so that any monk who has transgressed may confess and receive his punishment. Other rules deal with transgressions of a lesser nature.

FACT

Most Buddhist schools still stress celibacy, although some groups, particularly in Tibet and Japan, have relaxed this discipline. In other areas, young men can join a monastery for a short time, but do not have to vow to remain celibate for the rest of their lives.

Meditation

Meditation, which has carved out a secular place for itself in the Western world, has been part of the practice of many Eastern religions, including Buddhism and Hinduism, for centuries. Meditation can open the door to subtle perceptions, which can change conviction and character, and the daily practice of meditation nourishes the roots of the personality. According to medical literature, meditation calms the emotions, strengthens the nerves, and even lowers blood pressure. However, wonderful though that might be for health, it is not the prime reason a Buddhist practices meditation.

Because the Buddha reached his enlightenment through meditation, the practice is the most important aspect of Buddhism. The Sanskrit word, "samadhi," recognized in both Hinduism and Buddhism, means "total self-collectedness." It is the highest state of mental concentration that a person can achieve while still bound to the body. It is a state of profound, utter absorption, undisturbed by desire, anger, or any ego-generated emotion. Samadhi is an absolute necessity for attaining release from the cycle of rebirth.

Zen

Zen is one of the oldest traditional schools of Buddhism in Japan. It originated in China, where it's referred to as Ch'an Buddhism. Zen teaches that the potential to achieve enlightenment is in everyone, but lies dormant because of ignorance. This potential can be awakened by breaking through the boundaries of logical thought. A person must try to understand that words are only the surface of things and learn to get beyond words alone in order to understand the meaning of existence.

ESSENTIAL

The most famous *koan* is the question, "What is the sound of one hand clapping?" This riddle is not solvable using conceptual, rational thought. The purpose of this and other koans is to block reasons and permit a direct realization of reality.

Zen monks spend endless time, more than most people could handle, meditating on a phrase called a *koan*. A koan is a special kind of problem or paradoxical statement used as a meditation discipline. The effort to solve a koan is intended to exhaust the analytic intellect and the egotistic will.

Rituals and Customs

Buddhist monks and nuns generally get involved only marginally in the major rites (birth, marriage, and death), except for death. A monk would attend celebrations of birth and weddings or the bride and groom might visit the monastery and present gifts to the monk; in turn, the monk might offer a sermon. Marriage rituals are sometimes performed in the West today, but this is a new development.

Death in the Buddhist community, and in the Tibetan Buddhist community in particular, has been described as the science of dying—the rituals and beliefs around death are important and complex. A full account of these rituals and beliefs is available in the Tibetan Book of the Dead.

Pilgrimages form an important part of Buddhist ritual. Hundreds of sites draw pilgrims, who often come a very long way to reach a specific destination. While some of the sites might seem esoteric, many are shared by other religions such as Hinduism, Islam, and Christianity. Some locations are obvious, for instance, the Buddha's birthplace at Lumbini Grove; Bodh

Gaya, where he found enlightenment; Sarnath, where he preached his first sermon on the Four Noble Truths; and Kusinara, where he died.

The places, dates, and nature of Buddhist festivals are many and various. The important times in the life of the Buddha are obvious events to be celebrated. It's sufficient to say that a Buddhist festival is a colorful event with temple fairs and visits, alms giving and offerings at shrines, puppet shows, and theatrical and musical events.

CHAPTER 6

Christianity

Christianity arose from Judaism and rapidly developed as a faith with a separate identity, based on the teachings of Jesus of Nazareth, referred to as the Christ. There are many different denominations within Christianity. These have evolved over the years often because of disagreements about teachings or through different ways of worshiping. Most, however, agree on the basic tenets of the faith. The story of Jesus Christ's ministry and an early history of Christianity are contained in the New Testament of the Holy Bible.

Origins and Development

The founder of Christianity, Jesus of Nazereth (4 B.C.–A.D. 29) lived in Palestine during the height of the Roman Empire. In Palestine at the time of Jesus, the political situation of the Jews was chaotic. They had been in servitude for nearly 100 years, were extensively taxed by their masters, the Romans, and were suffering from increased internal conflict within their own ranks. The main source of this conflict was the rivalry between the Sadducees and the Pharisees.

The Sadducees were a priestly sect that had flourished for about two centuries before the Second Temple of Jerusalem was destroyed by fire in August A.D. 70. The sect was made up of aristocratic families and merchants, the wealthy elements of the population who clung to birthright and social and economic position. They tended to have good relations with their Roman rulers and generally represented the conservative view within Judaism.

Their immediate rivals, the Pharisees, claimed to be authorities on piety and learning. They were seen as a political party concerned with the laws of rabbinic traditions, especially its holiness code—including dietary laws and agricultural rules governing the fitness of food for Pharisaic consumption—and the observance of the Sabbath and festivals.

The core difference between the Sadducees and the Pharisees was the interpretation of the content and extent of God's revelation to the Jewish people. The Sadducees, because of their willingness to compromise with the Roman rulers, aroused the hatred of the common people.

A third group of Jews, the Essenes—a virtual monastic brotherhood of property-sharing communities devoted to lives of disciplined piety—considered the world too corrupt to allow Judaism to renew itself, so they dropped out of any conflict.

It was into this complex political-religious cauldron that Jesus added a further element of dissension.

Jesus Christ

Jesus was born in the Roman province of Palestine (present-day Israel, Palestine, and Jordan), probably just before the first century A.D., during the reign of Herod the Great. The term "Christ" comes from the Greek word *Xristos*, which can be translated as "the anointed one." It has the same meaning as *meshiach* or *messiah* in Hebrew. Christ is applied to Jesus as a title to indicate his status.

The Early Years

Jesus was born in a stable to Mary and Joseph of Nazareth, in Galilee. They had traveled to Bethlehem, near Jerusalem, because of a Roman census. Their son, Jesus, grew up as a Jewish boy and followed Jewish traditions. There is virtually nothing on record about his young life except that his father was a carpenter; it is presumed Jesus took up his father's profession. In the book of Luke, one of the books of the New Testament (the Christian portion of the Bible, consisting of twenty-seven books), Jesus was presented at the temple and interacted with the teachers there when he was twelve.

It wasn't until he was about thirty years old that Jesus emerged as a teacher himself. It was then that he left his life with his parents in Nazareth and began three years of travel throughout Judea. He never went more than ninety miles from his birthplace; he owned nothing, attended no school, and produced no written works. Nor are there objective records of his life. The records that are available in the New Testament, for instance, are often contradictory. What does seem to be reliable is that the ministry of Jesus commenced with his baptism by John the Baptist.

QUOTE

In the Authorized King James Version of the Bible, the Gospel According to Saint Luke 3:21–23, it is written: "Now when all the people were baptized, it came to pass, that Jesus also being baptized, and praying, the heaven was opened. And the Holy Ghost descended in a bodily shape like a dove upon him, and a voice came from heaven, which said, Thou art my beloved Son; in thee I am well pleased. And Jesus himself began to be about thirty years of age . . . ."

The Teachings of Jesus

Following his baptism, Jesus began to preach, teach, and perform miracles throughout Judea. As he did so, he recruited many disciples, including a core group of twelve referred to as the apostles. At the beginning of his ministry, Jesus restricted his work to his fellow Jews, but it wasn't long before Jesus broadened his preaching to include non-Jews, known as Gentiles.

Jesus' style of delivery is said to have been charismatic, with great moral authority. He spoke in the form of parables and of the coming of the kingdom of God. He was also a healer—raising Lazarus from the dead and curing a woman of an effusion of blood. The gospels record that he was a miracle worker, that he calmed the sea, changed water into wine, and fed the multitudes with only a few fish and loaves of bread. He was accused of challenging existing laws, while he insisted he fulfilled them. However, he often performed miracles on the Sabbath, which was a violation of Jewish laws.

As Jesus' fame and reputation grew, so did the resentment of the authorities. Perhaps it was Jesus' dramatic visit to a Jerusalem temple that sparked the authorities to take direct action. Merchants used the temple to conduct their business, and Jesus cast them out, saying that the temple was a house of prayer and not a den of thieves. When Jesus was questioned by Jewish leaders, his answers riled them. He claimed that he was the Son of God and that the highest commandment is to love God.

The Crucifixion

The most important celebration for Jews at that time was the Passover meal on the first evening of the festival. Supporters of Jesus had made arrangements for him and his followers to hold their celebration in an upper room they had prepared. At that meal, now called The Last Supper, Jesus' twelve disciples were in attendance. It was there that Jesus established the new covenant by instituting the Eucharist, also called Holy Communion or The Lord's Supper, by sharing bread with the words, "This is my body" and wine with, "This is my blood." He told the disciples to do the same in his memory.

In an effort to deal with Jesus and deliver him to the Roman justices, the Jewish authorities, who claimed Jesus was guilty of violating the law of Moses and preaching blasphemy, approached Judas Iscariot, one of the twelve disciples, and offered him thirty pieces of silver to betray Jesus. As arranged, Judas identified Jesus to the authorities by kissing him on the cheek in the garden of Gethsemane, where he was praying with his disciples.

Jesus was arrested and brought before Pontius Pilate, the Roman governor. On examination, Pilate couldn't find sufficient evidence against Jesus, but the large crowd demanded his execution. Pilate was forced to agree to the crucifixion of Jesus. According to the gospels, Pilate then took water and washed his hands before the multitude, saying, "I am innocent of the blood of this just person; see ye to it."

The Resurrection

As written in the gospels, Jesus was hanged on a cross to die. One of Jesus' followers requested and received permission to bury him. He laid Jesus' body in a cave and covered the opening with a heavy stone. This took place on a Friday, the day before the Sabbath. On the day after the Sabbath, women followers of Jesus went to prepare his body and discovered that the stone had been rolled away from the entrance to the cave. An angel then appeared and told them Jesus was alive, that he had risen from the dead.

Jesus revealed himself first to Mary Magdalene. Later, at Pentecost, Jesus appeared to his disciples and commanded them to make disciples of all nations, baptizing them in the name of the Father, the Son, and the Holy Spirit. During the weeks that followed, many who had known Jesus reported seeing him alive; they believed he had risen from the dead. Forty days after his resurrection, the disciples said they saw Jesus lifted up into heaven. That was the last time they saw him.

Central Beliefs

The belief that Jesus rose from the dead is central to Christians. As the Son of God, Jesus represents the person that all Christians must strive to be like. Christians believe that he was perfect and that he came to earth to teach God's plan. Christians, as well as Jews and Muslims, believe in one all-powerful creator—God. Thus, the most important belief for Christians is that the world and everything in it is an expression of God's power and love.

From the beginning of Christianity, followers have attempted to agree on statements of beliefs, called creeds. A creed is a set of principles or opinions especially as it refers to a religious philosophy of life. According to tradition, Jesus' twelve disciples wrote the Apostles' Creed, but it was actually developed in the early church to use with persons receiving instructions before they were baptized. The present text of the Apostles' Creed is similar to the baptismal creed used in the Church of Rome in the third and fourth centuries. In A.D. 325, a formal doctrine of Christian faith was adopted in Nicaea, referred to as the Nicene Creed. It gradually replaced other forms of baptismal creeds and was acknowledged as the official statement of faith used in the Roman Catholic, Anglican, and many Protestant churches.

FACT

Christians believe that Jesus died for their sins and that God's love has the strength to overcome the worst of human sin. God can forgive the sins of anyone who repents and wishes to lead a new life; hence, the expression "born again" applies to those who begin a new life following repentance.

Here is a modern English version of the Apostles' Creed:

I believe in God, the Father almighty, creator of Heaven and earth and of all things visible and invisible, and in one Lord Jesus Christ.

I believe in Jesus Christ, his only Son, our Lord.

He was conceived by the power of the Holy Spirit and born of the Virgin Mary.

He suffered under Pontius Pilate, was crucified, died, and was buried.

He descended to the dead.

On the third day he rose again.

He ascended into heaven, and is seated at the right hand of the Father.

He will come again to judge the living and the dead.

I believe in the Holy Spirit, the holy Catholic church, the communion of saints, the forgiveness of sins, the resurrection of the body, and the life everlasting.

Amen.

The Spread of Christianity

Christianity owes its initial dissemination to two men of vastly different backgrounds and personalities: Peter and Paul.

Peter

Peter's original name was Simon. He was a fisherman called to be a disciple of Jesus at the beginning of his ministry. He lived in Capernaum, where he and his brother Andrew were in partnership with James and John, the sons of Zebedee. It appears that Peter was not a well-educated man; he was untrained in Mosaic Law and it's doubtful that he knew Greek.

QUOTE

The story of how Jesus named Peter was reported in Matthew 16:18: "And I say also unto thee. That thou art Peter, and upon this rock I will build my church; and the gates of hell shall not prevail against it."

From all accounts in the New Testament, Peter was a man of strong emotions. He is depicted as rash, hasty, capable of anger, often gentle, but firm. He professed love for Jesus and was capable of great loyalty. Peter is invariably mentioned first in lists of the disciples and designated as the spokesman for the group.

Given the information from the gospels, it's not surprising that Peter should emerge immediately after the death of Jesus as the leader of the earliest church. Peter dominated the community for nearly fifteen years following the Resurrection. It was he who raised his voice and preached at Pentecost, the day when the church came into being. It was he who served as an advocate for the apostles before the Jewish religious court in Jerusalem. It was he who led the others in extending the church, going first to the Samaritans then to the Mediterranean coast where he introduced Gentiles into the church. When he accepted Gentiles and baptized them in the name of Jesus Christ without requiring the men to be circumcised, he encountered opposition from Jewish Christians and others. It didn't take long after that for his leadership in Jerusalem to come to an end.

How Peter's leadership ended is shrouded in uncertainty. Evidence that he lived in Rome and claims that he founded the Church of Rome or that he served as its first bishop or Pope are in dispute. The date of his death is unknown, and archaeological investigations have not located Peter's tomb.

Paul

Paul, on the other hand, was the powerhouse who fueled the growth of Christianity. It is safe to say that it was due to Paul more than anyone else that Christianity grew from a small sect within Judaism to a world religion.

Paul was first and foremost an enigma. His original name was Saul of Tarsus. A Jew, he inherited Roman citizenship, perhaps granted by the Romans as a reward for mercenary service. This might explain why he had two names: He used his Jewish name, Saul, within the Jewish community and his Roman name, Paul, when speaking Greek.

He had a strict Jewish upbringing and received training as a rabbi in Jerusalem under Gamaliel. Like most rabbis, he supported himself with a manual trade; in his case, tent making. He obviously grew into a man of some sophistication.

Although it is fairly certain that he never met Jesus while in Jerusalem, he learned enough about him and his followers to regard the Christian movement as a threat to Pharisaic Judaism, of which he was an enthusiast. He had become a member of the Pharisees, the Jewish sect that promoted purity and fidelity to the Law of Moses.

Paul's first appearance on the historical Jewish-Christian landscape was as an oppressor of the members of the newly founded church. Serious persecutions of Christians started with converts in Jerusalem, and Saul was a fierce advocate of the regime of persecution. So eager was Saul to pursue, threaten, and slaughter Christians that he went to the high priest to request letters to the synagogues of Damascus so that if he discovered Christians, whether they were men or women, he might bring them bound to Jerusalem. As he came near Damascus, it is written in Acts 9:

> *. . . suddenly there shined around about him a light from the heavens: And he fell to the earth, and heard a voice saying unto him, Saul, Saul, why persecutest thou me? And he said, Who art thou, Lord? And the Lord said, I am Jesus whom thou persecutest: it is hard for thee to kick against the pricks. And he trembling and astonished said, Lord, what wilt thou have me do? And the Lord said unto him, Arise and go into the city, and it shall be told thee what thou must do.*

Three years after his conversion, Paul went to Jerusalem to meet Peter and James. At the meeting, they recognized Paul as an apostle together with the founders of the church. In Jerusalem, Paul was accused of bringing a Gentile into the inner courts of the temple, beyond the barrier excluding non-Jews. He was arrested, partly to save his life from the mob. As a citizen of Rome, he was able to avoid trial and appeal to Caesar. He was taken to Rome and kept under house arrest for two years. Paul was eventually convicted of the charges against him. No reliable account of his death exists.

His letters, which were collected for general circulation, have become a standard reference for Christian teaching. In addition, Saul of Tarsus is probably the first example in religious history of a sinner who was truly born again.

Holy Writings

The holy book of Christianity is the Bible. It is divided into two segments: the Old Testament and the New Testament. The word "testament" means "witness." Generally speaking, the average Christian looks at the Old Testament—also known as the Hebrew Bible—as the part that concerns the Jews, their history, and their prophecies, and at the New Testament as the part that concerns Jesus and the apostles.

While that could be looked at as an oversimplification, it is nonetheless a very adequate way of approaching the Bible. There is no question that the Bible's impact has been, and continues to be, immeasurable. The survival of the Jewish religion, for instance, and its subsequent influence in the history of Western culture are direct results of Biblical writings.

The first complete Bible in English appeared in the late fourteenth century and has been retranslated into English dozens of times. In the modern world, missionaries have translated the Bible into nearly every written language in existence.

FACT

The designations "old" and "new" seemed to have been adopted after A.D. 200 to distinguish the books of the Mosaic covenant and those of the "new" covenant in Christ. The Old Testament is substantially the Hebrew Bible with its three divisions—law, prophets, and writings, amounting in all to twenty-four documents in the traditional Jewish reckoning. The New Testament comprises twenty-seven documents, written within the century following Jesus' death.

Some of the early Christian thinkers leaned toward the view that there was no need to have an Old Testament, but the dominant position conceded that Christianity needed to know about God's work on earth prior to Jesus, and the only place to get that knowledge was from the Old Testament.

FACT

In the early days of Christianity, various sects were vying for recognition. In this setting, much of what was written was later judged to be apocryphal, meaning of doubtful origin, invented, or mythical. These writings were subsequently denounced.

As for the New Testament and the way it evolved, it took several centuries for religious leaders to come to agreement on what information would be included. During the early years, there were many different versions and theologies of Christianity throughout the Mediterranean world and dozens of written gospels. Of the writings that Christian groups considered sacred, twenty-seven were chosen to become the New Testament around A.D. 380. These twenty-seven books were the four gospels (Matthew, Mark, Luke, and John), Acts, twenty-one letters or epistles, and the Revelation of St. John the

Divine. Many of the twenty-one letters or epistles were attributed to Paul. John, a close friend of Jesus, is credited as the author of Revelation, the last book in the New Testament. It describes his vision of the end of time—the Apocalypse and Jesus' return.

Many Christian worship services include a reading from the Bible, often called the lesson. Often, members of the congregation will take turns reading it from the pulpit or lectern.

Rituals and Customs

Different denominations celebrate varying rites, festivals, and sacraments. The Protestant churches tend to be less formal than the Orthodox and Roman Catholic ones. The following are the common rituals and customs performed in Christianity.

Prayer

It is prayer that forms the backbone of Christian religious life. Although specified periods for communal prayer are not set (unlike in some other religions), Sunday is usually the chosen day for Christians. This is not only the first day of the week, but also the day on which Jesus rose from the dead. The typical place for prayer is the church. However, Christians are also urged to pray regularly either in public or in private.

FACT

While prayers are said frequently for someone who is ill, prayers—whether by a group or individual—can cover almost every kind of need or occasion. They are used to thank God for his gifts, to ask for forgiveness, and to petition for blessings and favors.

Prayer has been described as a pilgrimage of the spirit; many people consider it the purest form of religious expression. It expresses the desire to enter into a personal and constant intimate relationship with God.

Baptism

Baptism marks the beginning of life as a Christian. It is the emergence of a new person upon whom a new name is conferred. It is the total annulment of the sins of the person's past, from which an innocent person emerges. At the baptism, the person becomes a member of the church and is incorporated into the body of Jesus Christ. Most Christian churches baptize babies, but some denominations baptize only adults. Some churches hold that when children baptized as infants reach adulthood, they must confirm their beliefs.

Historically, baptism was meant for adults who were capable of accepting the ancient liturgies themselves. The Roman Catholic Church in more modern times asked adults, parents, or godparents to make the decision on behalf of the infant, with the expectation that the child would accept the decision made.

Eucharist

Most formal churches, for example Orthodox, Roman Catholic, and Anglican, will include the celebration of The Last Supper in their services, sometimes called the Eucharist, Mass, or Holy Communion. Only a minister or priest is authorized to perform the ceremony.

Confirmation

Confirmation usually takes place in adolescence or adulthood. In some traditions, it is seen as a confirmation of vows the candidate could not make for herself as a child. In both Anglicanism and Lutheranism, confirmation is generally preceded by instruction in the catechism. Other Protestants deny that confirmation is a sacrament, but they do sometimes use the term to mark the transition of baptized members into full membership of the church, including the right to receive Holy Communion.

Marriage

Christianity has contributed to a spiritualization of marriage and family life. Marriage can be called the most intimate form in which the fellowship of believers is realized. In many traditions, there is respect for those who choose not to marry—monks, nuns, and Roman Catholic priests, for instance. But all Christians regard marriage as a serious step and a commitment, as marriage vows are made before God.

Death

Christians believe that death is not the end of life because Jesus taught and promised eternal life for all believers. At the funeral service, the body of the dead person is commemorated and comfort is offered to the bereaved. The deceased is committed into God's care; thereafter, the body is buried or cremated, depending on the wishes of the deceased or the tradition of the church.

Religious Festivals and Holy Holidays

It may surprise even devout Christians to learn that there are more than a dozen holy days of obligation in the Catholic Church. It is not Easter and Christmas that command the attention of the faithful; there are holy days in every season of the calendar.

- **Christmas Day:** Christmas is the feast of the nativity of Jesus, celebrated in Roman Catholic and Protestant churches on December 25. The observance of Christmas did not become widespread until the fourth century. The date was likely chosen for its proximity to the Epiphany, which in the East originally included a commemoration of the nativity.
- **Epiphany:** The word "epiphany" refers to a sudden understanding of something, usually of divine power. It is a prime Christian feast celebrated on January 6, also called Twelfth Day or Little Christmas.
- **Ash Wednesday:** Ash Wednesday is the first day of Lent, a period of preparation for Easter. On this day, ashes are placed on the foreheads of the faithful to remind them of death, the sorrow they should feel for their sins, and the necessity of changing their lives.
- **Palm Sunday:** Palm Sunday in the Christian calendar is the Sunday before Easter and the first day of the holy week. The palms recall the time of Jesus' entry into Jerusalem, riding upon an ass, when his followers shouted, "Hosanna" and scattered palms in his path.

- **Easter:** Easter is the chief Christian feast, commemorating the resurrection of Jesus after his crucifixion. In the West, Easter is celebrated on the Sunday following the first full moon after the vernal equinox. The Orthodox Eastern Church calculates Easter differently; thus, the Orthodox Easter comes several weeks after that of the West.

- **Ascension Day:** The Ascension signifies the departure of Jesus from the earth as related in the Gospels according to Mark (16) and Luke (24) and in Acts (1.1–11). The commemoration of Ascension Thursday, forty days after Easter, is one of the principal feasts in most Christian churches.

- **Pentecost:** Pentecost is a commemoration of an event that happened fifty days after the resurrection of Jesus (the word "Pentecost" comes from the Greek meaning "fiftieth"). The Holy Spirit, according to the Acts of the Apostles, descended on the disciples in the form of tongues of fire, accompanied by the sound of a rush of wind, and gave them the power of speaking in such a way that people of different languages could understand them. Pentecost is observed as the birthday of the church and the feast of the Holy Spirit.

- **Assumption of the Virgin Mary:** The Assumption is one of the principal feasts honoring Mary. It celebrates the Christian belief that, at the end of her life, Mary was physically taken into heaven.

- **All Saints' Day:** All Saints' Day is a feast day—celebrated on November 1 in the West—of the Roman Catholic and Anglican churches to honor all saints, known and unknown. In medieval England, the festival was known as All Hallows', hence the name Halloween (meaning "All Hallows' eve") for the preceding evening.

- **All Souls' Day:** On All Souls' Day, a feast of the Roman Catholic Church celebrated November 2, the church on earth prays for the souls of the departed faithful still suffering in purgatory.

CHAPTER 7

Catholicism

Catholicism is a branch of Christianity. Today, Roman Catholics throughout the world outnumber all other Christians combined. While Catholicism has its own rituals and customs, it is a form of Christianity and therefore follows the basic tenets outlined in the previous chapter.

History of Catholicism

Christianity became an accepted religious path when Constantine emerged as the political power of the Roman Empire. Constantine was sympathetic to the Christians because his mother was a member of the faith. It has been reported that Constantine himself experienced a conversion experience during a battle in A.D. 312 when he had a vision of a cross with the message "IHS," meaning "by this sign" in Latin. Constantine was victorious in the battle after receiving this vision. His rise to power continued until A.D. 323, when he became emperor and established his seat of power in Byzantium, later known as Constantinople (now Istanbul).

As Christianity spread throughout the empire, theological interpretations began to differ in the East and West. Councils were held to establish orthodoxy and try to eliminate heresy. These councils became increasingly politicized. In 1054, the divide between Rome and the Eastern churches became permanent. The Eastern part became the Eastern Orthodox Church; the Western part became the Roman Catholic Church, with headquarters eventually in the Vatican in Rome, Italy.

The Eastern Orthodox and Roman Catholic Churches divided primarily for two reasons. One was over the issue of the authority of the papacy. When it came to doctrine, however, the most important disagreement was over the nature of Jesus Christ as both human and divine. The Eastern Church emphasized his divinity, while the Western church emphasized that plus his humanity.

Probably the most decisive era in the history of Roman Catholicism was during the Protestant Reformation. On October 31, 1517, the German priest and theology professor Martin Luther (1483–1546) tacked his famous *Ninety-five Theses* on the door of the castle church in Wittenburg, Germany. Luther's bold act has come to symbolize the inception of the Protestant Reformation.

The Protestant movement threw almost all of Europe into war throughout most of the sixteenth and much of the early seventeenth centuries. As it turned out, the final division of Protestant and Catholic was determined mainly by the religious affiliation of the individual princes and kings who emerged victorious. France, for instance, remained Catholic, and the numerous city-states of Germany formed a patchwork of Protestant and Catholic enclaves.

The historical development of the Catholic Church has been fraught with complicated dissension, not the least of which was the claim that it was the successor of the church started by the apostle Peter. However, the references to Peter in the New Testament and his identification with the Church of Rome show so many contradictions that even among scholars there is no consensus regarding his role in the early church.

ESSENTIAL

There were political, economic, and moral factors that aided and abetted Luther's protests, notably the financial burdens imposed by Rome on outlying parishes, and clerical excesses—particularly the selling of so-called indulgences that helped citizens atone in advance for sins real and contemplated—aroused hostility toward the church.

The Roman Catholic Church conducted its liturgy in Latin well into the twentieth century; sweeping changes were made at the Second Vatican Council. Officially known as the twenty-first ecumenical council of the Roman Catholic Church, it was announced by Pope John XXIII on January 25, 1959. The work of the council continued under Pope Paul VI up until its completion on December 8, 1965. The council enacted sixteen documents detailing how the church would function going forward. One of the documents, titled "The Pastoral Constitution on the Church in the World of Today," acknowledged the changes that had taken place and the requirement for the church to relate to the needs of a modern culture.

FACT

Major changes were authorized in another of the sixteen documents, the "Constitution on the Sacred Liturgy." It allowed for church members' participation in the celebration of the Mass and sanctioned significant changes in the texts, forms, and language used in the celebration of the Mass and the administration of the sacraments.

The Hierarchy in Catholicism

Jesus Christ is the invisible head of the church, and by his authority, the Pope is the visible head. The hierarchy of the Roman Catholic Church is a structure of authority that weaves its way from pope to parish priest.

Pope

Over the centuries, the Bishop of Rome became the leading authority in both civil and religious matters and assumed the title "Pope" from the Latin *papa* and the Greek *pappas,* meaning "father." The pope is the successor to St. Peter, thus the shepherd of all Christians and the representative (or vicar) of Christ.

The pope's supremacy is grounded in Matthew 16:18–19, but this supremacy is not recognized outside the Roman Catholic Church. But the church holds that God will not permit the pope to make an error in a solemn official declaration concerning a matter of faith or morality. However, the First Vatican Council created the doctrine of papal infallibility, with the bishops voting 533 in favor and only two against. (Actually, some sixty bishops in the minority did not want to vote for the doctrine, and because they did not want to expose their dissent publicly by voting negative, they packed up and left Rome.) The pope is infallible when speaking *ex cathedra*—literally "from the chair" or his position of authority.

Despite the controversy concerning papal infallibility, the Pope is recognized as having supreme religious authority. The College of Cardinals elects a new Pope when the one in office dies.

Priests

Each local church is attached to a district called a parish. A priest runs the parish and is a liturgical leader and pastor. He is responsible for the administration of the sacraments, including the Mass. A priest hears confessions and assigns penance.

Bishops

A group of parishes in a region are called a diocese and are presided over by a bishop. Bishops are priests nominated by other bishops and appointed to their office by the Pope. Traditionally, a bishop was a teacher and leader of worship, but today a bishop is more of a manager and administrator.

Cardinals

Cardinals are bishops who have been chosen and elevated to this position by the Pope. They join the College of Cardinals, which is a group of approximately 120 bishops who have also been elevated to cardinal. Membership of the college is divided among those who hold office in the Vatican and those who are bishops in major cities in the world. The United States has eight cardinals.

The sacred College of Cardinals of the Roman Catholic Church is, in essence, the electoral college of the papacy. Its members are appointed by the pope. A cardinal's insignia resemble those of the bishop, except for a red, broad-brimmed, tasseled hat.

The Virgin Mary

The Virgin Mary is revered as the mother of God, and holds a unique devotional position in the Catholic Church. Catholics gave her the title Queen of Heaven. They believe that she rules over death in that capacity.

Based on the gospels of St. Matthew and St. Luke, Jesus Christ, who had no natural father, was conceived by Mary through the power of the Holy Spirit. Most Christian churches and Islam accept the virgin birth of Jesus.

Prayers to the Virgin Mary include the Ave Maria Prayer, which praises God and asks for intercession:

Hail Mary, full of grace!

The Lord is with thee.

Blessed are thou among women,

And blessed is the fruit of thy womb, Jesus.

Holy Mary, mother of God.

Pray for us sinners

Now and at the hour of our death.

Amen

Sin, Confession, and Penitence

The Catholic Church teaches that penance is a sacrament instituted by Jesus Christ. The church recognizes two kinds of sin: venial and mortal. Venial sins concern lesser offenses and carry lesser consequences. Mortal sins are obviously more dire, as are their consequences.

FACT

The term "sin" denotes an unethical act in religion. In particular, in Judaism, Christianity, and Islam it denotes disobedience to a personal God. By contrast, the term does not arise in belief systems such as Buddhism, where there is no personal deity.

It used to be that Catholics were instructed to observe a weekly rite of confession; however, this sacrament has declined in ritual observance, although it does remain an important part of a Catholic's spiritual life. To make an act of confession, the penitent has to enter the confessional box. This is typically a boxlike structure with a division creating two halves. There is a small, screened sliding door in the division. The penitent sits in one half, the priest in the other. However, today many Catholics have the option of a face-to-face confession in a reconciliation room. The principle remains the same; only the form has changed.

The penitent says to the priest, "Bless me father for I have sinned. It has been (however long) since my last confession." Then the penitent says what he considers to be his sins. The priest will ask if the penitent is sorry. The answer to this question is important, because if the penitent isn't genuinely sorry and does not make a firm commitment to change his ways, he won't be forgiven. After the sins have been confessed, the penitent then finishes by saying an Act of Contrition. The following is an example of an Act of Contrition prayer:

My God, I am sorry for my sins with all my heart. In choosing to do wrong and failing to do good, I have sinned against you whom I should love above all things. I firmly intend, with your help, to do penance, to sin no more, and to avoid whatever leads me to sin. Our Savior Jesus Christ suffered and died for us. In his name, my God, have mercy.

The priest will then give an admonition. Depending on the severity of the sins confessed, the penitent's penance might consist of several prayers. Then the priest will release the person, guilt free, with the directive, "Sin no more."

Holy Writings

The Roman Catholic Church bases its teachings on the Holy Bible. However, the Catholic canon differs from the Protestant version of the Bible. The Roman Catholic canon has forty-six books in the Old Testament; the Protestant version has thirty-nine. Both Bibles include twenty-seven books in the New Testament. This happened because of the questionable nature of certain texts. According to the Protestants, books of Tobit, Judith, and a few others were not inspired by God and therefore did not belong to the Scriptures.

The Ten Commandments hold an important place in Catholic teachings. Young Catholics are expected to memorize and understand them. They differ slightly from the Commandments as given in Exodus 20 in the Holy Bible because they have been simplified.

The Ten Commandments as they are taught to Catholics are:

1. I am the Lord your God. You shall not have strange gods before me.
2. You shall not take the name of the Lord thy God in vain.
3. Keep holy the Sabbath.
4. Honor your father and your mother.
5. You shall not kill.
6. You shall not commit adultery.
7. You shall not steal.
8. You shall not bear false witness against your neighbor.
9. You shall not covet your neighbor's spouse.
10. You shall not covet your neighbor's goods.

Sainthood

In the Roman Catholic Church, canonization is the process by which a person is declared a saint and is then included in the cannon of recognized saints. The process takes place in Rome, though dating to before the Middle Ages bishops canonized. Canonization is not required for martyrs—who are considered as saints upon death.

ESSENTIAL

One of the curious aspects of John Paul's pontificate has been the large number of canonizations during his papacy, which ran from October 1978 until his death in April 2005. By February 2002, the number of new saints was 455, with 1,277 beatified (or "blessed"). John Paul canonized some controversial figures, but his criterion seemed to be their living exemplary lives of Christian courage.

Beatification is the process preceding canonization. At this stage, the candidate is declared blessed and proof of two miracles is required. Until 1983, canonization procedures were akin to trials, during which the candidate would be defended by the church against a prosecutor, whose job it was to discount all evidence in favor of canonization. In this standoff, the spirited prosecutor was called *advocatus diaboli* (devil's advocate) and the defender *advocatus dei* (god's advocate). Of late, the devil's advocate position has been eliminated.

FACT

In July 1999, Archbishop Henry D'Souza from Calcutta began the process that led to the canonization of Mother Teresa. She died due to cardiac arrest in Calcutta, India, where she had worked with the "poorest of the poor" for five decades. Due to her efforts, her Missionaries of Charity now number over 4,000 nuns and 400 brothers who run homes, clinics, and schools in over 100 countries.

Despite the removal of the devil's advocate, the "burden of proof" of the would-be saint's qualifications may be more rigorous. For now, canonization requires proof of two additional miracles—in addition to the two considered in the beatification—in order to prove that the candidate's life was exemplary. In the Eastern Orthodox Church, canonization is usually effect by a synod of bishops.

Beliefs and Rituals

The Catholic Church has extensive rules; one such set of rules is called Precepts of the Catholic Church. While different sources may express them in varying ways, they essentially all come down to the same thing. Here is an example:

1. You shall attend Mass on Sundays and Holy Days of Obligation.
2. You shall confess your sins at least once a year.
3. You shall humbly receive the Lord Jesus in Holy Communion at least during the Easter season.
4. You shall observe the Holy Days of Obligation.
5. You shall observe the prescribed days of fasting and abstinence.
6. The faithful have the obligation of supporting the Church.

Another, even more extensive listing of rules, is the Canons. Canon Law is a complex system totaling 1,752 rules. They are regularly reviewed and updated. They define the internal structure and describe the rights and obligations of a Catholic religious life. The Canon Laws cover the gamut—from how and when marriages take place to the way in which church teachers are chosen.

The Seven Sacraments

The Catholic use of the word "sacrament" often causes confusion in the church. The accepted meaning is a religious ceremony or an outward and visible sign of inward and spiritual grace. The seven major sacraments of the Catholic Church are baptism, confirmation, holy Eucharist, holy orders, matrimony, reconciliation (or penance), and anointing of the sick. Of these seven, probably only two need further explanation—holy orders and anointing of the sick.

Holy orders is a sacrament reserved for the three separate levels of ordination—deacon, priest, and bishop. It is a sacrament whereby a person commits to serving the faith for life. When that commitment is made the church grants the recipient the responsibility and power to offer Mass, forgive sins, give blessings, administer other sacraments, and attend to the spiritual life of the people served.

ESSENTIAL

In the teaching of the Roman Catholic Church, purgatory is considered a place. But it is also a state; in particular, a state after death in which the soul destined for heaven is purified. One difference between purgatory and hell is that a soul in purgatory knows that its punishment is temporary; thus people pray for the dead person, knowing their prayers shorten the time the soul spends in purgatory.

Historically, anointing of the sick was called the last rites or extreme unction. The old rules reserved this sacrament for those about to die; today, it can also be used as a healing aid for the very ill, elderly, and frail. Timing is of the essence; having a "good death" is important, particularly to devout Catholics who wish to make their last confession to a priest and receive absolution. Once that's done, the dying person is anointed with consecrated oil.

Views on Controversial Topics

The Catholic Church opposes unrestricted abortion. The view of the Vatican is that as God is the originator of life, the conception of a child is a gift from him. The Church believes that life begins at the moment of conception; life is sacred and the fundamental value of life must be awarded to the soul in the womb. The Church allows abortion only if it is necessary to preserve the mother's life. Pregnancy resulting from rape, coercion, or ignorance has not been addressed. The Church only approves of birth control by natural means; it opposes artificial means such as pills, condoms, IUDs, foams, jellies, sterilization, and the noncompletion of the act of sexual union (*coitus interruptus* or the withdrawal method).

The Roman Catholic opinion on capital punishment has not yet received an absolute official directive, except that the Pope has certainly made strong statements against it. The Vatican proposes that life can be taken in cases of self-defense and a just war.

St. Thomas Aquinas, one of the principle saints of the Roman Catholic Church, addressed the requirements for a just war in his *Summa Theologica* (literally, the "sum of theology") in Part II, Question 40. There he writes:

In order for a war to be just, three things are necessary. First, the authority of the sovereign by whose command the war is to be waged. For it is not the business of a private individual to declare war, for he can seek redress of his rights from the tribunal of his superior.

Secondly, a just cause is required, namely that those who are attacked, should be attacked because they deserve it on account of some fault.

Thirdly, it is necessary that the belligerents should have a rightful intention, so that they intend the advancement of good, or the avoidance of evil. Hence Augustine says: "True religion looks upon as peaceful those wars that are waged not for motives of aggrandizement, or cruelty, but with the object of securing peace, of punishing evil-doers, and of uplifting the good."

CHAPTER 8

Prevalent Christian Faiths

The majority of the Christian denominations follow the established forms, beliefs, rituals, and customs of traditional Christianity; of course, there are exceptions to be noted. This chapter will concentrate on the earliest Christian faiths and their differences with the Roman Catholic Church.

Eastern Orthodoxy

Together with Roman Catholicism and Protestantism, Orthodoxy (at times called Eastern Orthodoxy and the Greek Orthodox Church) is one of the three principal traditions in Christianity. Orthodoxy evolved in 1054 following the climax of the major cultural, intellectual, and theosophical differences between the Roman Catholic Church and the Orthodox Church, called the Great Schism.

The schism can be traced to the Emperor Constantine (273–336), who moved the capital of the Roman Empire from Rome to Constantinople. Political matters came to a head in 1054, when Pope Leo IX excommunicated the patriarch of Constantinople, the leader of the Eastern Church. In turn, the patriarch condemned the Pope. Thus, the Christian church has been divided into the Roman Catholic West and the Eastern Orthodox East ever since.

What is the substance of the split? There were doctrinal and political factors aplenty. For one, there was the issue of the correct belief of the *filioque* clause ("filioque" is Latin for "and from the son"). In Roman Catholicism, the Nicene Creed includes the phrase, "And in the Holy Spirit, the Lord and giver of life, who proceeds from the Father and the Son." The words "and the son" were accepted in Rome around 1000 and adopted as part of the official doctrine. It is accepted by major denominations of the church, including the Roman Catholic, Anglican, and Protestant churches. But the adoption was offensive to the East. Their history made them more sensitive to the terminology of the Trinity. Their understanding of the matter emphasized the Holy Spirit, which descended *through* the son, not *from* the son.

Conflicts between East and West also resulted from their differences over the use of religious images. Christian worship included the veneration of pictures and statues symbolizing sacred figures from earliest times. Indeed, the humanity of Christ was a frequent theme of these works, and images of crucifixes were commonplace. Opponents such as Leo III the Isaurian (685–741) thought the use of such iconography led to idolatry and outlawed the veneration of icons in the eighth century. The policy came to be known as iconoclasm or icon breaking. Canon 36 of the Synod of Elivra in 305 was one of the earliest to prohibit images in the churches, "lest that which is worshipped and venerated is depicted on the walls."

Other bones of contention between West and East include the authority of the pope, different liturgical practices, and the issue of celibacy among priests. Orthodoxy allows for parish priests to be married.

Today, the Orthodox Church numbers about 225 million adherents.

Central Beliefs

Members believe the Orthodox Church was founded by Jesus Christ, and that it is the living manifestation of his presence. Orthodoxy further believes that the Christian faith and the church are inseparable, that it is impossible to know Jesus Christ, to share in the life of the Holy Trinity, or to be considered a Christian apart from the church, and that it is through the church that an individual is nurtured in the faith.

"Orthodoxy" means "the state of being orthodox, what is authorized or accepted as right and true." The Orthodox Church stresses "right belief and right glory." Essentially, Orthodox adherents' beliefs are very similar to those of other Christian traditions. For instance, they recognize seven sacraments—baptism, confirmation, holy Eucharist, confession, ordination, marriage, and holy unction—but express them slightly differently than other faiths.

When death occurs, the Orthodox Church believes the person's soul, being immortal, goes to God who created it. Immediately after death, the soul is judged, called the Particular Judgment. The final reward takes place later, at the time of the General Judgment. During the time between the Particular and the General Judgment, called the Intermediate State, a soul has a foretaste of the blessings or punishments accorded.

The church today is an invaluable treasury of rich liturgical tradition handed down from early Christianity. There is grandeur in the works of art and music and mystery in the Orthodox icons. Many of the churches are rich in history, the Church of Constantinople for one. Others are relatively young, such as the Church of Finland. Some are large, like the Church of Russia; some are small, like the Church of Sinai.

The international organization of the Orthodox churches is one of autocephalous (self-governing) branches. The churches hold the same dogmas and faiths, although the principle of "authority with freedom" prevails. Each church is independent in internal organization and follows its own particular customs. The Orthodox Church acknowledges that unity does not mean uniformity. In America, where Orthodoxy is relatively young, there are a number of dioceses and archdioceses linked directly to one of the auto-cephalous churches.

FACT

Each Orthodox Church is led by a synod of bishops. The president of the synod is known as the Patriarch, Archbishop, or Metropolitan. Among the various bishops, the ecumenical Patriarch of Constantino-ple is accorded a place of honor and is regarded as the "first among equals."

The administration of the church is spiritual and civil in character. The laymen in the church are prominent not only in the election of candidates to the priesthood but also in the sharing of the spiritual and administrative affairs of the church. Laymen share these duties with the clergy and have a responsibility for the discipline of the membership of the church. They also have the right to participate in the tasks of the church in teaching, mission, and charitable obligations.

There is no one person who leads or speaks for the church, nor do all its members act separately; they are seen as a whole, the one "Mystical Body of Christ."

Holy Writings

Scriptural authority is stressed, and there is an insistence upon the gospel, which is considered the foundation of the faith. It has been quoted that "scripture is fixed, it is the ground and pillar of our faith."

The Bible, therefore, is highly regarded by the church; a portion of it is read at every service. The church sees itself as the guardian and interpreter of the scriptures. The content of the Old Testament is seen as preparation for the coming of Jesus. The New Testament, with its four gospels, twenty-one epistles, the Acts of the Apostles, and the Book of Revelation, are all accepted and part of the church. (As you will see, this is not always the case with other religions.)

Protestantism

The term "Protestantism" refers to various forms of Christianity originating during the Reformation. The Reformation—essentially a movement for theological and moral reform in the Western Christian Church during the sixteenth and seventeenth centuries—was an incomparable catalyst for change that gave birth to a number of different types, such as Lutheranism, Calvinism, Anglicanism, Presbyterianism, Methodism, Congregationalism, and Baptism.

There was deep dissension within the Roman Catholic Church, which led to liberal Catholic reform earlier in the century. However, the traditional beginning of the Reformation occurred when Martin Luther, a German Roman Catholic priest, posted his Ninety-five Theses for debate on the door of the Castle Church in Wittenberg, Germany, on October 31, 1517, the eve of All Saints' Day.

Luther was a pastor and professor at the University of Wittenberg. In his theses, he attacked what he saw as the theological root of corruption in the life of the Church. He insisted that the Pope had no authority over purgatory and that only the scripture was authoritative; his critique was against the doctrine of the Church. In essence, he said that the Church was acting as a mediator or filter between the individual and God. To the Reformers, the Church seemed to be a transaction in place: The people would attend Mass, make confessions, do penance, and so on, and the Church would give approval and access to God's pleasure.

Another part of the argument was that because Catholics lived in fear of failing to provide what the Church said God required and their only dispensation was via the Church, church leaders had both political leverage and the ability to exert terror and compliance over the general populace.

Like many others, Luther complained of the terrible state of affairs of the Church. He railed against the avarice and simony connected with attaining offices in the Church. After a time, he became convinced that the Gospel itself was at stake—that the Church was actually perverting the Gospel of Jesus Christ by teaching people that heaven could be purchased by good works.

Understandably, this attack didn't sit well with the Roman Catholic establishment, and Pope Leo X excommunicated Luther in 1521.

Lutheranism

Lutheranism, a major Protestant denomination, started with the thoughts of the German Augustinian monk Martin Luther. It may only be legend that Martin Luther nailed ninety-five theses to the door of the castle church at Wittenberg, but it is no legend that his protest provoked a general revolt against the Papacy. Luther believed the church had lost sight of its central teachings, most importantly that of justification—God's act of declaring a sinner righteous by faith alone, not though any act or work.

ESSENTIAL

Martin Luther (1483–1546) was a German theologian who was the principal initiator of the Protestant Reformation in Europe. He did this by challenging the Christian Church, especially on the idea of buying indulgences. An indulgence was the putting off of a temporal punishment still due for a sin that has been absolved.

Martin Luther's teachings spread through Germany and Scandinavia and, in the eighteenth century, to America and the rest of the world. Lutheranism is the state religion of many north European countries. Lutherans see their movement centered in the understanding that, thanks to the saving activity of God in Jesus Christ, they are themselves "justified by grace through faith." Lutherans, like most Protestants, base their teachings not on churchly authority but on the divinely inspired Bible.

Central Beliefs

Lutherans believe that all human beings are sinners, in bondage to the power of Satan because of original sin. Their faith, therefore, is the only way out. Worship is firmly based on the teachings of the Bible, which Luther insisted was the only way to know God and his will. The Bible was the divine word, brought to man through the apostles and prophets.

Unlike the practice of the Roman Catholic Church, Luther conducted worship not in Latin, but in the language of the people. Apparently, the use of the vernacular enhanced the delivery and acceptance of the sermons, to say nothing of the rest of the service. Because of this serious change, access was granted not only to the highly educated members but also to the general population. Luther also reduced the established seven sacraments to two: baptism and the Lord's Supper. Infant baptism was considered God's grace reaching out to the newborn, and as such, a symbol of unconditional love. Congregational participation in worship was encouraged, particularly through the singing of the liturgy and of hymns, many of which Luther himself wrote.

FACT

Luther became obsessed about what to do to get deliverance from an angry god. According to a popular story, in 1505 he was returning from school and was thrown from a horse during a thunderstorm. Terrified, he promised St. Anne, the patron saint of minors, that he'd become a monk.

It is estimated that Lutheranism throughout the world constitutes the largest of the churches to come out of the Reformation. Lutherans number about 70 million worldwide, with approximately 10 million in the United States and Canada.

Calvinism

John Calvin (1509–1564) was the leading French Protestant reformer and the most important second-generation figure of the Reformation. A highly educated man, Calvin studied Greek, Hebrew, and Latin in order to improve his studies of the Scriptures. As such, he tilted toward humanism and rebelled against conservative theology. In 1533, he experienced, in his words, a "sudden conversion" and turned all his attention to the cause of the Reformation.

Because of internal religious strife in France, Calvin went to Basel, Switzerland. The same thing eventually happened in Switzerland that happened in France, and he was expelled from the country. Years later, he returned to establish the Geneva Academy for the training of ministry students. In the mid-1560s, he produced what became his masterpiece, "Institutes of the Christian Religion," which systematized Protestant thought and became the single most important statement of Protestant belief. In the book, which he finished in 1536 and later revised and supplemented, he diverged from Catholic doctrine by rejecting papal authority. He also explained his positions on justification by faith alone and predestination.

What has come down as Calvinism is a philosophy that expressed the sovereignty of God's will in predestination. Calvinism held that those God specifically elects are saved and that individuals can do nothing to effect this salvation. The term "Calvinism" is also used as a system of doctrine accepted by the Reformed churches, such as Presbyterianism.

Central Beliefs and Holy Writings of Protestantism

Jesus Christ and the Bible formed the authoritative base of the faith. The Protestant churches were organized with biblical supremacy. They believed in what might be called a democracy of believers—every Christian could communicate directly with God without having to go through the intermediary of a priest or saint. Thus, the Protestant principle is that the church is not God, nor are priests, pastors, or ministers; only God is God and He alone should be worshipped.

The Reformation rebelled against what was called "fixed prayer," prayers that had been composed by others to be remembered by rote and later regurgitated at the appropriate time and place. Freedom from the strictures of the Roman Catholic Church was emphasized, and people were encouraged to pray frequently and directly from the heart and not the head. Protestants recognize two sacraments: baptism and Holy Communion (the Eucharist). There have been variations in sacramental doctrine among Protestants over the years, but these two have become virtually universal.

The New Testament, especially the letters and writings of Paul, captured the Protestant sense of having discovered a religious hero, a mentor who exemplified their philosophy. Paul was brought up in one strict faith. He tried to please God, but failed. Then he went through a period of self-doubt about his worthiness. Protestants saw Paul's conversion through an epiphany with Jesus and his acceptance of Christ as a savior as the perfect example of the Protestant theology of justification by grace through faith. In other words, God didn't have to be satisfied to forgive and accept.

The literature of the Reformers shows that they did not believe that good works by themselves produced God's appeasement or salvation. Rather, good works inevitably flowed from the forgiven heart and were the consequence of the person's life. The law of God measured human frailties and judged them.

The other side of this belief presented Protestant leaders with a dilemma: When people were saved, it was to God's credit; when they were not, it was their own fault—it couldn't be both ways. Some leaders saw themselves solving the problem in Biblical terms by stressing God's loving relationship to humanity in sending his own Son, Jesus Christ, to suffer on their behalf.

ESSENTIAL

One might say that the Protestant ethic formed what was later referred to, particularly in the United States, as the work ethic. High value was given to honesty, hard work, and thrift. In the Calvinist view, these attributes were seen as the underpinnings of eternal salvation. Sociologists have argued that the Protestant ethic contributed significantly to the beginning and later development of capitalism.

Diversification of Protestantism into Modern Society

Protestantism increased the importance of the laity. In most denominations, they exercise more control over the hiring and firing, if necessary, of their pastor. They have a hand in church policy and offer advice on secular concerns. They also help lead worship and get involved in many other activities of the church. Some of the laity even participate in various church conferences, where they help set policy. Protestantism has led the way in providing women with the ability to become ministers. Today, in many of the denominations, there are even female bishops.

Protestantism became strong in northwestern Europe, England, and English-speaking America. Through the missionary movement, it spread to all parts of the world and joined Roman Catholicism as a minority presence in Asia and Africa. Protestantism became part of the history of the North Atlantic nations. While there are more Protestants than Catholics in the United States, Catholicism is the single largest church.

The Protestant heritage of separation led to diversity, which in turn contributed to the vast array of denominations within it.

Anglicanism

The Anglican Church is the established Church of England. It is recognized by the state, with the British monarch as the titular head. The Anglican Church was created in the sixteenth century during the Protestant Reformation. King Henry VIII (1491–1547) became Supreme Head of the English Church in 1534. Henry VIII wished to get an annulment from his first wife, the aging Catherine of Aragon, so that he could marry Anne Boleyn in an effort to produce a son for the throne of England. However, Pope Clement VII refused to grant the annulment.

In short, King Henry took over the English church, broke with Rome, and created the Anglican Church. He was then able to have the Archbishop of Canterbury, Thomas Cranmer, pronounce the marriage to Catherine null and void, leaving him free to marry Anne Boleyn.

FACT

Though King Henry had established this new church in order to wed Anne Boleyn, he had actually already done so in secret. Incidentally, Anne Boleyn gave birth to a daughter, the future Queen of England, Elizabeth I.

The Church of England spread throughout the British Empire, spawning sister churches throughout the world; part of this colonial expansion and influence spread into India and North America. All this together made up the Anglican Communion as it is today, a body headed spiritually by the Archbishop of Canterbury, which has about 80 million adherents, making it the second largest Christian body in the Western World.

Central Beliefs and Holy Writings

The Anglicans meld features from both Protestantism and Catholicism; they prize traditional worship and structure and operate autonomously. They have few firm rules and great latitude in the interpretation of doctrine. They consider the Bible to be divinely inspired, and hold the Eucharist, or the Lord's Supper, to be the central act of Christian worship. They recognize both the Nicene and Apostles' Creeds. (See Chapter 7.) Anglicans have a reputation for respecting the authority of the state without submitting to it; likewise, they respect the freedom of the individual.

The Book of Common Prayer (1662) is a major influence not only on the faith but also on English society in general and is used by churches of the Anglican Communion. Since its publication in the sixteenth century, it continues in various editions as the standard liturgy of most Anglican churches of the British Commonwealth. Most churches outside the Commonwealth have their own variants of the prayer book.

Expansion

The expansion of Anglicanism is directly related to British colonization. The Church of England's great missionary societies went out into all the English colonies and promoted Christian knowledge. They were instrumental in creating a decentralized body of national churches that were loyal to one another and to the forms of faith inherited from the Church of England.

The scope of the missionary work was immense, and Anglicanism spread from Nigeria to Kenya, South Africa, India, and Australia. It also traveled east to China and Japan. The first American bishop, Samuel Seabury, was consecrated in Scotland in 1784. The Anglican Church of Canada created its own organization in 1893.

The Episcopal Church in the United States came into existence as an independent denomination following the American Revolution. Since members of the Anglican Church were required to swear allegiance to the King, it became necessary for American followers to establish their own church. It now has about 2 or 3 million members in the United States. Isaac Newton was an Anglican clergyman and theologian, as were some of the founders of the Royal Society, one of the world's oldest and most prestigious scientific societies.

The Episcopal Church continues this tradition. The church routinely requires its clergy to hold university as well as seminary degrees. For more than twenty years, the American Episcopal Church has ordained women to the priesthood. In 1988, it elected the first Anglican woman bishop, Barbara Harris.

Baptists

The Baptists are a denomination of Protestant Christians holding a distinctive belief with regard to baptism—adults are baptized by total immersion in the water—and by the autonomy of their own congregation. Baptism is the right of purification by water. The ceremony of baptism regenerates, freeing a person from sin and making him part of the church.

The Baptists—once nicknamed the Anabaptists—trace their origins to the English church established in Amsterdam by John Smyth (1554–1612). They were recognized as dissenters from the Anglican Church. Smyth baptized first himself, then the others. In 1611, certain members of this congregation returned to London and established a church there under Thomas Helwys.

America's first Baptist church was established in Providence, Rhode Island, with the help of Roger Williams, who founded the city of Providence. Williams (1603–1683) was a minister of the Church of England who, because of his separatist views, fled to America in search of religious freedom. In time, this theologian was notable more for his religious tolerance than his alignment with one church.

ESSENTIAL

Baptists were instrumental in the fight for religious freedom in England and the United States. Their convictions about the liberty of the individual played a role in securing the adoption of the "no religious test" clause in the U.S. Constitution and the guarantees embodied in the First Amendment. "God is too large to be housed under one roof," said Roger Williams.

He became a minister in Salem, Massachusetts, where he upset the civil authorities who subsequently banished him. Williams then bought land from the Narragansett Indians. Other colonists joined him, and together they set up one of the first settlements in the country established on the principle of complete religious freedom. Eventually, through extensive missionary work, the Baptist church spread throughout the world.

Baptists are well known as evangelists. The Association of Baptists for World Evangelism (ABWE) was founded in August 1927 in the home of

Marguerite Doane in Rhode Island. In keeping with the Baptist philosophy of independence, the ABWE states that it is an independent Baptist mission agency with a missionary presence in over forty-five countries.

The Baptist churches operate democratically because they believe every other form of church government infringes on their beliefs. Individual members have an equal right to voice their convictions and to vote according to their consciences when the congregation makes decisions.

Baptists see the Old and New Testaments as their final authority; the Bible is, they say, to be interpreted responsibly. Of the edicts they embrace, pluralism of race, ethnicity, and gender, and the acknowledgment that there are individual differences of conviction and theology feature strongly. However, they are opposed to homosexuality and are firmly antiabortion.

Congregationalists

Congregationalism is a form of church organization in which each local church is independent. The concept derives from the belief that Jesus Christ is the sole head of his Church, and thus congregationalism mimics the original form of the church's organization.

In England, the Congregationalists were known as Separatists or Independents. They can be traced back to the sixteenth century followers of Robert Browne, who broke from the Anglican Church.

The Pilgrims who came to America in 1620 and settled in Plymouth Colony were Congregationalists, and the religion became widely established and blossomed in New England. As the country grew, Congregational churches were established in newly opened frontier regions, and were allowed freedom of worship. Theologically, they fall somewhere between Presbyterianism and the more radical Protestants. Emphasizing education, the Congregationalists played a significant role in founding the universities of Harvard (1636) and Yale (1701). The denomination maintains the right of each individual church to self-government and to its own statement of doctrine.

In its home country, England, Congregationalism has declined, but not as markedly in the United States. Even so, it has not expanded at the same rate as other religions. In 1931, Congregational churches were united with the Christian Church under the name General Council of the

Congregational and Christian Churches of the United States. In 1957, many Congregational churches united with the Evangelical and Reformed Church to form the United Church of Christ.

Congregational philosophy, ideas, and practices have influenced many other churches and have been a major factor in shaping the institutions and general culture of the United States. There has always been a strong urging to preach the faith because the Word of God, as declared in the scriptures, has great importance to Congregationalists.

Baptism and the Lord's Supper are considered the only sacraments instituted by Christ. Infants are baptized by sprinkling, not immersion. The Lord's Supper is usually celebrated once or twice a month.

Methodism

Methodism is a protestant movement founded by an Anglican priest, John Wesley (1703–1791), who stressed the individual believer's personal relationship with God. With his brother Charles, Wesley led a devout and scholarly group in Oxford whose prayer and bible meetings counterbalanced the worldliness of student life at Oxford.

Wesley went to the American colony of Georgia to act as a priest to the settlers. There he would sign hymns and hold fellowship meetings. He organized his followers into "societies" with emotional class meetings. If followers failed to attend meetings, they couldn't remain members.

He preached far and wide, from settlements to the frontiers. During his fifty-year ministry, he is said to have traveled 250,000 miles, mostly on horseback, and delivered 50,000 sermons. The religious revival which he spirited—known as the Great Awakening—created Methodism and caused the Anglican Church to reassess its own evangelism.

Wesley had wanted his followers to remain within the Anglican Church, but after his death, Methodism rejected the authority of the church. The church grew very rapidly, but schisms developed, and eventually the issue of slavery split the Methodist Church into two. In 1845, the Methodist Episcopal Church and the Methodist Episcopal Church, South were organized. The church in the South lost its black members during the Civil War. After the Civil War, both churches grew rapidly.

In 1939, the Methodist Church was formed and the Methodist Protestant Church joined in the same union. At that time, the Central Jurisdiction was formed for black members and existed alongside other jurisdictions. In 1968, the Central Jurisdiction was abolished and black Methodists were integrated into the church.

The United Methodist Church was created on April 23, 1968, when Bishop Reuben H. Muller of the Evangelical United Brethren Church and Bishop Lloyd C. Wicke of the Methodist Church merged at the General Conference in Dallas, Texas, to form the United Methodist Church. The combined church then had 11 million members, which made it one of the largest Protestant churches in the world.

FACT

An increasing number of women have been admitted to the ordained ministry and to denominational leadership as consecrated bishops. In 1980, Marjorie Matthews was the first woman elected to the Church's episcopacy.

As with many Protestant denominations, the Methodist Church recognizes and practices two sacraments: baptism and the Supper of the Lord. The UMC looks upon humans as sinful creatures estranged from God who have wounded themselves and others. As humans have wreaked havoc throughout the natural order, they stand in need of redemption.

The Methodist Church has an extensive, worldwide missionary organization. Missionaries are trained to carry their religion and philosophy throughout the world using a global communications network. They also explore and sustain ecumenical cooperation with other missionaries.

The equality of the sexes within the church is established. The church affirms the right of women to equal treatment in employment, responsibility, promotion, and compensation. An official statement reads: "We affirm the importance of women in decision-making positions at all levels of Church life."

CHAPTER 9

Prevalent Christian Faiths, Part Two

Christianity has many more branches in addition to the most common ones introduced in the previous chapters. In this chapter, you will explore some very familiar, and in most cases newer, Christian faiths.

Presbyterians

A Presbyterian is a Protestant Christian who opposes state intervention in religious affairs and advocates the primacy of the Bible as a rule of faith. The first Presbyterian Church to be organized on a national basis was in sixteenth-century France.

In 1876, the Presbyterian Church of England was formed by a merger. Various factions from English and Scottish congregations came together and adopted the Presbyterian system of church government. Its history is a rocky one, and didn't come close to real stability until 1972, when it merged into the United Reformed Church in England and Wales. Similarly, in 1983 the American Presbyterian Churches' headquarters in New York City and Atlanta, Georgia, merged to end a North-South split that dated from the Civil War.

Mergers seem to have been the historic norm in the Presbyterian Church; it didn't consist of just those mentioned above, but was present through the years with the North America Church, the Southern Church, the Cumberland Church, the Secession Church, and the Synod of Ulster. Perhaps this isn't surprising, considering the church was a blend of New England Puritans—the Scottish, Irish, English, and Welsh. Actually, the Cumberland Presbyterian Churches, which were founded on the American Frontier in the early 1800s, have two heritages, one from the 1800s and a new version that came about in 1906. It has survived all the upsets, and today is centered in Memphis, Tennessee.

It should come as no surprise to learn that the church avoids highly centralized authority in the government.

Foundations of Faith

Presbyterians believe in the Trinity: God the Father and Creator, Jesus Christ his Son, and the Holy Spirit. The Bible is considered the foundation of their faith, and they acknowledge the common creeds of the church (Apostles' and Nicene Creeds). They hold that they are saved "by faith alone, by God's grace only, through scripture only." The sacraments are two: baptism for infants and adults and the Lord's Supper, open to all baptized Christians.

The churches are governed by elders—the word "Presbyterian" means "elder"—who are elected by their congregations. Similarly, the congregation elects and ordains pastors. Elders and pastors from all the churches are gathered to form presbyteries for mutual support and cooperative governance. It is a policy of the church that they seek community with all Christian churches.

Stands on Controversial Issues

The Special Committee on Problem Pregnancies and Abortion recommended in 1992 that the General Assembly approve a paper and adopt it as policy. The report stated that it affirmed the ability and responsibility of women, guided by the scriptures and the Holy Spirit, in the context of their communities to make good moral choices regarding problem pregnancies. There were strong recommendations that all Presbyterians work for a decrease in the number of problem pregnancies, thereby decreasing the number of abortions.

It considered the decision of a woman to terminate a pregnancy morally acceptable, though certainly not the only or required decision. Further, the report stated that there may be possible justifying circumstances including medical indications of severe physical or mental deformity, conception as a result of rape or incest, or conditions under which the physical or mental health of either woman or child would be gravely threatened. The report went on to say that it did not wish to see laws enacted that would attach criminal penalties to those who seek abortions or to appropriately qualified and licensed persons who perform them in medically approved facilities.

In 1997, all members voted on the issue of ordination of homosexuals. The result was to bar any members who were sexually active outside marriage from the office of clergy, elder, or deacon. The church's Book of Order was specifically amended to address the church's deep division over homosexuality.

In June 2001, a move intended to include lesbians, homosexuals, bisexuals, and transgender people as candidates for ordained ministers, elders, or deacons took place. A decision was made to change the language in the Book of Order to do away with any prohibition of sexual minorities. That decision has to be ratified by the majority of the denomination's local governing bodies, the presbyteries.

Amish Mennonites

It might be surprising to some that the people known as the Amish in America date to a Protestant group founded in the Netherlands in the sixteenth century. The Amish were followers of Anabaptist leader Jakob Ammann, a seventeenth-century elder whose teachings caused a schism among members in many parts of Europe. His followers were called the Amish.

Persecution drove many Mennonites to emigrate from Holland and Switzerland starting in 1663. The Mennonite beliefs still include adult baptism (usually between the ages of sixteen and twenty-five), pacifism, and an overarching rejection of worldly concerns in favor of withdrawal from society.

Ammann was difficult due to his oppressive strictures and orders. He took issue with Swiss Mennonite leaders for their lack of discipline and split off to form his own group. He introduced the washing of feet into services and taught the plainness of dress and habit that became a staple of the Amish way of life.

The Amish migration to North America landed them in eastern Pennsylvania, and their settlement remains in that part of the country. Schisms again occurred after 1859 between the Old and the New orders, resulting in the formation of smaller churches or amalgamations within the Mennonite Church.

FACT

Amish children attend public elementary schools, but not high schools. This practice has caused problems because of school attendance laws. Some Amish have gone to jail rather than allow their children to attend high school. In fact, the Amish shun education past the eighth grade, believing that their learning to that point provides a sufficient preparation for their lifestyle.

Following the eighth grade, children work on their family's farm or business until they marry. Although they pay school taxes, the Amish have fought to keep their children out of public schools. In 1972, the Supreme Court handed down a landmark unanimous decision that exempted the Old Order Amish and related groups from state compulsory attendance laws beyond the eighth grade. Amish students do have access to higher education by enrolling in their own colleges, seminaries, and Bible schools.

Each Amish settlement is generally comprised of some seventy-five baptized members. If a group becomes any larger, a new group is formed because members meet for services in each other's homes; they have no church buildings. Each district has a bishop, two to four preachers, and an elder. Holy Communion is celebrated twice each year. Services are conducted in a mixture of English and palatine German, known as Pennsylvania Dutch.

Adults are baptized when they are admitted to formal membership, generally around seventeen to twenty years of age. The Amish believe in the Trinity and affirm the scriptures, particularly the New Testament.

ESSENTIAL

To better grasp the Amish way of life, you should bear in mind two ideas. One is their rejection of *hochmut* (pride, arrogance, haughtiness) and their prizing of *demut* (humility) and *gelassenheit* (calmness, composure; but perhaps better translated as "submission" or "letting be"). This concept also signals an aversion to self-promotion and a rejection of individualism in favor of community life.

The Amish are notable for their "plain" customs, which even today include homemade clothing without buttons; hooks and eyes are used instead. A familiar sight is of men wearing broad-brimmed black hats and full beards without moustaches. The women wear bonnets and modest dress, including long dresses with capes over the shoulders, shawls, and black shoes and stockings. No jewelry of any kind is ever worn. The mode of dress dates to their early traditions established in Europe.

They live without telephones or electric lights. The Amish drive horses and buggies rather than automobiles, and they shun modern farm machinery, although they have a reputation for being excellent farmers.

There are now about 500,000 full members, about 225,000 of whom are in the United States and Canada.

Christian Science

Mary Baker Eddy (1821–1910), a frail woman deeply interested in medicine and the Bible, founded the Church of Christ, Scientist in 1879. Eddy wrote a book, *Science and Health with a Key to the Scriptures,* and the teachings of Christian Sciences were grounded in the principles of the book. She stressed the elimination of sin and healing of the sick through prayer alone. This was grounded in the principle of the "allness of Soul, Spirit, and the nothingness of matter."

This spiritualism extends to humanity and the universe. The reality of truth and goodness implies the unreality of evil and error. The Church of Christ, Scientist teaches that God is divine mind. Only mind is real; thus, matter, evil, sin, disease, and death are unreal illusions.

Physical suffering is an illusion, the philosophy continues, and can be conquered by the spirit-filled mind. However, a person who is not grounded in prayer or an understanding of God can attain this realization.

QUESTION

Can Christian Scientists go to their own doctor or a hospital for medical care?
Christian Scientists say that they always have freedom of choice in caring for themselves and their families. If an individual departs from the use of Christian Science by choosing some other kind of treatment, she is neither condemned by the church nor dropped from membership.

Eddy had a stern Calvinist upbringing, which she rebelled against. In her search for good health, she experimented with alternative healing methods: homeopathy and suggestive, charismatic therapeutics as practiced by Phineas Parkhurst Quimby. Following Quimby's death, she increased her studies toward finding a universal spiritual principle of healing in the New Testament. Her recovery from a serious illness in 1866 deepened her commitment to religious healing.

Study and prayer are basic requirements of the denomination, as is the readiness of members to meet the challenges of Christian healing. All Christian Science churches maintain reading rooms for this purpose.

Christian Scientists say that healing comes through scientific prayer or spiritual communion with God. It is specific treatment. Prayer recognizes a patient's direct access to God's love and discovers more of the consistent operation of God's law of health and wholeness on his behalf. They know God, or Divine Mind, as the only healer. A transformation or spiritualization of a patient's thought changes her condition.

Those members who indulge in a full-time healing ministry are called Christian Science practitioners and are listed in a monthly directory. They usually charge their patients a nominal amount.

The spiritual aspect of healing has come under direct criticism by the medical profession. There have been cases in which the law has stepped in to force conventional medical treatment, particularly when a child is involved.

FACT

The church is known worldwide and has a well-earned reputation of excellence for its international daily newspaper, *The Christian Science Monitor,* which is published in Boston, Massachusetts. Mary Baker Eddy started the publication in 1908, and it was in print a century later in 2008 with a circulation of 56,000. But revenues declined and it moved from print to online the following year.

Three books—*Healing Spiritually* and *A Century of Christian Science Healing,* both published by The Christian Science Publishing Society, and *Spiritual Healing in a Scientific Age* by Robert Peel give detailed accounts of purported healings.

Membership figures for Christian Science have been unavailable since 1936, when there were 250,000 members in North America.

Jehovah's Witnesses

The Jehovah's Witnesses were founded in Pittsburgh in 1872 by Charles Taze Russell (1852–1916). The Witnesses, who are known for their proselytizing on American streets and door to door, have little or no association with other denominations, nor with secular governments. A millenarian movement, the Jehovahs interpret the Bible literally, reject the Trinity, and assert the millennium will begin after a final battle (Armageddon), after which the witnesses will rule with Christ.

Among other beliefs, they hold that world powers and political parties are the unwitting allies of Satan. They refuse to salute the flags of nations or to perform military service; they almost never vote. They reject other churches as ruled by Satan.

The belief grew from the International Bible Students Association founded in Pittsburgh, Pennsylvania. A successor to Charles Taze Russell, Joseph Franklin Rutherford, aimed to have Jehovah (Yahweh) reaffirmed as the true God and to identify those who witness in his name as God's specially accredited followers. It was Rutherford's successor, Nathan Homer Knorr, who directed a group of Witnesses to produce a new translation of the Bible.

They are a high-intensity faith group that expects a dedicated commitment from its members. Jehovah's Witnesses are in over 200 countries and may number as many as 7 million adherents.

Scripture

Publishing activities have formed a major part of the belief's work, including books, tracts, recordings, and the successful semimonthly magazines *Watchtower* and its companion publication *Awake!*, which are claimed to have a circulation of over 10 million distributed in eighty languages.

ESSENTIAL

The Witnesses are known for controversial beliefs. These include a refusal to serve the military and a rejection of blood transfusions, even when they are required to save a life. They acknowledge a group of elders who are authoritative on matters of their way of life, and governments have no such authority.

Beliefs

The goal of their belief is the establishment of God's Kingdom, the Theocracy (or government by God). They believe that this will come about after Armageddon, based on their interpretation of the Biblical books of Daniel and Revelation, which they used to make apocalyptic calculations. Pastor Russell determined that 1874 would be the year of Christ's invisible return. He also figured that 1914 would be the year of Christ's Second Coming and the end of the Gentiles. Apparently, making prophecies is not done in this way anymore, which isn't surprising considering the track record. Nowadays, analysis is based on modern life and current events.

Jehovah's Witnesses insist that Jesus Christ is God's agent and that through him man will be reconciled to Jehovah. The Bible is considered to be infallible and the revealed word of God. Their own version of the Bible is called New World Translation of the Holy Scriptures. Biblical scholars have disagreed sharply about what they claim are distortions in the translations.

As far as hell and the inevitability of eternal life are concerned, Jehovah's Witnesses dismiss both. Many believe that death is total extinction.

Witnesses meet in churches called Kingdom Halls. There are appointed members called Overseers or Elders; there are also Presiding Overseers and Service Overseers. Members are baptized by immersion, and must adhere to a strong moral code. Members refuse stimulants. Divorce is not approved of, except on the grounds of adultery.

A much-criticized condition of membership is the prohibition against blood transfusions. Even the storing of one's own blood for auto transfusion, generally done prior to major elective surgery, is not permitted. Witnesses believe that any blood that leaves the body must be destroyed. In 1967, they stated that organ transplants are a form of cannibalism and are to be shunned. This directive was reversed in 1980 and left up to personal conscience, a policy of little value to those members who needed transplants to save their lives during the thirteen years of prohibition. There have been many court cases over the claims of the deaths of children, mothers, and other adults who might possibly still be alive had a transfusion been given.

Rituals and Customs

Only one day of celebration is acknowledged: Memorial of Christ's Death at the time of Passover. They believe that Jesus was born on October 2. Neither that date nor any so-called pagan holidays—Christmas, Thanksgiving, Independence Day, Halloween, birthdays—are celebrated. There is no Sabbath; all days are regarded as holy.

All positions of authority are reserved for men.

As most people know, doorstep preaching is a very visual part of Jehovah's Witness practices. In addition to those activities, members are expected to spend five hours a week at meetings in Kingdom Hall.

The Church of Jesus Christ of Latter Day Saints: The Mormons

The Mormons are the members of a Christian Millenarian movement, also known as the Church of Jesus Christ of Latter Day Saints. In 1823, Joseph Smith (1805–1844) claimed to have visions and published his mystical writings as the Book of Mormon (1829). The book was a curious admixture of religious concepts and mythical history, including the far-flung belief that Native Americans (who apparently underwent experiences similar to those written in the Old Testament) were, in fact, the lost tribe of Israel.

Like other Christian denominations, the Mormons embrace Millennialism (the Latin root means "one thousand years"), maintaining that a Golden Age is coming, during which Christ will reign. Still, Mormon beliefs diverge sharply from orthodox Christianity, which they view as a corrupt faith. Mormon beliefs include an expectation of a Second Coming of Christ, baptism of adults, and belief in prophecy.

They accept a highly American form of Millenarianism. In particular, they hold that Jesus Christ was revealed to early immigrants in America, and they would found a new Jerusalem there.

Smith organized the first Mormon community in Fayette, New York, but soon encountered persecution, not to mention disagreements within the community, and he headed west to Ohio, then to Missouri, and finally in 1840 to Nauvoo, Illinois. His opposition only grew after he sanctioned polygamy. In June 1844, following a general breakdown in order, Smith was lynched and assassinated by a mob in Carthage, Illinois. Leadership of the Mormons then passed to Brigham Young, who led them to Utah. Polygamy was renunciated by the church in 1890.

Way of Life

The Mormon way of life is distinguished by order and respect for authority, church activism, strong conformity with the group, and vigorous proselytizing and missionary activities.

As an example of the strictness of the faith, the official pamphlet "Dating and Courtship" calls passionate kissing prior to marriage a sin. The church advises young people not to engage in any behavior with anyone that they would not do with a brother or sister while in the presence of their parents.

The church also discourages interracial dating. The edict is that unless the young people who do marry outside the temple repent quickly, they cut themselves off from exaltation in the celestial Kingdom of God.

As for military service, the church considers it a duty of its members. However, any member can opt for conscientious objection, but not by giving the church as a reason for it. The church discourages conscientious objection, and, in fact, endorses a corps of chaplains who serve in the United States armed services.

Mormons believe that faithful members of the church will inherit eternal life as gods, and even those who had rejected God's law would live in glory.

The Church of Latter Day Saints is world famous for its genealogy repository, the Family History Library in Salt Lake City. It boasts more than 2 billion names and is considered the finest such repository in the world. The church has made available, free to church members and nonmembers alike, over 600 million names for research purposes on its Family Search website on the Internet. It encourages its members to trace their ancestors as a religious obligation. This service is now available to anyone.

Adventists

Commonplace in Christian theologies is the belief in a Second Coming. According to this notion, Christ will return from heaven to earth in accord with the Messianic prophecy that claims he will resurrect the dead, render a last judgment of the dead, and establish a Kingdom of Heaven on Earth. Thus, "Adventists" subscribe to this notion of the "Second Advent of Jesus."

The term "Adventist" is used interchangeably with the "Seventh-day Adventist Church." The Seventh-day designation serves as a reminder that their Sabbath is distinguished by its observance on Saturday, the seventh or last day of the week, instead of a Sunday Sabbath. In fact, the Adventists, like Jews, observe the Sabbath from Friday sunset to Saturday sunset. According to the creation story in the Bible, Saturday was instituted by God as the day of rest, and the commandment concerning Sabbath rest is part of God's eternal law.

Adventism is one of a group of Protestant Christian churches with a belief in the Second Coming, with firm roots in the Hebrew and Christian prophetic tradition. They believe that when Christ returns he will separate the saints from the wicked. The founder of the faith, William Miller (1782–1849), was a Baptist preacher. His followers were called Millerites. Miller came to the conclusion that Christ would arrive sometime between March 21, 1843, and March 21, 1844. Though he was encouraged in this view by some clergymen and followers, Miller was also accused of being a fanatic because he insisted that Christ would arrive on schedule with a fiery conflagration.

Christ did not appear as predicted, so Miller set a second date: October 22, 1844. So great was the expectation of Christ's arrival that Millerites changed their ways of life, and, in many cases, abandoned their possessions and joined Miller in awaiting the arrival. That day passed quietly, too, and followers suffered what was called the Great Disappointment by Adventists. Nevertheless, Millerites persisted; they believed Miller had set the right date, but it had been interpreted incorrectly. Some members of the faith independently believed that Christ's advent was still imminent, although they didn't set a new date.

Later, Adventists reinterpreted the events of 1843–1844 and claimed that something had occurred in the invisible realm, where Jesus lived with his Father. So Adventists again expected Jesus to come. Times of great religious experiment ensued, and Adventists promulgated vegetarian and other measures to improve health.

In the mid-1990s, membership numbered 733,000 in the United States, but the worldwide figure has swelled to nearly 5 million.

Quakers

The Quakers, a Christian group, are also known as the Society of Friends, thus members are called Friends. George Fox (1624–1691), a nonconformist religious reformer, founded the movement in England. The name "Quakers" likely derives from their trembling at the discovery of God during meetings. They held that the trembling would lead to the purification of all Christendom.

Fox had a vision and heard a voice that told him, "There is one, even Jesus Christ, who can speak to thy condition," which motivated him to become a preacher. He believed in an "Inner Light"—the presence of God's spirit within each individual. The existence of the Inner Light means that everyone has direct access to God. Fox reasoned that there was no need to have a church or a priest to act as a go between. Nor did people need elaborate formal structures of creed and sacraments or liturgy or clergy. Rituals, creeds, and dogmas were also superfluous, and there was no need to dress up in church garments.

None of this sat well with the infamous Oliver Cromwell and his Puritan government. As a result, Fox and his followers faced persecution. By 1660, there were more than 20,000 Quakers in Scotland, Wales, and the American colonies. They continued to grow in number, despite severe punishments from 1662 to 1689 for refusing to take oaths, attend Anglican services, or pay tithes.

The philosophy of intense concern for others was developing; it has continued to the present day and is a bulwark of the movement. The early Quakers agitated for an end to slavery and improvement in the treatment and conditions in mental health institutions and penitentiaries. Their philanthropic tendencies and pacifism are well known. Quaker pacifists make an absolute personal stand against war. They refuse to register for selective service and thus forfeit conscientious objectors' status.

When the Quakers came to the United States, they didn't fare any better than they had at home. They were looked at as witches, and many were hanged. They eventually settled in Rhode Island, known for its religious tolerance. As time went by, they became accepted as a denomination. Nevertheless, they distanced themselves from society in general, which was evidenced by their simple clothing and their way of speaking—they used "thee" and "thou" instead of "you."

The Revolutionary War sparked resentment against the Quakers again because they refused to pay military taxes or to join in the fighting. Some of them were even exiled. After the war, their attitudes toward helping improve society and the people in it gained ground. Quaker organizations sprang up in opposition to slavery and poverty, and they formed the Underground Railroad, which was specifically set up to help runaway slaves escape to the northern states and Canada.

Disagreements developed and two schisms eventually resulted in the formation of four groups: the Hicksites, a liberal group mainly in the eastern states; Gurneyites, an evangelical group that had pastors; Wilburites, a more traditional sect; and Orthodox, a Christ-centered group.

Central Beliefs

Quakers are one of the least ritualized religions. Spiritual soul searching is a common element, culminating in a closeness with God. Much stress is made on the Inner Light, which has mystical aspects to it in that members receive an immediate sense of God's presence.

Meetings are held to worship God and wait for his word. Generally, members will sit in a circle or a square, facing each other. In some American meetings, there may be a pastor to lead it. Sometimes the meetings are silent; at others, members express a new understanding that has come to them. Men and women are equal in the faith. Whenever a "message" comes out of these meditations that might require action, it is put to the group, considered, and if there is consensus, acted on. The action to be taken generally has a strong social bias to it; something has to be put right irrespective of the consequences to the group or individual members. Thus, courage and conviction are paramount.

Quakers have no stated creed or ritual, but they do have an agreement, regarding the philosophy and beliefs of the faith. These include: worship is an act of seeking, not asking; the virtues of moral purity, integrity, honesty, simplicity, and humility are to be sought after; there shall be concern for the suffering and unfortunate; and true religion is a personal encounter with God. Quakers refuse to take oaths, believing that since one should tell the truth at all times an oath is irrelevant. They feel that taking an oath implies that there are two types of truthfulness: one for ordinary life and another for special occasions.

The individuality of the Quakers is seen in their belief, or lack of one, in life after death. Very few believe there is eternal punishment in hell. They see all life as sacramental with no difference between the secular and the religious. No one thing or activity is any more spiritual than any other. Baptism, in the accepted sense, is not a practiced sacrament; Quakers believe in the "inward baptism of the Holy Spirit" (Ephesians 4: 4–5).

Quakerism in Today's World

Meetings are held all year in North America. These include the Friends United Meeting, (about fourteen meetings each year); Friends General Conference (some 500 meetings); and Evangelical Friends International and the

Friends World Committee for Consultation, which is an international group in London, England. Today, Quakerism has spread to Africa and Europe.

Quakers have practically and visually contributed to the promotion of tolerance, peace, and justice more than most Christian denominations. In 1947, the Society of Friends was awarded the Nobel Peace Prize. It was awarded to the American Friends Service Committee and the (British) Friends Service Council for their active work in ministering to refugees and victims of famine.

FACT

Most of the early suffragist leaders in America were Quakers. In the nineteenth century, American Friends founded colleges such as Earlham, Haverford, and Swarthmore. Individual Friends founded Bryn Mawr College, Cornell University, and Johns Hopkins University. Friends' schools tend to emphasize science.

Unitarians

The Unitarians may hold the distinction of being the most undogmatic of all religious sects. Unitarians draw from the sixteenth-century Protestant Christian thinkers who rejected the doctrine of the Trinity and stressed the unity of God. Their outlook is sanguine: their religion is based on freedom, reason, and a belief in the goodness of human nature. The Unitarians have often been considered heretics because they want to choose their faith, not because they are rebellious.

The word "Unitarian" is a shortened version of Unitarian and Universalism. The roots of the Unitarianism beliefs were formed in Transylvania, now the border area of Hungary and Romania. The church was influenced by Ferenc David (1510–1579), himself a convicted heretic. David, a Transylvanian Nontrinitarian and Unitarian preacher, taught that prayers could not be addressed to Jesus, since Jesus was only a human and not divine. David died in prison. However, the church he founded in 1568 is the world's oldest surviving Unitarian body. His legacy of tolerance is captured in a remark often quoted by modern-day Unitarians: "We need not think alike to love alike."

A similar Unitarian movement developed in England in the seventeenth century with a number of dissenter churches. Indeed, the early history of the movement is rife with dissension. Some members wanted to change the name to Free Christian—a title suggesting the unfettered way those members approached their vision and version of religious thought. The movement prospered and eventually became the British Unitarian Association.

The first Unitarian Church was founded in London by Theophilus Lindsey in 1773. Lindsey, like Joseph Priestley, one of the "rational dissenters" against the established church, soon encountered spirited opposition. Holding Unitarian views was a legal offense in Britain for the next forty years, until 1813, and the movement, perhaps as a consequence of the opposition, has never attracted many British adherents.

The origins of the movement in the United States developed slowly in New England out of Congregational autonomy, which stressed moderation, reason, and morals over spiritual revivalism. In 1825, following yet another schism between various sects of the movement, the American Unitarian Association was formed.

The movement stressed free use of reason in religion and believed that God existed in one person only; they did not believe in the Trinity, and, as did Ferenc David, they also denied the divinity of Jesus Christ. They had no creed and individual congregations varied widely in religious beliefs and practices. For instance, Thomas Starr King is credited with coming up with a definition that endeavored to show the difference between Unitarians and Universalists: "Universalists believe that God is too good to damn people, and the Unitarians believe that people are too good to be damned by God."

From the early days the movement embraced the marginalized members of society, including the Universalists, in 1863 becoming the first denomination to ordain a woman to the ministry: Olympia Brown. They affirmed that God embraced everyone and that dignity and worth are innate to all people regardless of sex, color, race, or class.

The influence of Unitarianism in America is evidence by four American presidents (John Adams, John Quincy Adams, Millard Fillmore, and William Howard Taft) being Unitarians.

CHAPTER 10

Islam

Islam is the religion of Muslims, revealed through Muhammad, the prophet of Allah. In effect, Muhammad, as God's messenger, was to the origins of Islam what Moses was to Judaism. An Arabic term meaning "submission to God," Islam originated in Arabia in the seventh century. While the distribution of Islam throughout the world generally covers Africa, the Middle East, and sections of Asia and Europe, it is becoming a growing religious factor in the United States as well. More than 6 million Muslims reside in the United States.

Muhammad

The founder and prophet of Islam, Muhammad (570–632 C.E.) was born in Arabia. At the age of forty, he was selected by God (Allah) to be the prophet of true religion. He heeded the command to preach and spread the word, preaching openly against idolatry and of the oneness of Allah or God.

Muhammad's parents were of the Hashim clan, of the Kuraish tribe. Once laborers, tribal members acquired the Kaaba in the fifth century and became one of the most prominent and powerful tribes in central Arabia. Muhammad was orphaned soon after his birth and raised by an uncle, Abu Talib.

As an adult, Muhammad became a respected and successful trader. On a trading journey to Syria, he was put in charge of the merchandise of a rich middle-aged widow named Kahdija. She was so taken with him that she offered herself in marriage. She eventually bore him six children, two sons and four daughters. The best known of these children was his daughter Fatima, who became the wife of Muhammad's cousin Ali, who was regarded as Muhammad's divinely ordained successor.

Muhammad was known for his charm, courage, impartiality, and resoluteness. He was considered a man of virtuous character who epitomized what would later become the Islamic ideal. His personal revelation came while he was meditating in a cave outside the city of Makkah (or Mecca) when he was forty years old. He had a vision of the angel Gabriel, who said, "Recite." Muhammad refused three times until the angel said, "Recite in the name of thy Lord who created." The words that were given to Muhammad declared the oneness and power of God, to whom worship should be made, and the judgment that all must face.

The Koran called Muhammad the "unlettered prophet." This makes his recitation more credible, the thinking goes, for if he was unable to read or write he could not have changed the words of Allah, but received the revelation directly. Indeed, Allah says to Muhammad in the Koran, "Never have you read a book before this, nor have you transcribed one with your right hand. Had you done either of these the unbelievers might have justly doubted." (29:48)

Following his revelation, Muhammad began preaching. It was a turbulent time of military conquest and political expansion throughout the area, and Muhammad met with opposition. He and his followers fled the persecution and migrated to Medina, where his teachings began to be accepted and the first Islamic community was founded.

FACT

Arabia in the seventh century was polytheistic, hosting many religions, including Christianity, Buddhism, Judaism, and Zoroastrianism. Geographically, it covered an area that bordered on the Byzantine Christian Empire, Yemen, and the boarders of the Zoroastrian Persian Empire. Muhammad traveled widely and studied with followers of other tribes and religions, among them Syrian Christians and many Jews.

The major achievements of Muhammad were the founding of a state and a religion. He was politically successful, created a federation of Arab tribes, and made the religion of Islam the basis of Arab unity. He died in 632 in Medina.

What followed was an amazing expansion of the Muslim faith throughout a large part of the world from Spain to Central Asia to India, Turkey, Africa, Indonesia, Malaya, and China—the same areas where the Muslims were very active traders. But the expansion was also due to suppression of alternate religious faiths. Jews and Christians were given a special status; they had to pay a tax to maintain their religious autonomy. Other religions were given a different choice: Accept Islam or die.

In the early days of the faith, Islam became a part of both the spiritual and temporal aspects of Muslim life. There was not only an Islamic religious institution but also Islamic law, state, and other government institutions. It wasn't until the twentieth century that the religious and secular were formally separated. Even so, Islam actually draws no absolute distinction between the religious and temporal parts of life; the Muslim state is by definition religious.

Central Beliefs

Islam is a monotheistic religion—Allah (God) is the sole god, the creator, sustainer, and restorer of the world. The overall purpose of humanity is to serve Allah, to worship Him alone, and to construct a moral lifestyle. The

Five Pillars of Islam were set down as the anchor for life as a Muslim. A Muslim should express belief in them and uphold them in daily life.

The five pillars are:

1. **Profession of faith**. There is no God, but God; Muhammad is the prophet of God. Sometimes a variation is used: There is no God, but God and Muhammad is his prophet.
2. **Prayer**. A Muslim must pray five times a day facing Mecca: before sunrise, just after noon, later in the afternoon, immediately before sunset, and after dark.
3. **The Zakat**. Each Muslim must pay a *zakat* (an obligatory tax paid once a year) to the state government.
4. **Fasting**. A Muslim must fast for the month of Ramadan (the ninth Muslim month). Fasting begins at daybreak and ends at sunset. During the fasting day eating, drinking, smoking, and sexual intercourse are forbidden.
5. **Hajj**. "Hajj" means "pilgrimage." A Muslim must make a pilgrimage to Mecca at least once in his lifetime, provided he is physically and financially able.

Holy Writings

The Qur'an or Koran is the holy book of Islam. According to one Muslim tradition, it was written by God and revealed to Muhammad by the angel Gabriel from his first revelation at forty until his death at sixty-two. In another of the many traditions regarding the writing of the Qur'an, Muhammad had the revelations written down on pieces of paper, stones, palm leaves, or whatever writing materials were available. He indicated to the scribes the context in which the passages should be placed.

After the prophet's death, it was decided to find people who had learned the words by heart and to locate written excerpts from all parts of the Muslim Empire. The resulting information was edited to complete a correct edition of the work. Thus, an authoritative text of the Qur'an was eventually produced. It is held in very high regard; its Arabic language is considered unsurpassed in beauty and purity. To imitate the style of the Qur'an is a sacrilege.

The Qur'an is the primary source of every Muslim's faith and practice. It deals with the subjects that concern all human beings: wisdom, beliefs, worship, and law. However, it focuses on the relationship between God and his creatures. It also provides guidelines for a just society, proper human relationships, and equal division of power. The Qur'an also posits that life is a test and everyone will be rewarded or punished for their actions in the next life. For example, on the last day, when the world comes to an end, the dead will be resurrected and a judgment will be pronounced on every person in accordance with their deeds.

ESSENTIAL

Mecca is the birthplace of Muhammad and is the most sacred city in Islam. According to tradition, Muslims around the world must face Mecca during their daily prayers. Every year, during the last month of the Islamic calendar, more than 1 million Muslims make a pilgrimage or hajj to Mecca. Muslims are obliged to make the hajj once in their lifetime.

Another source of Islamic doctrine is the Hadith (a report or collection of sayings attributed to the prophet and members of the early Muslim community). The Hadith is second only to the authority of the Qur'an. It is considered the biography of Muhammad created from the long memory of the members of his community. Hadith was a vital element during the first three centuries of Islamic history, and its study gives a broad index into the philosophy of Islam.

To the non-Muslim, the Hadith is an introduction to the world of Islam with almost encyclopedic inclusiveness. Provisions of law are the primary element, dealing with the moral, social, commercial, and personal aspects of life and the theological aspects of death and final destiny. The content of the Hadith has the kind of minutia found in the Talmud, the body of Jewish civil and ceremonial law and legend.

There is evidence of the impact on Islam of Jewish and Christian philosophies and theology, particularly as they relate to the last judgment. Together, the Qur'an and the Hadith form the basis of Islamic law.

Worship and Practices

The Qur'an forbids the worshiping of idols, which means Muslims are not permitted to make images either of Allah or of the prophet. Some Muslims object to any form of representational art because of the inherent danger of idolatry. For this reason, mosques are often decorated with geometric patterns.

A great sin in Islam is something called shirk, or blasphemy. The Qur'an stresses that God does not share his powers with any partner. It warns that those who believe their idols will intercede for them will find that they and their idols will become fuel for hellfire on the Day of Judgment.

Different grades of shirk have been identified in Islamic law. The shirking of custom includes all superstitions, such as the belief in omens. The shirking of knowledge, for instance, is to credit anyone, such as astrologers, with knowledge of the future.

Many of Muhammad's restrictions in the Qur'an were explicit in establishing distinctions between Arabs and Jews as shown, for example, in his dietary rules, which borrowed heavily from the Mosaic Law. The most radical difference between the Qur'an and Mosaic laws has to do with intoxicating beverages. Jews frown on alcoholic beverages, but they do not forbid them entirely; wine is an important element in many Jewish rituals and feasts. However, Muhammad absolutely forbade the use of such beverages.

Prayer and Mosques

Prayer has been described as the act of communication by humans with the sacred or holy. The Islamic Qur'an is regarded as a book of prayers, as is the book of Psalms in the Bible, considered to be a meditation on biblical history turned into prayer. Prayer obviously takes as many forms as there are religions.

Muslims are expected to pray five times a day at definite times, wherever they happen to be. In addition to that practice, on Fridays all Muslim men are also expected to attend the mosque for the after-midday prayer. Friday is not an identifiable holy day in the manner that Christians and Jews, for instance, consider the Sabbath. In Islam, business may go on as usual before and after the midday prayers.

Islam teaches that the whole world is a mosque because a person can pray to God anywhere. Islam makes no distinction between what is sacred and the everyday; however, every mosque has an area with a water supply so that the devout may wash their hands, feet, and face before prayer. Muslims may use sand for washing if water isn't available.

FACT

The first mosques were modeled on Muhammad's place of worship, which was the courtyard of his house in Medina. The first mosques were just plots of earth marked out as sacred. At the mosque, the worshipers align themselves in rows, spaced so they may kneel and bow without touching those in front of them.

There is no prescribed architectural design for mosques. They generally have a minaret in an elevated place, usually a tower, for the crier or muezzin to proclaim the call to worship. The muezzin stands at either the door or side of a small mosque or on the minaret of a large mosque. He faces each of the four directions in turn: east, west, north, and south. To each direction, he cries:

Allah is most great.

I testify that there is no God but Allah.

I testify that Muhammad is the prophet of Allah.

Come to prayer.

Come to salvation.

Allah is most great.

There is no God but Allah.

The muezzin's call to worship is followed by the imam, who leads the community prayers, and then the khatib, who often preaches the Friday sermon. Sometimes the imam performs all three functions. The imam is not a priest; although he can't perform any rites, he usually conducts marriages and funerals. The imam generally acts as a leader of the local Muslim community and gives advice about Islamic law and customs. Imams are picked for their wisdom.

Islam does not use liturgical vestments in the way many religions do; instead, it has universal regulations governing dress. For example, all who enter a mosque must remove their footwear, and all individuals on a pilgrimage must wear the same habit, the *hiram*, and thus appear in holy places as a beggar.

Inside a mosque, no representations of Allah or humans, plants, or animals are allowed. Women who attend, particularly in America, should wear a head scarf (*hijab*) and avoid wearing jewelry, particularly any that might depict people or animals or Jewish or Christian religious imagery. Modesty should be the guiding factor; Muslim girls and women cover their hair completely.

While women may attend prayers in a mosque, they are seated in a separate area, often upstairs if there is one, in a gallery so that neither sex is distracted.

ESSENTIAL

The imam—the title means the spiritual leader of the entire community—is an individual with religious training who is learned in the Koran. On Fridays, the leader often gives a sermon that addresses political and religious problems or points of interest.

All Muslim prayer is made facing Makkah (Mecca). When prayers are held congregationally, people stand in rows shoulder to shoulder with no gaps or reserved spaces. All are considered equal when standing before God. Muslim prayers are memorized; new members of the faith generally have someone to guide them until they commit the prayers to memory.

Rituals and Customs

Birth is not observed in any established routine manner; local traditions vary greatly. Many Muslims wish that the first sounds a baby hears is the call to prayer whispered in each ear. Boys must be circumcised between the ages of seven days and twelve years.

Marriage in Islam is considered God's provision for humanity; no value is given to celibacy. Parents are responsible for choosing marriage partners for their children; marriage is considered to be a joining of two families, not just two people. However, the Qur'an says that the girl must give her consent and not be forced into marriage.

Marriage is a contract between a man and a woman, not a religious rite. Although it does not have to be performed in a mosque with an imam in attendance, it must be conducted according to Islamic law with two male Muslim witnesses. Nevertheless, marriage is seen as a state blessed by God.

Divorce is allowed, but it is certainly discouraged. Islamic law allows a man to have more than one wife; in traditional Islamic societies, this is one way of trying to make sure that women can have the protection of family life. However, the Prophet Muhammad advised that unless a man feels able to treat the wives equally, he should marry only one.

Observant Muslims believe that their deaths are predetermined by Allah as part of His design. Therefore, death should not be feared, for the deceased will go to Paradise. To overdo mourning would show a mistrust of God's love and mercy.

FACT

Muslims believe in the resurrection of the body. Accordingly, they bury their dead quickly, giving all due care to treat the body with respect. The body is washed and shrouded in linen and then buried quickly, usually in a day.

In Islam, on the Day of Judgment Allah will raise all the dead and judge them. The good will go to Paradise, the others to the fire.

Aside from being ritually washed and wrapped in a linen shroud, all Muslims, regardless of sect, are dressed in the standard grave clothes, which number three: an upper shroud, a lower garment, and an overall shroud. Only martyrs are buried in the clothes in which they die, without their bodies or garments being washed. As evidence of their state of glory, the blood and dirt are on view.

Festivals and Celebrations

There are few major Islamic festivals in the year. However, local Muslim communities have their own traditions, which add to the year's festivities.

Muharram is the first month of the year in Islam. New Year's Day is not a major holiday. Ramadan, a month of fasting, is the ninth month of the Muslim year. Adult Muslims do not eat, drink, smoke, or have conjugal relations from dawn to sunset. Children under the age of puberty are exempt, although they make a limited fast.

ESSENTIAL

Muslims follow a different calendar than the one observed in the western world. The Islamic calendar is lunar, and unlike most other lunar calendars, is not adjusted to keep in step with the solar year. Thus, Muslim dates tend to change constantly in relation to the western solar calendar. Years are counted from the Prophet Muhammad's move to Medina in 622. The year 2000 was 1420/21 A.H. (in the year of Hegira).

Lailat ul-Qadr, also known as The Night of Determination, is believed to have occurred around the twenty-seventh, but is now considered one of the last ten nights of Ramadan. Many Muslims spend these days and nights in the mosque so they will be in prayer on The Night of Determination when Allah makes decisions about the destiny of individuals and the world as a whole.

Eid ul-Fitr celebrates the end of the month of fasting and lasts for three days. Prayers are offered, special foods prepared, and gifts are exchanged.

Eid ul-Adha, known as the Feast of Sacrifice, celebrates the willingness of Abraham to sacrifice his son Isaac when God asked him to. God commanded a lamb be sacrificed instead of Ishmael. The sacrifice of a lamb is an important part of the festival.

Al-Isra Wal Miraj is the night of the ascension of Muhammad to Heaven to meet with Allah. It is celebrated on the twenty-seventh day of the seventh month. It is said the prophet set out the disciplines of the daily prayers.

Muhammad-Maulid al-Nabi celebrates the birth of the prophet Muhammad. It is held on the twelfth day of the third month and is a highly popular festival that draws thousands of visitors who join in processions and prayers.

Developments of Modern Islam

To be a Muslim, or at least a reasonably devout one, is a way of life. Whereas other religions usually have at least an implied division between the secular and the religious, that is not the case with Muslims. Daily life is where Islam resides—the religion is about a way of living. The Qur'an and the Hadith provide the guidance to carry that out.

Islamic Law

Islamic law is founded on the Shari'ah that is based on the Qur'an, the Hadith, and the advice and wisdom of scholars. Allah is seen as the supreme lawgiver. The integration of this philosophy is directly related to the demographics of the country where Islam is being practiced. In countries where Muslims are in the minority, the integration of religion and secular activities will be less than where Muslims are in the majority. Money comes under the guidance of the Qur'an, which forbids usury and the charging of interest, though it approves making a fair profit. Naturally, this can be difficult to implement in a world market. In the Qur'an, business dealings and their outcome are described as "seeking the bounty of God." Wealth should first be used for the support of family then shared with those in need. The Qur'an also forbids gambling.

Jihad

Jihad in Arabic means "fighting" or "striving." In Islam, it is a doctrine that calls upon believers to devote themselves to combating the enemies of their religion. The term has been used in more recent times to describe a "holy war," even though this is not its literal meaning. Historically, the term was applied to wars between various Muslim sects and non-Muslim ones.

Family Life

Family life is an essential part of the Muslim way of living; all family members should care for one another. The Prophet Muhammad made particular reference about a man taking care of his mother. Animals, too, are to be respected and treated in ways that do not violate their lives in the family or community. Animals used for food must be slaughtered in the correct way. Pig meat and alcohol are strictly forbidden.

Sunnis and Shiites

Of the two main groups within Islam, Sunni Muslims compose 85–90 percent of all adherents and Shiite Muslims about 10–15 percent. In the late twentieth century, the Sunni made up the majority of Muslims in all nations except Iran, Iraq, Bahrain, and perhaps Yemen. All told, they numbered nearly 1 billion. Sunni Muslims view themselves as the traditional, mainstream, pragmatic branch of Islam; in fact, they became known as the orthodox element in Islam. This claim, however, is in dispute, since all orientations in Islam are a result of the common Islamic origin.

Religious and Political Differences

In early Islamic history, Shiite Muslims were the more political of the two groups. When problems arose over the rightful successors to Muhammad, the Sunni said the first four caliphs were Muhammad's rightful successors, whereas the opposing minority, the Shiites, believed that Muslim leadership belonged to Muhammad's son-in-law, Ali, and then to his descendants. This disagreement led to continuous internal wars that proved to be largely unsuccessful from Ali's point of view. However, Ali's status was eventually recognized and he became a major hero of Sunni Islam.

In contrast to the Shiites, who believed that the leadership of Islam was determined by divine order or inspiration, the Sunni regarded leadership as the result of the prevailing Muslim political realities. Historically, the leadership was in the hands of the foremost families of Mecca. For the Sunni, balance between spiritual and political authority afforded both the correct exercise of religious order and practical maintenance of the Muslim world.

Sunni orthodoxy placed strong emphasis on the majority view of the community. Over the years, this perspective provided them the opportunity to include matters that were outside the root teaching of the Qur'an. Thus, the Sunni have earned the reputation of being religiously and culturally diverse.

The religious and political differences between Sunni Islam and Shia Islam have been fraught with enmity and dissension throughout history. Today, Iran is the bastion of Shia Islam—its state religion—and the majority of Iranians are Shiites. Even so, people in Iran do practice other religions, such as Judaism, Christianity, and even Zoroastrianism, an ancient faith that predates Judaism. Shia adherents also live in Syria, East Africa, India, and Pakistan. Overall, Shiites comprise somewhere in the region of 80 million people, or a tenth of all Muslims.

Shiites maintain that only those in the bloodline of Muhammad are the legitimate heirs of Islam. Shia Islam is often called "twelver" because Iranians generally recognized only twelve imams or supreme religious leaders following the death of Muhammad. The twelfth of these is Mardi, the so-called hidden imam, who is still alive in some celestial state. The ayatollahs, highly respected scholars and teachers of Shia Islam, stand in for Mardi as they interpret the words of Muhammad.

Religious Practices

The religious practices of the Shiites are different from those of the Sunni. For devout Shiites, a pilgrimage to Mecca is the most important religious practice, but they also visit the tombs of the eleven earthly imams, and Iranians frequently cross the boarder into Iraq to visit the tomb of Ali.

In the twentieth century, Shiites became a major political force in Iran, where they deposed a secularist monarchy, and in Lebanon, where they led resistance to Israeli occupation in the south during the 1980s and 1990s.

The Shiites, from a western point of view, would probably be considered the more conservative of the two main factions in Islam. Their doctrine has always firmly revolved around the Qur'an, and in modern times, they have become the chief voice of militant Islamic fundamentalism.

CHAPTER 11

Confucianism

Confucianism, which means "teaching of the scholars," is an ethical code and spiritual philosophy founded on the teaching of Confucius (551–479 B.C.E.), the best known and most influential thinker in Chinese history. He was honored in Chinese chronicles as the Great Master K'ung or K'ung Fu-tzu. In the West, he is simply known by the Latinized "Confucius." Confucianism is more a worldview than a world religion. It is a social ethic, a political ideology, and a scholarly tradition.

Origins and Development

Confucianism was started in China between the sixth and fifth centuries B.C.E. and has been followed by the Chinese people for over two millennia. A major part of the belief is an emphasis on learning as well as a source of values.

Confucius was an educator and transmitter of knowledge rather than a creative thinker. In accepting students, he applied no class distinctions, accepting the poor as well as the rich. One of his inestimable contributions was the redefinition of key terms in Chinese life and thought along ethical and humanistic lines. For instance, the term *chun tzu*, meaning "son of a ruler" or person of noble birth, was extended by Confucius to refer to anyone who was benevolent and modest of speech, regardless of background.

FACT

The Four Books—The Analects, The Great Learning, The Mean, and The Book of Mencius—refer to ancient Confucian texts that were used officially in civil service exams in China for over 500 years. They introduced Confucian literature to students who then progressed to the more difficult texts, the Five Classics: The Book of History, The Book of Poems, The Book of Change (I Ching), The Spring and Autum Annals, and The Book of Rites.

The influence of Confucianism has spread across many other countries, including Korea, Japan, and Vietnam. Confucianism is now regarded seriously in the United States, where the culture has gone far beyond the derogatory stereotypical image of the Charlie Chan detective movies of the 1930s and 1940s and their fortune-cookie sayings. Confucianism made its mark extensively in Chinese literature, education, culture, and both spiritual and political life.

Confucius lived in a time of political violence, setting the stage for a teacher with the ability to dispense a spiritual philosophy that would generate restorative thoughts of social and ethical calm, and who saw perfection in all people. It is said he initially attracted over 3,000 students, some of whom became close disciples.

Confucius

Confucius was born in the small state of Lu in 551 B.C.E., in what is now Shan-tung Province. As a thinker and teacher, Confucius made an important contribution to political thought, with his insistence on the connection between ethics and politics. He thought that government included a moral responsibility and was not primarily the manipulation of power.

He was born into an aristocratic family that had seen much better times. His father died when he was only three years old, and his mother educated him at home. By the time he was a teenager, he inquired about everything and had set his heart on learning. He started as a keeper of stores and accounts, but moved on to other minor posts in government. However, he had difficulty finding a good job even though he was ambitious and willing to do anything. He never gave up his first love—learning. He found teachers who would school him in music, archery, calligraphy, and arithmetic. From his family he had learned the classics: poetry, literature, and history.

When he was nineteen, he married a woman of a similar background to his own. Not much else is known about her. They apparently had a son and daughter.

The Teachings of Confucius

All Confucius's learning qualified him to teach, which he started to do in his thirties. He became known as the first teacher in China whose concern was providing education for all. The rich had tutors for their children; he believed everyone could benefit from self-education. He defined learning as not only the acquisition of knowledge but also the building of character.

A major point in his teaching was filial piety, the virtue of devotion to one's parents. He considered it the foundation of virtue and the root of human character. Interestingly, the male attitude toward sex was strict. The purpose of sex was to conceive children, preferably sons. Sexual excess on the part of a ruler was given as a valid reason to take the right to rule from him.

Proper social behavior and etiquette were considered essential to right living. An ethical view is set forth in the Analects, a collection of moral and social teachings that amount to a code of human conduct. Many of the sayings were passed on orally. Here are some examples:

Clever words and a plausible appearance have seldom turned out to be humane.

Young men should be filial when at home and respectful to elders when away from home. They should be earnest and trustworthy. Although they should love the multitude far and wide, they should be intimate only with the humane. If they have any energy to spare after so doing, they should use it to study culture.

The gentleman is calm and peaceful; the small man is always emotional.

In his attitude to the world the gentleman has no antagonisms and no favoritisms. What is right he sides with.

If one acts with a view to profit, there will be much resentment.

One who can bring about the practice of five things everywhere under Heaven has achieved humanity . . . courtesy, tolerance, good faith, diligence, and kindness.

ESSENTIAL

Confucius concentrated his teachings on his vision, *Jen*, which has been translated in the most complete way as: love, goodness, and human-heartedness; moral achievement and excellence in character; loyalty to one's true nature; then righteousness; and, finally, filial piety. All this adds up to the principle of virtue within the person.

Confucian Literature

The most important Confucian literature comprises two sets of books. The major one is the Five Classics. While Confucius may not have personally written them, he was associated with them. The Five Classics contain five visions: I Ching (Classic of Changes); Shu Ching (Classic of History); Shih

Ching (Classic of Poetry); LiChi (Collection of Rituals); and Ch'un-ch'iu (Spring and Autumn-Annals). For 2,000 years, their influence has been without parallel in the history of China.

When Chinese students were studying for civil service examinations between 1313 and 1905, they were required to study the Five Classics; however, before they reached that level they tackled the Four Books, which served as an introduction to the Five. The Four Books have commentaries by Chu Hsi, a great Neo-Confucian philosopher who helped revitalize Confucianism in China. Confucian Classics, as they were called, became the core curriculum for all levels of education.

FACT

The I Ching, one of the Five Classics of Confucianism, combines divinatory art with numerological techniques and ethical insight. There are two complementary and conflicting vital energies: yin and yang. Enthusiasts have claimed that this Classic of Changes is a means of understanding and even controlling future events.

The Reputation of Confucius

The edicts of Confucius did not go without criticism, much of it based on what was seen as his idealism and unrealistic attitudes. Confucius said that, unlike Buddhist belief, karma was not a force in the progress of man resulting from moral goodness or the lack of it; rather, it was destiny. Confucianism taught that a person should choose what to do in a single-minded manner, without taking into consideration what the outcome may be. Is human nature fundamentally good or bad? Confucius didn't have an answer. As time went by, the positive view became the orthodoxy.

Confucius developed his ambition to become active in the teaching of politicians. He wanted to put his humanist ideas into practice and saw government employees as the best conduit. In his early forties and fifties he became a magistrate, then eventually a minister of justice in his home state of Lu.

Confucius's pronouncements on the cultivation of the gentleman are in the Analects or "Selected Sayings," (Lun Yu), the earliest parts of which were composed shortly after his death. They provide an insight into his ideal of the Superior Person. He said:

> *If there is righteousness in the heart, there will be beauty in the character. If there is beauty in the character, there will be harmony in the home. If there be harmony in the home, there will be order in the nation. If there be order in the nation, there will be peace in the world.*

ESSENTIAL

Confucius was asked for advice on how to induce people to be loyal. He answered, "Approach them with dignity, and they will respect you. Show piety toward your parents and kindness toward your children, and they will be loyal to you. Promote those who are worthy, train those who are incompetent; that is the best form of encouragement."

The reputation of Confucius grew, as did the number of his disciples. Trouble came, of course, because he generated the enmity of those who opposed his teachings and growing influence. His political career was short-lived, and at the age of fifty-six when he realized his influence had declined, he moved on and tried to find a feudal state in which he could teach and give service. He was more or less in exile, but his reputation as a man of virtue spread.

When he was sixty-seven years old, he returned home to teach, write, and edit. He died in 479 B.C.E. at the age of seventy-two.

Rituals and Customs

As Confucianism does not have all the elements of a religion and is primarily an ethical movement, it lacks sacraments and liturgy. However, the rituals that occur at important times in a person's life became part of the movement. Confucianism recognizes and regulates four life passages—birth, reaching maturity, marriage, and death. At the root is the ritual of respect: A person must exhibit respect to gain respect.

Birth

The Tai-shen (spirit of the fetus) protects the expectant woman and deals harshly with anyone who harasses the mother to be. The mother is given a special diet and is allowed to rest for a month after delivery. The mother's family is responsible for coming up with all that is required by the baby on the first-, fourth-, and twelfth-month anniversaries of the birth.

Marriage

There are six stages that couples go through in the marriage process:

- **Proposal**. The couple exchange the year, month, day, and hour of each of their births. If any unpropitious event happens within the bride-to-be's family during the following three days, the woman is believed to have rejected the proposal.
- **Engagement**. After the wedding day has been chosen, the bride announces the wedding with invitations and a gift of cookies made in the shape of the moon.
- **Dowry**. This is carried to the groom's home in a solemn procession. Gifts equal in value to the dowry are sent to the bride by the groom.
- **Procession**. The groom visits the bride's home and brings her back to his place, with much fanfare.
- **Marriage and reception**. The couple recite their vows that bond them together for a lifetime, toast each other with wine, then take center stage at a banquet.
- **Morning after**. The bride serves breakfast to the groom's parents, who then reciprocate.

Death

At death, the relatives cry aloud to inform the neighbors. The family starts mourning and puts on clothes made of coarse material. The corpse is washed and placed in a coffin. Mourners bring incense and money to offset the cost of the funeral. Food and significant objects of the deceased are placed into the coffin. A Buddhist or Taoist priest, or even a Christian minister, performs the burial ritual. Friends and family follow the coffin to the cemetery, bringing a willow branch, which symbolizes the soul of the person who has died.

The branch is later carried back to the family altar where it is used to "install" the spirit of the deceased. Liturgies are performed on the seventh, ninth, and forty-ninth days after the burial, and on the first and third anniversaries of the death.

FACT

On Confucius's death, his students compiled his thoughts in Spring and Autumn Annals. Mencius spread the values of Confucianism throughout the known world. With the increasing popularity in Confucius, his disciples and followers left sacrifices in temples dedicated to him. The People's Republic of China banned the ritual sacrifices in 1906.

Diversification into Modern Society

Not long after Confucius's death, his followers split into eight separate schools, and all of them claimed to be the legitimate heir to the legacy. Many superior disciples surfaced though, including Tseng-tzu, Tzu Kung, and Tzu-hsia. They were instrumental in continuing the teachings and legacy of Confucius. The man who had the greatest influence on Confucianism and its continuance is Mencius, known as the Confucian intellectual.

Mencius sought social reform in a society that had become oriented almost totally for profit, self-interest, wealth, and power. It was the philosophy of Mencius that a true man could not be corrupted by wealth. Rather than challenging the power structure head on, Mencius offered a compromise of right living and wealth. That way the wealthy could have their cake and eat it and preserve protection for themselves and their families. Mencius's strategy was to make the urge for profit and self-interest part of a moral attitude that emphasized public spiritedness, welfare, and rightness. This attitude of acknowledging human nature and its desire for success and self-improvement in shaping the human condition might today be thought of as surprisingly modern, particularly when one considers when it was said.

Mencius was followed by Hsun-tzu (300–230 B.C.E.), one of the most eminent of noble scholars. Unlike Mencius, Hsun-tzu taught that human nature is evil because he considered that it was natural for men to go after gratification of their passions. His attitude, as opposed to that of Mencius, was that learning produced a cultured person who, by definition, became a virtuous member of a community. Hsun-tzu's stance was a tough, moral reasoning. He believed in progress, and his sophisticated understanding of the political mindset around him enriched the Confucian heritage. Confucians revered him as the finest of scholars for more than three centuries.

The influence of Confucianism on China in particular was largely due to the power of its disciples and of the written works of not only Confucius but also his followers. The vitality of the Confucian ethic permeated much of the basic elements of societal thought and political action in the eastern hemisphere that was unprecedented. But in modern times it began to wane, due to the rise of Marxism-Leninism in 1949 as the official ideology of the People's Republic of China. Confucianism was pushed into the background. In spite of that, the upper crust of that society kept a publicly unacknowledged link that amazingly continued to influence aspects of behavior; it had an effect on the attitudes at every level of life. Confucian roots run extremely deep.

In other regions, especially Japan, Korea, Taiwan, Singapore, and North America, there has been a revival of Confucian studies. Thinkers in the West have been inspired by the philosophy and have begun to explore what it might mean today. Even in China, exploration is taking place between what might be a fruitful interaction between Confucian humanism and other kinds of political practices. There are six different schools of Confucianism: Han Confucianism, Neo-Confucianism, Contemporary Neo-Confucianism, Korean Confucianism, Japanese Confucianism, and Singaporean Confucianism.

CHAPTER 12

Taoism

The word *Tao* signifies "path" or "way." Taoism is a Chinese system of thought and until the twentieth century, one of the three major religions of China, along with Confucianism and Buddhism. In English, Tao is pronounced "dow." The Tao is a natural force that makes the universe the way it is. It has also been referred to as "the way of heaven."

Origins and Development

The foundation of Taoism, the second of the great Chinese traditions, is attributed partially to Laozi (Lao Tzu) and his written material called the Dao De Ding or Tao Te Ching ("The Way and its Power"). He advocates the philosophy of disharmony or harmony of opposites, meaning there is no love without hate, no light without dark, no male without female—in short, yin and yang. Collectively, the writings called Tao Tsang are concerned with the ritual meditations of the Tao. Adherents of the philosophy are called Taoists.

FACT

Little is known about the life dates of Lao Tzu; he is sometimes placed in the sixth century and sometimes in the fourth. What is beyond doubt is that the book attributed to him, the Tao Te Ching, is a work held in the highest regard not only in China but in many parts of the world.

Taoism is generally seen as a balance to Confucianism, rather than in opposition to it. Taoism seeks harmony with the nature of things through a humble submission to the Way Tao, which for Taoists is the ultimate metaphysical principle of being. In its way, Confucianism also seeks a harmony with nature, but with Confucianism this is achieved by enacting rituals and ceremonies deemed conducive to it. Where Confucianism is ceremonial, Taoism is intuitive and meandering.

Taoist thought permeated the Chinese culture the same way Confucianism did, and the two are often linked. Taoism became more popular than Confucianism, even though Confucianism enjoyed state patronage. Taoism was based on the individual and tended to reject the organized society of Confucianism. The traditions became so well entrenched within China that many people accepted both of them, although they applied the concepts to their lives in different ways.

Taoism wasn't a religious faith when it began; it was conceived as a philosophy and evolved into a religion that has a number of deities. Lao Tzu, who many credit as the founder of Taoism, was so revered he was often thought of as a deity or a mystical character.

Nonaction

A key Taoist concept is that of nonaction or the natural course of things. It is a direct link to yin and yang. Yin (dark/female) represents cold, feminine, and negative principles. The yang (light/male) represents warmth, masculine, and positive principles. Yin (the dark side) is the breath that formed the earth. Yang (the light side) is the breath that formed the heavens. When civilization gets in the way, the balance of yin and yang is upset. A western person might remark that one needs to get out of one's own way to get anywhere. However, yin and yang are not polar opposites; they are values in people that depend on individual circumstances. What is cold for one person may be warm for another. Yin and yang are identical aspects of the same reality.

The study, practice, and readings of yin and yang have become a school of philosophy in its own right. The idea is for the student to find balance in life where yin represents inactivity, rest, and reflection and yang represents activity and creativity. The basic feature of Taoism is restoring balance. Extremes produce a swinging back to the opposite. Therefore, there is a constant movement from activity to inactivity and back again.

ESSENTIAL

Buddhism was the other religion close to Taoism, and it held sway with people in the same way that Confucianism did. However, Buddhist notions of the nonexistence of the individual ego and the illusory nature of the physical world didn't square with Taoism; in fact, Taoists were opposed to them. Taoism and Buddhism did share common ground, however, as with the practice of Zen.

It's not easy to define Taoism in any formal way because its philosophy doesn't have a concrete system. While it shares many of the same ideas about man, society, and the universe as Confucianism, its attitude tends to be more personal and metaphysical. Taoism must be experienced, and thus words like "power" and "energy" are frequently used to describe what actually can't be measured in any scientific form. That said, it's interesting that Taoism had a bent toward science, especially medicine. Taoist faith healers contributed to medical knowledge and literature with the production of the medical book The Yellow Emperor's Esoteric Classic, which included experiments with natural ingredients such as plants and minerals.

Interest in science reflected the Taoist emphasis on direct observation and experience of the nature of things. But there is a sort of contradiction of terms because a tremendous amount of the work was based not on scientific discovery but intuitive thought and experience. It is said that much of the knowledge died with the men who discovered it, for they did not share it with future generations.

Lao Tzu

Lao Tzu's birth date is unknown, with scholars placing it between 600 and 400 B.C.E.; it is most likely close to the sixth century. In his biography, *Records of the Historian,* it is said that he was a contemporary of Confucius (there is some evidence that he may have met and instructed Confucius on one occasion) and once served as curator of the dynastic archives until retiring to the mythical K'un-lun Mountains. Thereupon he transmitted his teachings to a border guard who compiled the Tao Te Ching. The name "Lao Tzu" signifies "old person" or "old philosopher."

The Tao Te Ching, purported to contain Lao Tzu's great teachings, is a compilation. Most scholars agree that the sayings were gathered over many years, with some ascribed to Lao Tzu and others to his disciples. The work is a collection of pithy aphorisms or sayings that express the ideas that make up his teachings.

The Tao Te Ching has been referred to as a "wisdom book." Here is a sampling:

There is nothing better than to know that you don't know.

Not knowing, yet thinking you know—

This is sickness.

Only when you are sick of being sick

Can you be cured.

The sage's not being sick

Is because she is sick of sickness.

Therefore she is not sick.

Central Beliefs

The Taoist philosophy is at once oblique and difficult, poetic and aphoristic. The Taoists rejected the Confucian idea of regulating life and society, saying it's better to be concerned with a contemplation of nature. They believed that by doing nothing they could accomplish everything and harness the powers of the universe. Here is another passage from the Tao Te Ching:

The Tao abides in non-action,

Yet nothing is left undone.

If kings and lords observed this,

The ten thousand things would develop naturally.

If they still desired to act,

They would return to the simplicity of formless substance.

Without form there is no desire.

Without desire there is tranquility.

In this way all things would be at peace.

The Taoist sage has no ambitions so he cannot fail.

Those who never fail always succeed.

And those who succeed are all-powerful.

The Tao has been described as the origin and mother of the Ten Thousand Things—a standard phrase to show that everything exists. One achieves without force. One gives life without possessing the things one has created. This is the essence of naturalness. One cannot grasp this philosophy with the intellect. One becomes aware, but unable to define.

FACT

At the main entrance of many Taoist temples is an elaborately colored container. It is for joss sticks (incense sticks), which are placed there to be lit. The rising incense symbolizes prayers offered to heaven. On either side of the container will be carved dragons; similarly, there will be dragons on the roof of the temple. These symbolize strength, energy, and life force.

The idea of a personal deity is foreign to Taoism, as is the concept of the creation of the universe. The Tao—a natural force—constrains the universe to act as it does. Yet nature is full of deities; the most familiar are those connected with childbirth, wealth, and health. But a Taoist does not pray as the Christians do, for they believe there is no god to hear the prayers or act upon them. On the contrary, the way to seek answers is through inner meditation and outer observation. Their beliefs can be summed up thus: The Tao surrounds everyone and everything so everyone must listen to find enlightenment.

Taoists have an affinity for promoting good health. They believe that there are five elements: water, fire, wood, metal, and earth. Everything outside of and inside of your body belongs to one of these elements. When the five elements are balanced within your body, you are healthy, if they out of balance you will experience disease of some kind. Each person should nurture the chi (breath) that refers to the spirit, energy, or life force within everything. There are Yoga-style and Tai Chi exercises to help accomplish this.

The art of *wu wei*—action through no action or do without doing—should be practiced. One way of looking at this is to imagine standing still in a flowing river and letting what is opposing do all the work. By standing still, you appear to move against the current by not moving against it. To an outsider, it would appear that you were taking no action, but in fact, you have taken action before others have foreseen such a need. It follows that you should plan in advance and consider what to do before doing it.

The essential belief of Taoism is that the only permanent thing in life is change. Taoism says that because everything is changing, people are tempted to look ahead to find something that is permanent. Once they do that, a person ceases to be aware of the present. When that happens, the tendency is for the present to be interpreted in terms of the past. Taoism says a person should be in the reality of the now—the present moment.

ESSENTIAL

Traditional Chinese medicine believes that illness is caused by blockages or lack of balance of the body's chi. The practice of Tai Chi balances this energy flow. Through the gradual building of your inner energy you can discover how soft overcomes hard. Tai Chi is known as an internal art because of its emphasis on internal Chi power rather than on external physical power that helps restore balance.

The world is as it is. If it is perfect, then that is what is, not what people imagine it should be. That being so, any change will make things less than perfect. The enemy of human perfection is the unnatural, which includes the forced, premeditated, and socially prescribed.

Writings

The major piece of literature in Taoism is Lao Tzu's Tao Te Ching, though it hasn't been established that Lao Tzu was the sole author. There are no references in the work to other persons, events, places, or even writings that could provide any evidence to assist in placing or dating the composition. The fact that the author or location of the work can't be authenticated is somehow in keeping with the philosophy of Taoism; the work exists and that is everything.

The essence of the book is pure simplicity: One should accept what is without wanting to change it. Study the natural order and go with it, rather than against it. The effort to change something creates resistance. Everything nature provides is free; a person should emulate nature and consider everyone as an equal.

If people stand and observe, they will see that work proceeds best if they stop trying too hard. The more extra effort you exert and the harder you look for results, the less gets done. The philosophy of Taoism is one of being more than doing.

The Tao Te Ching was compiled in an environment rife with widespread disorder, wanton self-seeking rulers, and rampant immoral behavior. The popularity of the work has been, and remains, widespread. An amazing number of translations have been produced, more than for any other literary work except the Bible. There have been eighty English translations alone.

FACT

> One example of the use of harmony and meditation is the practice of *Feng Shui.* The literal meaning is "wind and water," which are the natural elements that shape the landscape. A Feng Shui expert can advise how to get the best results in a home or office by establishing the most advantageous alignment of space and furnishings to allow the most positive and harmonious flow of chi.

Chuang Tzu

Chuang Tzu was a great Taoist sage who lived around 327 B.C.E. He is best known for the book that bears his name, the Chuang Tzu, also known as Nan-hua Chenching (The Pure Classic of Nan-hua). It is thought to have once comprised thirty-three chapters, although there may have been more. As with many works from antiquity, controversy abounds over what the author wrote and what others contributed. However, scholars agree that the first seven chapters of the Chuang-tzu were written by the author alone.

He wrote other books highly critical of Confucianism. On the other hand, he was seen as being a great influence on the development of Chinese Buddhism. Buddhist scholars considered Chuang Tzu to be the primary source for Taoist thought and they drew heavily from his teachings. Overall, he was considered the most significant and comprehensive of the Taoist writers.

Apparently, when he was near death, there was talk of an elaborate funeral. Chuang Tzu dismissed the idea and said that all creation would make offerings and escort him on his way. His disciples replied that they were afraid that the crows and buzzards might eat him if he wasn't properly prepared. Chuang Tzu replied, "Above the ground it's the crows and the kites who will eat me, below the ground it's the worms and the ants. What prejudice is this, that you wish to take from the one to give to the other?"

ESSENTIAL

The following example of the value of living naturally comes from Chuang Tzu. He said that a drunk could fall from a moving carriage without hurting himself, whereas a sober person would be injured by the same fall. The reason is that the drunk is "united" and his body reacts naturally. The sober person, perceiving danger, tenses himself and is thus vulnerable.

Rituals and Customs

The religious aspects of Taoism are related more to shamanism than typical worship. In fact, Taoism shares strong elements of shamanism in its belief in the existence of two worlds: the physical and the spiritual. Taoist priests usually look after temples in urban areas. Monks and nuns live in temples located in sacred mountains. In general, monks and nuns are permitted to marry. Their work ensures the worship of the sacred texts, of which there are some 1,440 books.

In Taoism, there is a strong element of the ways and means of achieving immortality. Throughout life, adherents study and practice exercises designed to increase the flow of chi energy. The search is concerned with chi and its supply, meaning a need to create a greater reservoir of breath (chi). The essence of this is not that you would get younger but would live longer. Some adherents will become experts in meditation to the point where they become one with the Tao. A quote from the Chuang Tzu provides a good clue to the Taoist attitude toward life and death:

Birth is not a beginning; death is not an end. There is existence without limitation; there is continuity without a starting point.

Existence without limitation is space. Continuity without a starting point is time. There is birth, there is death, there is issuing forth, there is entering in. That through which one passes in and out without seeing its form is the Portal of God.

Birth and Death

Birth is a time for casting horoscopes. A month after the birth a naming ceremony is held. Death combines elements of Taoism, Buddhism, and Confucianism regarding life after death. Funeral rites have to be performed correctly for the dead to join the family ancestors. There is a belief that the soul is judged by the King of Hell. After the body is buried, paper models of money, houses, and cars are burnt to help the soul in the afterlife, perhaps by paying for a release from the King of Hell. After about ten years, the body is dug up. The bones are cleaned and reburied, often at a site chosen by a Feng Shui expert.

Festivals

Taoists and Buddhists share four major Chinese festivals. In addition, the Taoists celebrate many others throughout the year including the Taoist vegetarian and fasting days.

Chinese New Year is the major festival, also known as the Spring Festival. It is a time of great excitement and joy, not to mention abundant food and gifts and roving bands of musicians that parade through the streets. Families reunite and give lavish gifts to children. Traditionally, it is the time when new paper statues of the kitchen god are put up in houses. The door gods, who defend the house against evil spirits, are also replaced with new ones and good-luck sayings are hung over the doorways.

The high point of the season is New Year's Eve, when every member of every family returns home. A sumptuous dinner is served and children receive gifts of red envelopes containing lucky money. Firecrackers and whistles go off everywhere.

In preparation for the events, every house is thoroughly cleaned so the New Year will start off fresh and clean. Hair must be cleaned and set prior to the holiday; otherwise, a financial setback would be invited. Debts should also be settled so that the coming year can start off with a clean slate.

Following various religious ceremonies, the eleventh day is a time for inviting in-laws to dine. The Lantern Festival, on the fifteenth day after New Year, marks the end of the New Year season.

The Dragon Boat Festival is celebrated with boats in the shape of dragons. Competing teams row their boats forward to a drumbeat in an effort to win the race. Celebrated in June, the festival has two stories about the history of its meaning. The first one is about the watery suicide of an honest young official who tried to shock the emperor into being kinder to the poor. The race commemorates the people's attempt to rescue the boy in the lake from the dragons who rose to eat him. It is viewed as a celebration of honest government and physical strength.

QUESTION

How did the Taoists and Confucians get along together?
Confucians looked at Taoism as emotional, irrational, and magical. The Taoists looked at the Confucians as bureaucratic and imperialistic. But, it was the Confucian system that shaped China for over 2,000 years.

The third great festival is the Hungry Ghosts Festival. Taoists and Buddhists believe that the souls of the dead imprisoned in hell are freed during the seventh month, when the gates of hell are opened. The released souls are permitted to enjoy feasts prepared for them so they will be pacified and do no harm. Offerings and devotions, too, are made to please these ghosts and even musical events are staged to entertain them.

The Mid-Autumn Festival is also called the Moon Festival because of the bright harvest moon, which appears on the fifteenth day of the eighth lunar month. The round shape of the moon means family reunion, so, naturally, the holiday is particularly important for members of a family.

CHAPTER 13

Shinto

Shinto is the religion of Japan. The word "shinto" came from the Chinese words *shin* and *tao* ("the way of the gods/spirits"), a translation of the Japanese phrase *kami-no-michi*. *Kami* is the spiritual essence that exists in gods, human beings, animals, and even inanimate objects. The Shinto believe that the world is created, inhabited, and ruled by kami. The religion was named in the eighth century, after Buddhism was introduced, to distinguish the two.

Origins and Development

The Shinto religion is as old as the Japanese people. It has neither a founder nor sacred scriptures. Adherents believe that the world is created, inhabited, and ruled by kami, varied spirits running the gamut from those that reside in trees, rocks, oceans, and entire mountain ranges to spirits that act as guardians to various trades such as fisherman, laborers, or entire villages.

ESSENTIAL

There's no real way to describe kami other than the emotions it evokes: wonder, fear, and awe. Buddhists regard the kami as a manifestation of various Buddhas, but the Shintos believe that the Buddha is another kami or nature deity.

Shinto is one of two religions practiced by the Japanese people, the other being Buddhism. The two faiths have not always seen eye to eye on doctrine, but the differences haven't altered their peaceful coexistence.

Shinto was affected by the influx into Japan of Confucianism and Buddhism in the sixth century. Unlike the migration of other religions to foreign locations, this one did not cause conflict and disruption, at least for some years. Instead, both arrivals melded into the culture and a cross-fertilization of religious and cultural influences took place.

During the first century of Buddhism in Japan, it had a great influence on the arts, literature, and sciences and was the dominant religion of the upper classes. Buddhism evolved and merged with many aspects of Shintoism to incorporate the worship of kami. Buddhist priests then began to run many Shinto shrines and Shinto priests were demoted to the lower steps of the hierarchy ladder.

From earliest recorded times until the later part of the nineteenth century, Shinto and Buddhism coexisted without incident. The intermingling of Buddhism and Shinto even extended to sharing some rituals. For instance, Buddhists supervised the preaching and conducting of funeral services; Shinto priests oversaw the birth and marriage rituals. This didn't last forever, of course; eventually the Shinto priests wanted to establish and preserve their own identity. As a result, the Shinto priests began to assert their own ancient traditions in contrast to the foreign, more sophisticated Buddhist practices.

In 1868, things changed when the Emperor Meiji ascended to the throne. The Emperor used Japan's myths—linking the sun goddess to the emperor—to promote being worshiped as a living god. He then put Shinto shrines and priests under governmental control; State Shinto became the national religion. Then the discord started. Buddhist estates were seized, temples were closed, and Buddhist priests were persecuted.

FACT

Interestingly, Shinto could not coexist with Catholicism that arrived in the form of European missionaries. Initially, the guests were welcomed. However, the influx of more missionaries and their message proclaiming loyalty to a pope in faraway Rome began to anger the Shinto. In 1587, Christian missionaries were banned from Japan. For the next fifty years, many initiatives were enacted to abolish Christianity from the islands of Japan.

The state was divided into two: Shrine Shinto (Jinja Shinto) and Sectarian Shinto (Kyoha). Jinja was the larger group of the two and was the original form of the religion. A third sect called Folk Shinto (Minkoku) also developed; it was not an organized sect and was centered in agricultural and rural families. Shinto has had a proclivity to form subsects; altogether, there are more than 600 of them. However, when State Shinto evolved it promulgated nationalistic and racist overtones. In State Shinto, priests became civil servants. Many of them opposed the regime, but to no avail; State Shinto became mandatory throughout Japan.

State Shinto played a very significant role in Japanese society during its involvement in the Second World War. It wasn't until the defeat of Japan that it was officially discredited and banned by decree of the Allied occupation forces. Nevertheless, many Shinto followers apparently still held that the emperor was divine and a direct descendent of the sun goddess Amaterasu.

After the Second World War, Shinto was completely separated from the state and returned to being a nature-based, community-oriented faith. The shrines no longer belonged to the state, but to the Association of Shinto Shrines.

Central Beliefs

Shinto is very deeply rooted in the Japanese culture and traditions. It is an optimistic faith, believing all humans are fundamentally good and evil is caused by evil spirits. Its rituals are directed toward avoiding evil spirits through rites of purification, offerings, and prayers. Shinto lacks a fully developed theology; it has no concepts that compare to Christian or other beliefs concerning the wrath of God or the dogma of separation from God due to sin. All humanity is regarded as kami's child, so all life and human nature is sacred.

The absolute essence of Shinto philosophy is loyalty. It is of greater importance for a follower of Shinto to demonstrate loyalty than to do good deeds for others. A follower is absolutely loyal to the family, his superiors, his job, and so on. That doesn't mean that Shinto followers don't think about others. On the contrary, they would see the philosophy of loyalty as being the ultimate thought for others. So strong is the concept of loyalty that a person who commits *hara-kiri* (suicide by cutting one's own stomach) does so to prove loyalty after having failed to meet the Shinto code of conduct.

ESSENTIAL

The sun goddess Amaterasu is the closest that Shinto comes to having a deity. Her name means literally, "that which illuminates heaven."

Traditions are preserved through the family. A love of nature is sacred; close contact with nature is equated to close contact with the gods. Natural objects are worshiped as sacred spirits; for instance, rocks, birds, beasts, fish, and plants can all be treated as kami. Physical cleanliness is paramount, which is why followers of Shinto frequently take baths, wash their hands, and rinse out their mouths.

There are three Shinto sects—Shrine Shinto, Sectarian Shinto, and Folk or Popular Shinto. Shrine Shinto revolves around the more than 100,000 shrines throughout Japan. Sectarian Shinto has five subsects: Pure, Confucian, Mountain, Purification, and Redemptive. The Purification Shinto performs rites of purification to purify the soul, mind, and body from evil. All the sects are concerned with the environment and the cleansing of pollution. Pure Shinto fosters nationalism and is opposed to foreign influences. Loyalty to the state is a central element. Confucian Shinto follows the ethics of Confucianism. Redemptive or Faith-Healing Shinto believes in a divine source such as the sun goddess.

Folk Shinto, the most diverse form of Shinto, involves superstition, the occult, and ancestor worship. Thousands of deities are part of Folk Shinto and many adherents have rituals that are centered on the *kami-dana* (kami shelf), a small shrine used for daily worship. Memorial tablets made from wood or paper are inscribed with the names of an ancestor. At special life-cycle events such as births, marriages, and anniversaries, candles are lit and the head of the family offers food and flowers to the deities.

Parishioners of a shrine believe in their kami as the source of life and existence. All the deities cooperate with each other. To live a life in accordance with the will of a kami is gives mystical power to the recipient and provides power and the approval of the particular kami.

FACT

In some shrines, statues of the kami are present, but images are not commonly found. The foremost Shinto shrine in Japan is the grand shrine of Ise, Amaterasu's chief place of worship. The most common representation of the kami in a shrine is a mirror, which is what Amaterasu left behind to represent her presence.

Sacred Texts

There are no holy writings in Shinto, but they do possess some 800 myths, some of which have been enshrined. Shinto literature tends to be based on the interpretation of mythology. Two major texts form the basis of the Shinto sacred literature: the Kojiki (Records of Ancient Matters) and the Nihon (Chronicles of Japan), written in 712 and 720 respectively. These derive from oral traditions and were passed on and compiled. Apparently, because of the lack of a Japanese alphabet at that time, they were written in Chinese characters to represent Japanese sounds.

Of all the myths' subjects, the most famous and important one is about the sun goddess Amaterasu Omikami (Great Divinity Illuminating Heaven). One myth states that she was born from the god Izanagi when he used water to purify his left eye after a visit to the nether world. Another says she was born after intercourse between Izanagi and Izanami (Nihon Shoki 720 C.E.). She was the sun goddess and assigned to rule the High Celestial Plain. Later, she sent her grandson, Ninigi no Mikoto, to pacify the Japanese islands, having given him a sacred mirror, sword, and jewels that became the Imperial Regalia. Her great-grandson became the first Emperor Jimmu.

ESSENTIAL

The Kojiki contains myths, legends, and historical information on the imperial court. The entire writings were re-evaluated by Moto-ori-Norinaga, who wrote the complete Annotation of the Kojiki in forty-nine volumes.

Worship and Practices

Shinto does not have a schedule of regular religious services. Followers decide when they wish to attend a shrine. Some may decide to go when there is a festival, of which there are many, or on the first and fifteenth of each month. Of course, some Shinto go every day.

A devotee attending a shrine follows a ritual. First, she must cleanse the mouth and hands (purity is a vital part of Shintoism). If a person has been in contact with blood—for instance, a menstruating woman—she is forbidden to enter. When a person enters the shrine area, she passes through a *tori* (bird), a special gateway to the gods that demarcates the finite world from the infinite world of the gods. Once inside the shrine, worshipers can buy a prayer board. Some have prayers printed on them or a depiction of an animal. Adherents believe that animals are messengers of the gods.

Once she approaches the shrine, the worshiper claps her hands together to let the kami know of her presence, then makes an offering of money, which is put into a box in front of the shrine. It is appropriate to bow twice deeply, clap the hands twice, bow deeply once more, and pray. When a priest is present in the shrine, he will bang a drum to alert the kami of his presence. In a purification ceremony, the priest will deliver prayers and then pass a purification stick over the head of the worshiper to draw out all the impurities.

FACT

Japan has over 80,000 Shinto shrines. Some, particularly in outlying districts, are tiny; others, elaborate and large. The small shrines seldom have a priest; the local people look after the shrine, opening the shrine doors at dawn and closing them at dusk.

Rituals and Customs

Shinto priests perform the rituals and are usually supported by young ladies (*miko*) in white kimonos. The young ladies must be unmarried; often they are daughters of priests. There are also a few female priests.

A newborn child is taken to a shrine to be initiated as a new adherent somewhere between thirty and 100 days after the birth. When boys are five years old and girls three years and seven years of age, they go to the shrine to give thanks for kami's protection and pray for healthy growth. This is done at the Shichi-go-san (Seven-Five-Three) festival on November 15. Another festival for young men to commemorate their twentieth year is celebrated on January 15.

Festivals

Japanese festivals are designed to express pride and patriotism. The New Year festival requires much preparation. Houses are cleansed of evil influences and the kami-dana is provided with new tablets, flowers, and other items. Special foods are prepared, and houses are decorated with flowers, straw, paper, pine branches, and bamboo sticks.

A Girl's Festival is held each March 3; it is intended to honor family and national life. The Boy's Festival is held each May 5 and is meant for families to announce to the community their good fortune in having male children.

A festival of the dead called Bon is held in the middle of the year in which souls of dead relatives return home to be fed by their families. At the conclusion of the feast, farewell fires light the way for the relatives on their journey home. As the majority of Japanese are both Shinto and Buddhist, they have their funerals in the Buddhist manner. Only those who adhere exclusively to Shinto will follow the Shinto ceremony and services.

The most famous Japanese festival is the ancient Cherry Blossom Festival, held in early spring. Obviously, it is the celebration of the cherry blossom trees, which can frequently be seen on the grounds of shrines or on holy mountains. This festival is another example of the Shinto reverence for nature.

New Year's Day is the largest festival. It draws millions to shrines all over the country. There will be much praying and asking for blessings of the kami, and the celebration will mark the beginning of an auspicious new year.

CHAPTER 14

Sikhism

Sikhs reject the assertion that Sikhism is a reform movement of Hinduism and Islam. Rather, they claim it came from the divine inspiration of Guru Nanak and the nine gurus who succeeded him. All sects follow the belief in one God and the teachings and scriptures of the ten gurus.

Origins and Development

Sikhism was founded by Guru Nanak in Punjab (Panjab), India, in the late fifteenth century. An adherent of the faith is called a Sikh, which means "follower" in Sanskrit. There are roughly 19 million Sikhs, the majority in Punjab in the northwestern part of India. About 2 million have emigrated to live and work in the United States, Europe, or in parts of what used to be the British colonies.

Sikhism is a young religion; it is also a monotheistic one. Sikhs believe in one God called Waheguru (great teacher). Scholars think Sikhism evolved as a Hindu reform movement or as a mixture of Hinduism and Islam. The Sikhs reject that theory and claim their religion grew out of the divine inspiration of Guru Nanak and the nine gurus who came after him.

Nevertheless, Nanak was born a Hindu in Punjab in 1469. Just as many predicted that Siddhartha Gautama would become a Buddha, so did people predict that Nanak would praise God and teach many others to do the same. As a youth, he worked for a local Muslim politician, and it's recorded that he impressed everyone with his wisdom and learning. He was part of a group that would sit by the side of a river to pray and discuss religion. He meditated frequently and discussed religious notions with Hindus and Muslims. In time, he formed a group of friends, united by their spiritual concerns, who would gather along a river to pray and worship together.

FACT

There are stories told about Nanak's childhood and his amazing abilities. At school, he was taught the classical lessons in addition to Persian and Arabic languages and Muslim literature. His teacher realized he had reached the point where there wasn't any more he could teach him; he was learning from Nanak.

At one point he was absent from this routine for three days. When he came back, he didn't speak for a day. When he did, he said, "There is neither Hindu nor Muslim, so whose path shall I follow? I shall follow God's path. God is neither Hindu nor Muslim and the path I follow is God's." There are other reports on what Nanak might have said, but the essence of having received enlightenment seems to be reliable.

After his revelation in his late twenties, he left his wife and two sons to travel in search of truth and wisdom. After about twenty years, he acquired farmland and settled in central Punjab, where he founded the town of Kartarpur and became Guru Nanak. The Sikh religion was born and Nanak was its first guru.

The Path of Guru Nanak

Guru Nanak followed the not-unusual path of the prophets who preceded him. He would forego a job with the governor for a life of traveling and teaching. He taught in far outlying areas and set up communities of followers along the way. In time, he became known as Guru ("teacher") Nanak. Part of his teaching was that public rituals are not the essence of worship and that God is ill defined by any one religion. He spoke out against what he saw as inequities (the Hindu caste system, for example), stressing that all people were equal.

ESSENTIAL

Nanak's childhood friend, Mardan, a professional musician, accompanied him on his travels. Nanak liked to sing and did so in the form of hymns. So he and Mardan entertained the local populace while getting the message out. As part of his message, Nanak wore a mixture of Hindu and Muslim clothes when he and Mardan toured.

Many of the Hindu and Muslim audiences became followers of the fledgling religion. As he gathered followers around him, his spiritual ideas bore fruit and his composed hymns, which were written down, eventually became the core of the Sikh sacred text, the Adi Granth ("original book").

In the final phases of his life, Guru Nanak returned from all the traveling to his established Sikh community at Kartarpur and settled down with his wife and sons. It was time for him to consider a successor and most people thought he would appoint one of his sons. But his insistence on the principle of equality that he had been teaching for years and had made part of the religion made him choose Lehna, a man who had become an ardent disciple. Nanak blessed Lehna and gave him a new name, Angad, meaning "part of me." He anointed him with a saffron mark on his forehead. When Guru Nanak gathered his followers together for prayers, he invited Angad to occupy the seat of the Guru. In that way, Guru Angad was ordained as the successor to Guru Nanak.

The myth goes that when he died, Guru Nanak asked for flowers to be placed on either side of him, from the Hindus on his right and from the Muslims on his left. He explained that those whose flowers remained fresh the next day would have their way. He then asked his disciples to pray, and he lay down and covered himself with a sheet. In the early hours of the next morning, September 22, 1539, Guru Nanak merged with the eternal light of the Creator.

After Nanak's death, his followers lifted the sheet covering him and found nothing except the flowers, all of which were fresh. The Hindus took theirs and cremated them. The Muslims took theirs and buried them.

Central Beliefs

To understand how the Sikhs developed it helps to get to know The Ten Gurus. The word "guru" normally means "teacher," but when the Sikhs speak of the Guru, they mean God, the Great Teacher. Pieces of Sikh history can be related to a particular guru; each one of them had an influence on the beliefs of the religion, and some of them had political influence. The period from the first to the last guru was likely the mid-1500s to the late 1600s. Each guru appointed his successor.

The Ten Gurus in historical order are:

1. **Guru Nanak** (1469–1539) was founder of the Sikh religion.
2. **Guru Angad** (1504–1552) was a Hindu before turning to Sikhism. Born Bhai Lehna, he made pilgrimages every year and became a close disciple of Guru Nanak, who eventually anointed him. He devised a script used for writing the Sikh scriptures. His work is found in the Guru Granth Sahib—the Holy Book.
3. **Guru Amar Das** (1479–1574) collected the hymns of Guru Nanak and added his own. He developed the custom of the *langar,* the communal meal, which was devised as a social kitchen to remove caste distinctions and establish social harmony among his followers.

4. **Guru Ram Das** (1534–1581) was the son-in-law of Guru Amar Das. He founded the city of Ramdaspur, now known as Amritsar, which became the Sikh holy city to which he initiated pilgrimages. The construction of the Golden Temple began during his time. He also contributed to the Guru Granth Sahib. In particular, he wrote the Sikh wedding hymn.

5. **Guru Arjan** (1563–1606) was the youngest son of Guru Ram Das. He compiled the Adi Granth, the most important segment of the Guru Granth Sahib, and completed the building of the Golden Temple. He made the Sikhs very popular and such a presence that the Muslim Mughals came to see the Sikhs as a growing menace. The emperor had him tortured and killed.

6. **Guru Hargobind** (1595–1644), the son of Guru Arjan, instilled a sense of Sikh militancy and tried to organize the Sikhs and the Hindus against the Mughals and was imprisoned for a short time. He perfected the dress code introduced by his father and started the tradition of wearing two swords, one signifying his political authority, the other his religious authority.

7. **Guru Har Rai** (1630–1661), grandson of Guru Hargobind, supported the elder brother of Emperor Aurangzab in a conflict and as a reprisal the Mughals held his son hostage. He had a reputation for medicine and opened hospitals where treatment was provided free.

8. **Guru Har Krishan** (1656–1664), known as "the boy guru," was the second son of Guru Har Rai and succeeded his father at the age of five when his brother was still being held hostage by the Mughals. The emperor summoned the boy guru to Delhi and kept him under house arrest. He contracted smallpox and died.

9. **Guru Tegh Bahadur** (1621–1675) was the second son of Guru Hargobind. Tegh Bahadur ("brave sword") was not his original name, it was given to him by his subjects because of his resistance to Emperor Aurangzab. He gained a reputation for feeding the hungry, and he wrote many hymns that are now in the Guru Granth Sahib. He predicted the coming of the Western powers to the Indian subcontinent and the downfall of the Mughals. He was beheaded after refusing to accept Islam.

10. **Guru Gobind Singh** (1675–1708), the tenth and last guru, was the most famous after Guru Nanak. He organized the Sikhs to oppose the tyranny of the Mughals and established a military defense group known as the

Khalsa (the brotherhood of the pure), which still remains. The Khalsa are considered a chosen race of soldier-saints willing to give up their lives to uphold their faith and defend the weak. Guru Gobind Singh gave all Sikhs the name *singh* ("lion") for men and *kaur* ("princess") for women, to do away with all traces of the caste system. He also decreed that the writings of the Guru Granth Sahib would be the authority from which the Sikhs would be governed. The book is treated as if it were a living thing; wherever it is moved, it is attended by five Sikhs who represent the Khalsa. In his efforts to oppose the Mughals, he lost his two sons and was finally assassinated. He has been called "the most glorious hero of our race."

Sikhism is based on the discipline of purification and the overcoming of the five vices: greed, anger, false pride, lust, and attachments to material goods. At the end of a person's life, the good and the bad conduct are balanced out and the result determines the family, race, and character of the person when reborn. There is no direct belief in heaven or hell as places, but those who have been selfish or cruel in the current life will suffer in their next existence. Those who acted with compassion and honesty will be better off in their next incarnation. The soul develops as it passes through the many incarnations until it becomes united with the infinite one.

FACT

Sikhs developed a warrior attitude because of the violence against them by the Mughals. This attitude was reinforced when the Khalsa was founded and the five tenets known as Ks were instituted—*kesh* (uncut hair), *kangha* (comb), *kirpan* (sword), *kara* (steel bracelet), and *kachch* (short pants for use in battle). As a result, Sikhs wear long uncut hair with a comb in it and a steel bracelet on the right wrist. The sword and short pants are reserved for battle.

Sikhs are opposed to the idea of austere asceticism; rather, they emphasize the ideal of achieving saintliness as active members of society. Sikhism prohibits idolatry, the caste system, and the use of wine or tobacco. Stress is placed on the importance of leading a good moral life that includes loyalty, gratitude for all favors received, philanthropy, justice, truth, and honesty.

Holy Writings and Worship

There is only one canonical work, the Adi Granth (First Book), also known as the Guru Granth Sahib, compiled by Guru Arjan in 1604. There were at least three versions of the book, but the one recognized as authentic was revised by Guru Gobind Singh in 1704. The Adi Granth has about 6,000 hymns composed by the first five Gurus. Other contributors to the book include Bhakta saints and Muslim Sufis.

The Adi Granth occupies a focal point in all Sikh temples. The *gurdwara* (doorway to the Guru) contains a cot under a canopy. A copy of the Adi Granth is placed on cushions within the gurdwara and covered by elaborate decorations. All who enter the gurdwara in the temple must cover their heads, take off their shoes, and wash their feet. Services may take place at any time; there is no special time of worship. Worshipers will bow in front of the Guru Granth Sahib and during services prayers will be said, there will be a sermon, chanting of hymns, and finally a communal meal. In accordance with the principles of equality in Sikhism, men and women share the tasks of preparing and serving the langar that is made available after most services to anyone who wishes to indulge.

The chief gurdwara is the magnificent Harimandir (the Golden Temple) at Amritsar in Punjab state. However, in the average gurdwara there may be readings, Sikh music, study classes, and even physical activities.

FACT

The Dasam Granth (tenth book), a compilation of writings ascribed to Guru Gobind Singh, is not paid the same reverence as the Adi Granth. There is some disagreement about the authenticity of the contents.

In their homes, most Sikhs set aside a room for a gurdwara to hold a copy of the Guru Granth Sahib. Daily readings are part of the duties of the household. Many Sikhs will recite verses during their daily activities. Because not every person or family has the accommodations to set aside a separate room for the Guru Granth Sahib, they instead have a copy of excerpts, known as the Gutkha, from which to say morning and evening prayers.

Rituals and Customs

Births and naming are carried out in different ways by different faiths. The Christians have christening, the Jews circumcision, and the Sikhs have the naming ceremony.

After the birth, the parents take the child to the gurdwara. Hymns are sung that express gratitude for the birth of a baby. The Adi Granth is then opened at random and the child is given a name beginning with the first letter of the first word on the left page. The parents take time to reflect then choose a name. Then more hymns are sung.

Marriage

Marriage can still be arranged between the families of the bride and groom. But Sikhs now accept the right of the man or the woman to reject the person chosen for them. However, marriage is still seen as the joining of two families.

Traditionally, the bride wears red and gold, with her head covered with a red scarf, her hands and feet decorated with patterns, and a good deal of gold jewelry. The groom sports a colored turban and scarf and carries a long sword.

The Sikh conducting the marriage ceremony explains the ideals of marriage to the couple. The bridegroom's sister (or other prominent female in his life) drapes a long scarf around the groom's shoulders and places the right end in his hand. The father of the bride then takes the left end of the groom's scarf and arranges it over the bride's shoulders and puts the left end in her hand.

A wedding hymn, the *Lavan* of Guru Ram Das, is sung. While that is happening, the couple walks around the Guru Granth Sahib four times. As they finish each circuit, they bow to the holy book. The families follow the couple to show support for them. The bride and groom are then free to go to their new home.

Death

Death could be a new beginning for a Sikh because they believe in the cycle of reincarnation. It is not necessary to mourn excessively since the deceased lives on in another body.

Hymns may be read by family and friends from the Guru Granth Sahib and prayers for the peace of the soul will be said, followed by evening prayers. The period of mourning usually lasts ten days. During that time, relatives visit to offer their condolences. The body is washed and dressed before the service. In India, it may be cremated on a funeral pyre, but taking the body to the crematorium is also acceptable. The ashes are usually scattered in a river or the sea. If the ceremony takes place in India, the ashes are scattered in a sacred river, such as the Ganges.

Festivals and Ceremonies

Many ceremonies are held to celebrate the births and deaths of the ten gurus, two to commemorate the deaths of martyrs, and a festival for the anniversary of the Baisakhi, the date the Khalsa was founded, which was originally a harvest festival. The five major observances include Baisakhi, the birthdays of Gurus Nanak and Gobind Singh, and the martyrdom of Gurus Arjan and Tegh Bahadur.

Diversification into Modern Society

The history of the development of the Sikhs over the past 500 years has at times been tumultuous and bloody. The involvement of the British only propagated the violent fighting between the Sikhs and the Hindus. The subcontinent was partitioned into India and Pakistan in 1947. The Sikh population was divided equally on both sides of the boundary line. In 1984, Indian troops attacked the Golden Temple, where militants had established their headquarters. There was considerable damage and the militants were driven out. It is believed that the angry reaction of the Sikhs led to the assassination of the Indian Prime Minister Indira Gandhi by Sikh members of her bodyguard later that year. The reaction to that dreadful event led to riots and the massacre of many Sikhs.

The separatist movement has the establishment of an independent Sikh state to be called Khalistan (Land of the Pure) as its goal.

CHAPTER 15

Newer Faiths

The faiths explored in this chapter share an unusual and exciting flavor. Most are newer faiths, having derived from faiths established before them. While not major religions, they are well dispersed throughout the world and illustrate the wide mosaic of faiths that exist.

Hare Krishna

Hare Krishna, also called the International Society for Krishna Consciousness (ISKCON), was founded in the United States in 1966, making it one of the world's youngest religions. Krishna was the eighth and principal avatar of Vishnu in the Hindu religion, and this religious sect has strong Hindu affiliations. The movement first appealed to counterculture youths, many of whom were runaways.

The Krishnas became a common sight on the streets of major cities, usually dressed in bright saffron-colored Hindu clothes with shaven heads, smiles on their faces, a copy of the Bhagavad Gita in hand, and a proselytizing spirit in their voice. They were often chanting and playing Indian finger cymbals. The chants are called a mantra, which is a repeated vibration of sound that many believe cleanses the mind. Their main activity was soliciting contributions from passersby, something many people called begging. They were frequently prohibited from public areas, particularly airports.

QUOTE

The words of Krishna in the ninth chapter of the Gita offer highest praise for Bhakti Yoga as a means to the highest spiritual attainments. Krishna says, "Fill they mind with Me, be My devotee, sacrifice unto Me, bow down to Me; thus having made thy heart steadfast in Me, taking Me as the Supreme Goal, thou shalt come to Me." (9.34)

People are thought of as souls composed of Krishna's highest energy. To achieve peace and happiness, adherents are urged to seek Krishna. Krishna consciousness is not imposed on the mind; rather, it is already inside waiting to emerge. Followers are advised that chanting "Hare Krishna" is a way of seeking Krishna directly.

Chanting in order to draw closer to God is an idea dating to the fifth century B.C.E. and the publication of the Bhagavad-Gita or Gita for short. Chanting or singing the names of the Lord is known as *bhakti*, meaning "devotion" or "participation." Swami Vivekananda described Bhakti Yoga as, "the path of systematized devotion for the attainment of union with the absolute."

On the streets, the Hare Krisha devotees could be found chanting:

Hare Krishna, Hare Krishna,

Krishna Krishna, Hare Hare,

Hare Rama, Hare Rama,

Rama Rama, Hare Hare.

"Hare" means "praise," so the devotees got the name Hare Krishnas because of their praise of this avatar.

This chanting is but one component of the Bhakti approach to God. The leader Srila Prabhupada also expected his Hare Krishna devotees to lead ascetic lives, not eat meat, and eschew alcohol and drugs. They were also to remain celibate, save for the procreation of children within marriage.

The official seven-point goal of the Hare Krishna consciousness movement was given by Srila Prabhupada at the time of ISKCON's incorporation in July, 1966 in New York City. The goals are:

1. To systematically propagate spiritual knowledge to society at large and to educate all people in the techniques of spiritual life, in order to check the imbalance of values in life and achieve real unity and peace in the world.
2. To propagate consciousness of Krishna, as revealed in Bhagavad-Gita and Srimad-Bhagavatam.
3. To bring members of society together with each other and nearer to Krishna, the prime entity, thus developing the idea within the members, and humanity at large, that each soul is part and parcel of the quality of Krishna.
4. To teach and encourage the *snkirtan* movement, congregational chanting of the holy names of God, as revealed in the teachings of Lord Sri Caitanya Mahaprabhu.
5. To erect for the members and for society at large, holy places of transcendental pastimes dedicated to the personality of Krishna.
6. To bring members closer together for the purpose of teaching a simpler and more natural way of life.

7. With a view toward achieving these six purposes, to publish and distribute periodicals, magazines, books, and other writings.

According to Lord Sri Caitanya Mahaprabhu, that God consciousness does not depend on caste or church membership. He was opposed to any social, religious, or racist prejudice. The purpose of chanting the name Krishna was a method to enable anyone to become Krishna conscious.

Srila Prabhupada

Srila Prabhupada, founder of the Hare Krishna movement, was born in Calcutta in 1896 and died in 1977. In 1922, he met his spiritual master, Srila Bhaktisddhanta Sarasvati Thakur, and became his initiated disciple. Meanwhile, he formed a successful pharmaceutical business to maintain his family.

In 1950, he left his home and family and dedicated the rest of his life to teaching. In 1959, he renounced material life and wrote three volumes of the Srimad-Bhagavatam in English. He became convinced that the United States would be the best marketplace for his preaching, so he moved there. Eventually, he rented a small storefront at 26 2nd Avenue in New York City. Devotees began to gather, which led to the incorporation of the movement. He held chanting sessions and gave lectures. He distributed *prasadam* (food that has been offered to the Supreme Lord; devotees eat only what has been offered first to the Lord, because to do otherwise would be to ingest sin), and he started the first Sunday feasts.

ESSENTIAL

Adherents of ISKCON are vegetarians and serve vegetarian meals in their restaurants, temples, and through the Food for Life programs for the homeless, hungry, or disadvantaged. The society has sold over 10 million copies of its vegetarian cookbooks.

Once the New York devotees became established, Srila Prabhupada moved to San Francisco, where the hippies flocked to join the movement. They were attracted by the philosophy of spreading spiritual love and peace. Some of the devotees became disciples and were sent to preach the message in other parts of the world and to establish Krishna Conscious centers. They went first to London, and then spread out to Berlin and India.

Prabhupada died in 1977. By then he had built a foundation and aided the expansion of a religion that encompassed well over 100 centers throughout the world and was said to have written more than fifty volumes of transcendental literature. He established a publishing house (The Bhaktivedanta Book Trust), which has become the world's largest publisher of Vedic literature. He also built a scientific preaching academy (The Bhaktivedanta Institute).

Central Beliefs

Reincarnation is a pillar of the faith. Hare Krishnas believe that our current lives are not the only ones we will live and that our soul or self has no beginning and no end; this essence within travels from one incarnation to the next. They propose that during life we move from childhood to middle age to old age, but only the body changes, not the inner self or the soul.

Death is only a transition; we continue the cycle with birth in another body. How we behave in one life will affect what we become in the next.

QUESTION

Do Hare Krishnas have churches?
Not as such—they have temples that are essentially communes. Unmarried men and women live separately; married couples have other quarters. Members support the temples by soliciting funds and selling publications. Spiritual masters initiate new members and oversee the spiritual life of the temples. Members of the temples dress in Hindu clothes.

The official statement of the faith proposes a society that moves toward a more natural economy with smaller, self-sufficient economic units based on simple living and high thinking. They envisage an environment that reduces the urge to excessive exploitation, thus leading to the nonmaterial happiness of the soul. They feel that without raising desires from the materialistic to the spiritual, the basic impetus toward environmental destruction will remain.

Holy Writings

The original Bhagavad-Gita forms the basis of Hare Krishna's required study; however, Srila Prabhupada produced his own translations and editing of the work. He wrote and published fifty volumes of transcendental literature. His major books include Bhagavad-Gita as It Is and Srimad Bhagavatam. Adherents are encouraged to read Srila Prabhupada's selected literature daily.

Pentecostalism

Pentecostalism is a movement that likely began in Los Angeles in 1906. Now a worldwide Christian movement, Pentecostalism emphasizes the experience of spirit baptism, evidenced by spiritual healing and ecstatic speaking in "tongues," or *glossolalia*. The term "Pentecostalism" derives from "Pentecost," the Greek name for the Jewish Feast of Weeks, celebrated on the fiftieth day after Passover.

There are many references to the Jewish feast in the Bible. Some Jews stay awake the night before Pentecost studying the Torah, signifying their commitment to accept the Torah all over again. During the morning service of Pentecost, the Book of Ruth is read because it too is set at harvest time. Ruth tells of a Gentile woman's acceptance of the Torah, forming a parallel to the acceptance of it by the Israelites at Sinai.

Early Christians believed that Pentecost commemorated the day the Holy Spirit descended in fulfillment of the promise of Jesus. It is written in Acts 2:2–13:

> And suddenly a sound came from heaven like the rush of a mighty wind, and it filled the house where they were sitting. And there appeared to them tongues as of fire distributed and resting on each one of them. And they were filled with the Holy Spirit and began to speak in other tongues, as the Spirit gave them utterance. Now there were dwelling in Jerusalem Jews, devoted men from every nation under heaven. And at this sound the multitude came together, and they were bewildered, because each one heard them speaking in his own language. And they were amazed and wondered, saying, "Are not all these who are speaking Galileans:

And how is it that we hear, each of us in his own language?" And all were amazed and perplexed, saying to one another, "What does this mean?" But others mocking, said, "They are filled with new wine."

Pentecostalism arose out of Protestantism in the twentieth century, due to dissension over the rigid manner in which the established churches preached and organized the delivery of their way of interpreting the Bible.

Pentecostalists endorse a more literal interpretation of the Bible than mainstream Christians. Many churches have adopted specific passages as their guiding force. One such passage is found in Mark 16:15–20, where it is reported that those who receive baptism and find salvation will "cast out devils, speak in strange tongues; if they handle snakes or drink deadly poison they will come to no harm; and the sick on whom they lay their hands will recover." There are some churches that include the handling of deadly snakes and the drinking of poison as part of their worship services.

The new sect didn't think the way of the true Christians was memorizing prayers and creeds and adhering to hard and fast rules within an unwavering structure. The Pentecostalists sought a direct experience of God that would produce a sense of ecstasy, known as the baptism of the Holy Spirit. This baptism was seen as a second blessing.

Speaking in Tongues

It was in 1901 in Topeka, Kansas, during a service at the Kansas Bible College by Charles Fox Parham, that the movement got the first demonstration of a strange happening. A female participant was praying and suddenly began speaking what seemed to be a foreign language. Apparently, she was unable to speak English for three days afterward. This event had a dramatic effect not only on Parham but on the entire congregation. The demonstration was taken as a sign from God and the word quickly spread.

The speaking in tongues, known as glossolalia, was not universally accepted. In fact, it was the reverse for most people. As in the Biblical story in Acts, many people thought the speakers were full of different sorts of spirits; namely, that they were drunk. It wasn't just the fact of speaking in an unintelligible tongue that upset listeners, it was the emotional overtones that went with the delivery. The term "holy rollers" got its name from practitioners who were actually rolling down the aisles of the church in their ecstasy.

Adherents believed that speaking in tongues and the actions that accompanied this were a way of communicating directly with God. However, no reliable sources have established that an actual language was or is being uttered during glossolalia.

FACT

Women became active members in the Pentecostal movement. One of them, Aimee Semple McPherson, generated a big following from her tabernacle where she produced theatrically dramatic versions of biblical stories from the stage.

Expansion

Pentecostalism is now one of the fastest growing religious movements in the world. In the United States alone, it claims 9 million adherents; worldwide, the figure goes up to 400 million. No wonder it is sometimes referred to as "the third force of Christianity."

The movement first drew members from among the poor; the promise of equality for all was particularly attractive to the unfortunate. Thus, the movement became associated with the Bible Belt in the Southern states among poor whites and urban blacks. It then became increasingly popular with the middle classes around the country, and once the movement spread to the mainstream of society, members of churches such as the Episcopal, Lutheran, and Presbyterian adopted it, often in addition to their own religion.

The controversy split the movement and led to the formation of new sects within Pentecostalism. Three main movements evolved: Pentecostalism, Fundamentalism, and Evangelicalism. Other sects, particularly throughout the rest of the world, are emerging.

Beliefs, Worship, Writings, and Rites

Pentecostalism has not united into a single denomination in spite of believing in baptism of the spirit and common beliefs in selected doctrines of the Christian faiths. It has strong beliefs in the literal interpretation of the Bible and healing by the spirit.

The history of Pentecostalism shows that many adherents either added it to their original faith or left the original faith entirely. Literature is being gathered from Roman Catholics who have committed to Pentecostalism.

With the growth of Pentecostalism, the charismatic experience as it is called has expanded its presence into many parts of the world to such an extent it is being looked at by some as a new era of the spirit. The Pentecostalists envision the movement sweeping whole countries, cultures, and religions, including Catholicism, with a promise of changing Christianity. They have even coined a new name: Catholic Pentecostals. The Pentecostalist viewpoint is that there is confusion not only in Catholicism but also in Christianity. This opinion is not shared by the Roman Catholic Church or other Christian denominations.

ESSENTIAL

Opponents of the movement say that Pentecostal-style religion is not easily captured in a denominational form because it stresses the impulse of the moment and behavior such as speaking in tongues. Many point out that similar evangelical outpourings that took place in the 1980s ended with the disgrace of people like Jimmy Swaggart and Jim and Tammy Faye Bakker.

Pentecostalists describe themselves as believing in exorcism, speaking in tongues, faith healing, and seeking supernatural experiences. As with other developing religions, schisms have occurred, resulting in separate sects with their own variations of the basic belief. Some of the best known sects include:

- Church of God in Christ
- International Church of the Foursquare Gospel Church of God
- Church of God of Prophecy
- Pentecostal Holiness Church
- Fire-Baptized Holiness Church
- Pentecostal Free-Will Baptist Church
- The Assemblies of God
- The United Pentecostal Church

Rastafarianism

The origins of Rastafarianism go back to Marcus Garvey (1887–1940), who was born in Jamaica. Garvey preached that members would be going back to Africa. In fact, he founded the Back to Africa movement and preached that a future black African king would lead the people.

In 1930, Ras Tafari Makonnen was crowned king of Ethiopia (hence the name Rastafarianism). He claimed the title Emperor Haile Selassie I (Lion of the Tribe of Judah, Elect of God, and King of Kings of Ethiopia). Thus, Haile Selassie fulfilled the prediction of a black king. As far as the Rastafarians were concerned, he was the living God for the black race. They believed that he was the Jesus Christ that Christianity speaks of; the white man had tricked the world into believing that Jesus was a white man.

It was after Haile Selassie was crowned that Rastafarianism came into being. One of its early leaders was Leonard Howell, who was later arrested by the Jamaican government for preaching a revolutionary doctrine. Here are his six principles:

- Hatred for the white race
- The complete superiority of the black race
- Revenge on whites for their wickedness
- The negation, persecution, and humiliation of the government and legal bodies of Jamaica
- The preparation to go back to Africa
- Acknowledging Emperor Haile Selassie as the Supreme Being and only ruler of black people

On April 21, 1966, Haile Selassie visited Jamaica. Two things resulted from his visit: April 21 was declared a special holy day and Selassie strongly advised Rastafarians not to immigrate to Ethiopia. He said they should liberate the people of Jamaica first. Many people have since wondered about his motive for discouraging immigration.

Rastafarians (sometimes called Rastas) do not accept that Haile Selassie is dead. They believe that his atoms have spread throughout the world and live through individual Rastafarians. The Rastafarian name for God is Jah.

Central Beliefs and Holy Writings

The original belief system was so vague that figuring out the acceptable doctrine was largely a matter of individual interpretation. Rastafarians accept the Bible, but with reservations. They think that much of the translation into English has produced distortions, so that while the basic text may be in order, it should be viewed in a critical light. They have no holy scriptures apart from the Rastafarian interpretation of the Bible.

The doctrine of Rastafarians has similarities to Christianity in that they believe that God revealed himself in Moses, their first savior, followed by Elijah and then Jesus Christ. But sources differ; one of them, as has been claimed above, asserted that Rastafarians believed Haile Selassie was actually Jesus Christ. Others believe that the devil is actually the god of the white man.

ESSENTIAL

The expression "I and I" is frequently heard in the Rasta dialect. "I and I" recalls theologian Martin Buber's ideal of an "I-Thou" relationship as being of a higher sort than an "I-It" relationship. "I and I" means that all are absolutely equal. This means that people wouldn't say "You and I," but "I and I."

There are two symbols that exemplify and identify Rastafarians: dreadlocks and *ganja* (marijuana). Dreadlocks symbolize the Rasta roots. They are the antithesis of the blond look of the white man and his establishment. The way the hair grows and is tended represents the Lion of Judah (Haile Selassie). By association, this has come to represent priesthood. It should be noted that dreadlocks have been adopted by many black people who may not be adherents of Rastafarianism.

Ganja is the Rasta name for marijuana; it is used for religious purposes. Its religious justification is based on different verses from the Bible:

- "He causeth the grass for the cattle, and herb for the service of man." (Psalms 104:14)
- "Thou shalt eat the herb of the field." (Genesis 3:18)
- "Eat every herb of the land." (Exodus 10:12)

- "Better is a dinner of herb where love is, than a stalled ox and hatred therewith." (Proverbs 15:17)

It isn't obvious how the passages cited justify marijuana. Apparently, however, the use of marijuana is extensive, and not only for religious ceremony. The Nyabingi celebration, for instance, uses it for medicinal purposes, such as for colds. The use of ganja for religious rituals started in a cult commune set up by Leonard Howell in the hills of St. Catherine called Pinnacle, which overlooked the city of Kingston.

The growth of Rastafarianism is attributed to the worldwide acceptance of the Jamaican reggae artist Bob Marley, who became a prophet of the belief in 1975. He aided and abetted the movement with his music and was given a Jamaican state funeral when he died in 1981.

The movement spread mainly to black youth throughout the Caribbean, many of whom saw it as a symbol of their rebelliousness. The expansion also found believers in England and the United States.

The Church of Scientology

Scientology is a philosophical religion without a god or deity, developed by Lafayette Ronald Hubbard (1911–1986) as an extension of a bestselling book, *Dianetics: The Modern Science of Mental Health* (1950). The book detailed Hubbard's new form of self-help psychotherapy. The "Church" of Scientology urges that a person can get "clear" by overcoming physical and mental stress by a process of "auditing." The process clears the person of past painful experiences that block their achievement of happiness and self-realization.

Its founder, better known as L. Ron Hubbard, attended George Washington University, School of Engineering from 1930 until 1932, but withdrew without attaining a degree. He was a prolific author, writing literature on scientology, but also novels and short stories.

His Church of Scientology was formally established in the United States in 1954. It was subsequently incorporated in Great Britain and other countries. It is has been called a religio-scientific movement. The movement has generated considerable controversy, even extreme anger, with accusations of being discriminatory, dangerous, and vicious, fleecing its members, and harassing those who disagree with its philosophy and manner of operation.

Central Beliefs

The core of the movement is based on a system of psychology and the way the mind seems to work. The word "engram" is a constant part of the Scientology nomenclature. It is a memory trace that causes a permanent change in the brain and accounts for the existence of a memory not available to the conscious mind. However, it remains dormant in the subconscious and can be brought into consciousness when triggered by new experiences.

These new experiences are supplied in what Scientology calls an "audit," which is conducted by a trained auditor in a one-on-one session with a potential devotee. The auditor confronts the engram in order to bring it to the surface and clear or free the devotee's mind of it. The purpose is to free the mind of engrams and allow the devotee to achieve improved mental health and outlook.

The officially stated Scientology meaning of the word "engram" is "A recording made by the reactive mind when a person is unconscious." An engram is not a memory; it is a particular type of mental image that is a complete recording, down to the last accurate details, of every perception present in a moment of partial or full unconsciousness. "To become 'clear' indicates a highly desirable state for the individual, achieved through auditing, which was never attainable before Dianetics. A Clear is a person who no longer has his own reactive mind and therefore suffers none of the ill effects that the reactive mind can cause. The Clear has no engrams, which when restimulated, throw out the correctness of his computations by entering hidden and false data."

In addition to the personal mental freeing, Scientology lays great stress on a universal life energy, what they call thetan.

Worship and Practices

Scientology ministers perform the same types of ceremonies and services that ministers and priests of other religions perform. At a weekly service, a sermon may be given that addresses the idea that a person is a spiritual being. Scientology congregations celebrate weddings and christenings with their own formal ceremonies and mark the passing of their fellows with funeral rites.

Shamanism

A shaman is a man or woman of any age who can be benevolent or harmful. Because of their supposed contact with supernatural spirits, shamans have gained a reputation mainly for healing and curing (and even causing) illnesses, including mental illnesses, which are the result of evil spirits. Whether they are medicine men or witch doctors, shamans usually occupy a position of high respect and even power in a village.

It is almost certain that the history of shamanism goes back to prehistory. Even though the practice has strong elements of sorcery and magic, most scholars agree that it also has religious characteristics in that a shaman deals in identification with the supernatural, particularly as it relates to calling up and working with spirits.

The word "shaman" is said to have originated in Siberia. It is a name and sometimes a verb. It is not a religion as such, but is frequently part of or an adjunct to a religion, especially in Eastern religions and developing countries. In fact, shamans can be found virtually anywhere in the world. With the popularity of the New Age movements in the 1960s, shamanism gained considerable attraction and gave birth to a growing number of western shamans.

The Shaman's Position in the Tribe

Like doctors, shamans tend to specialize. As one would consult a doctor whose specialty treats one's particular ailment, the same goes for the shaman of choice. In both professions, there are also general practitioners. However, shamans have absolutely no medical qualifications, although they would no doubt proffer their spiritual power as the absolute qualification. Their specialized knowledge or powers are a result of heredity or supernatural calling.

The diagnoses of shamans, too, will be vastly different. For instance, a doctor might prescribe an analgesic for consistent headaches; a shaman would find out what possessed the patient, perhaps an evil spirit that needs to be cast out.

Though shamans are often members of a tribe, they rarely hold a position that could be considered prophetic. The tribal chief could occupy such a position, but the shaman—or medicine man in some regions—does hold a position of authority, and if consistently successful, awe. Historically, shamans may have been itinerant, going from village to village, particularly if they had built up a good reputation.

FACT

Shamans use their power to cure illnesses; they do not typically cause harm. The power of a shaman will be directly related to the power of his spirits. Some shamans may also be consulted to influence the weather, getting the rain to start or stop depending on the agricultural needs of the client.

Central Beliefs

The supernatural is the domain of shamans. While they may inherit the position, they must train to become one. Once the decision or "call" has been made, the supplicant has to embark on a period of intensive training that leads to initiation. Many myths describe the process. One claims that in order to become a great healer, the supplicant has to journey to the underground, suffer, and nearly die. He would often have an out-of-body experience and ascend to the sky. Essentially, this is accomplished by going into a trance. The shaman thus masters the ability to go beyond the physical body. Shamans may enter into the trance state through autohypnosis, the ingestion of hallucinogens, fasting, or self-mortification, during which they are said to be in contact with the spirit world.

The initiated shaman will display the appropriate accouterments, including masks, drums, and rattles, all of which are important elements of his image for the patients. Similarly, a modern-day doctor wears a white coat with a stethoscope hanging out of a pocket.

Shamans are able to move outside their physical bodies and into other spheres. Such journeys, as they are called, may take the shaman to other levels of existence. A shaman is the link between this world and other worlds and between the past and the future. This ability is considered a sacred trust to be used for the benefit of all. Shamans frequently fulfill the role of priest, magician, healer, and guide. A shaman lives on the edge of other realities; it takes a person of exceptional strength and courage, and one willing to undergo personal deprivations, to accomplish these duties.

ESSENTIAL

Shamanism forms a major part of the religious life of Eskimos. Healing is a predominant part of the shaman's way of life in the Arctic. The shaman is called an *angakok* in the Arctic, and it is said that their journeys have taken them to the moon in magic flight. Some angakok claim to have flown around the earth.

While believers hold to the power of the shaman, skeptics attribute any healing success to the placebo effect, even though they agree that altered states of consciousness exist. However, the placebo effect accounts for 30 percent of responses to all medication and suggestion.

Shamanism has grown considerably in the Western world, particularly in the United States, due in part to the growth of the New Age movements based in California.

CHAPTER 16

Tribal Native American and African Faiths

The spans of the American and African continents are so vast that it is impossible to generalize about their specific religions. One thing they have in common is that they are both tribal faiths. Each tribe possessed—and in some cases still possesses—its spiritual ceremonies and beliefs. The spread of missionaries and the influx of Western thought did much to diminish the wisdom of these ancient peoples. Nevertheless, their influence on modern religious study continues.

Native American Religions

It is almost impossible to characterize Native American religions as a whole because of their amazing diversity. Knowledge about the development of religion in the Native American tribes is imprecise. In fact, the word "religion" had no equivalent in any of the 300 Native American languages that existed at the time Columbus arrived on the continent.

FACT

The Lakota were nomadic, equestrian plains Indians who hunted buffalo and lived in tepees. They became famous for destroying Custer's forces at the Battle of the Little Bighorn in 1876. They followed the Seven Sacred Rites: the sweat lodge, the vision quest, ghost keeping, the sun dance, the making of relatives, puberty ceremony, and throwing the ball. With the exception of throwing the ball, which has been replaced by a practice known as *yuwibi,* all are still used in worship.

Their origins have been traced back some 60,000 years, but there is little in the way of early written material to provide reliable data. The various teachings, ways of life, and stories were passed on orally with all the drawbacks that are inherent in that form of communication, becoming tainted and more unreliable with each telling. There are common elements, though. Religions (used here in the sense that the immigrant Christians and Roman Catholics knew) were closely related to the natural world, which included supernatural and sacred spiritual worship and power.

The Influence of Outside Forces

The invasion of settlers from Europe during the nineteenth century wrecked the existing customs of the native people. Whole ways of life were radically changed, destroyed, or lost. For instance, during the Gold Rush days in California, in spite of the treaties made by the federal government providing clearly defined reservations, the miners would hold "Sunday shoots," where crowds of whites would attack Indian villages and kill as many people as they could. Entire tribes were massacred.

Christianity was frequently forced on the natives, with reprisals if it wasn't embraced. Although some of the natives accepted the religion voluntarily, many may have acquiesced for the sake of expediency: become a Christian and survive. Once the threat of physical survival disappeared there was a melding of beliefs, as happened with many other religions that came under the power of an invader. Thus, the beliefs in fixed doctrines, sacred texts, and moral codes and customs that were part of the European religious system were adopted by Native Americans and made part of their beliefs and values.

Central Beliefs

Individual beliefs were peculiar to individual tribes. Without becoming overly simplistic, generalities can be found across the diverse religions that existed. The knowledge of past information was passed on verbally from one generation to the next. Tradition, therefore, was a vital element specific to each tribe.

Many tribes would actually record events. The known method was using a specially prepared buffalo hide. Each year a figure or symbol illustrating the most memorable event would be painted on the hide. In time, the hide would become filled and it would be maintained for as long as there were people who could remember what the figures and symbols meant. For one year, there might have been a very good harvest of berries; in another the tribe might have moved to another location.

ESSENTIAL

The Apache occupied the southwestern part of the United States. They embraced the concept of supernatural power and carried out shamanistic ceremonies. Four is a sacred number; their songs and prayers occurred in quartets. Rites lasted for four successive nights. Their lifecycle rites included the rite for a child's first steps and a girl's puberty rite.

Since there was a limit on the amount of material that could be painted on any one hide, oral communication was the standard method of passing on stories, customs, and rituals. There might be a ceremony where these teachings were told to the other members of the tribe, particularly the young. No doubt the recounting of the exploits of local warrior heroes was popular.

In the belief system there was one great advantage in not having a tribal religion: there was no controversy between competing beliefs or religious schisms within groups/tribes, as was common among established religions. The geographical vastness of the country and the sparse population also played a role.

Native American Practices

The Native American Church, which became institutionalized in the twentieth century, has accepted some of Christianity's beliefs and has spread from coast to coast. The church includes some 100,000 adherents from over fifty North American Indian tribes, including American Indians and Eskimos. In some instances, traditional languages have been incorporated into Christian worship. It has received government support, particularly in the establishment of Indian schools.

The church is also known as Peyote Religion. "Peyotism" is based on the use of mescal, which is obtained from peyote cactus; eating it produces hallucinogenic effects. The drug was originally used for medicinal purposes and (occasionally) during warfare for divination.

Peyotism was especially popular among the disenfranchised, culminating in 1918 in the Native American Church. This cult would combine such indigenous elements as drumming, singing, visions, and the use of the sacred pipe with Christian practices of healing, prayer, and the chewing and sacramental eating of the non-narcotic hallucinogenic buds of the peyote plant in Saturday all-night rites. The rites occurred around an earthen altar and sacred fire in a peyote house or tipi, followed by a communal breakfast on Sunday morning.

The church's ethics include brotherly love, family care and support, and the avoidance of alcohol. Peyote produces visions during trance states, which were part of a Ghost Dance. Songs were sung, and the person in the trance might have a vision of an eagle or crow guiding her to the world of the dead. Part of the Ghost Dance provided information about the traditional culture the individual sought to retrieve.

Aside from peyote's purported hallucinogenic powers was its ability to bring peace and healing. In addition, it was an antidote against alcoholism and provided visions of the Peyote Spirit, often understood as Jesus. The false labeling of peyote as a narcotic led to its banning by tribal councils, missionaries, and government. Peyote was used extensively throughout many of the tribes; in 1997, the Native American Church estimated that there were about 225,000 adherents.

Rituals

The majority of Native American rituals revolved around the calendar and lunar and solar observations. Others were allied to the various subsistence needs; for example, hunting and harvesting. The Native American environment was symbolized by the ritual of the six directions: north, south, east, west, the zenith, and the nadir. The zenith was Grandfather (day). Sky is represented by Father Sun and the Thunderbirds. The nadir is Mother or Grandmother Earth. Grandmother Moon was female.

FACT

The Navajo live on the Navajo nation, a reservation in northern Arizona and New Mexico. They believe in powerful holy people, with whom they can live harmoniously. Twenty-four Navajo chants have been identified. One of the central chants is the Navajo creation myth that recounts what happened after their emergence on earth.

Different tribes had different rituals; nevertheless, the principle throughout the majority of the tribes was closely tied to nature and existence. For instance, the spirits and power of mountains, springs, lakes, clouds, flora, and fauna were seen as sacred.

The sweat lodge, fasting, and the sun dance were all part of Native American rituals. A sweat lodge is a structure made from saplings and covered by animal skins that generates moist air, like a sauna. There is a depression dug in the center of the lodge where hot rocks are placed. Water is thrown over the rocks, creating steam. Sweat lodges vary in size; some can hold as many as a dozen people. The purpose is for purification or spiritual renewal.

The Sun Dance

Fasting rituals are self-explanatory, but the sun dance is spectacular. A religious ceremony that originated with the Plains Indians, most notably the Sioux, the Sun Dance was held once a year in the early summer to celebrate and reaffirm beliefs about the universe and the supernatural.

Sometimes the dance was performed by individual tribes; other times a group of them would come together. There were elaborate preparations, and once the Sun Dance was under way, it continued for several days and nights. Dancers didn't eat or drink during the dance and many ended up in a frenzy of exhaustion; some even indulged in self-torture and mutilation. In 1904, the U.S. government outlawed the Sun Dance. Some tribes have tried to revive the dance in its original form.

Death

Birth, marriage, and death do not fit into a universal set of beliefs and rites. The various rites are meant to be indulged in by the relatives and the community. However, death is considered a transition, and many outcomes are possible following death. Some believe in reincarnation, others that humans return as ghosts, and others that the spirit goes to another world.

The Native American Church Today

Many Native Americans still cling to and express the values and traditions they were taught by their forefathers. Tribes of Native Americans continue their legal measures to reclaim lands they feel they have title to. Original languages are virtually extinct, but the Native American Church and its congregations are endeavoring to keep them alive and to re-establish a culture that has been virtually destroyed by its invaders.

African Religions

Attempting to analyze religions across the vast continent of Africa is a daunting task. The second largest continent in the world after Asia, Africa contains more than fifty countries. It possesses amazing geographical variation and cultural diversity. Each of its countries has its own history, ethnic group, and language. Many of the religious beliefs, customs, and rites evolved due to the environment in which the followers were born, grew up, and survived.

There is no single body of religious dogma for the continent, yet many similarities are found among all the countries. The simple common denominator is the belief in a single god or creator who is somewhere else. Even though in some instances there is a collection of gods, there is usually one supreme god who has domain over all. These other spiritual beings can be nature spirits and ancestors and are often called the Children of God. Sacrifices to lesser spiritual beings go to the Supreme Being. Many of the religious groups in various parts of the continent are on the decline.

The largest religious influence in Africa has been Islam, which came first to North Africa. Islam spread early on along the Mediterranean shores from Egypt to Morocco. Islamization of African was well advanced by the ninth century; Muslim dynasties were established in West Africa as early as the eleventh century in Takrur and Kanem.

ESSENTIAL

By the nineteenth century, Muslim mysticism—Sufism—was of considerable influence in Saharan and Sudanic Islam. Closely associated with Sufism in sub-Saharan Africa was the veneration of the Wali, the holy men of Islam, and the influence of the Muslim healing arts such as Quranic erasures and protective amulets, ornaments worn as a charm against evil.

The Arabs then brought the faith into the Sahara, where it was embraced by many western Africans.

People often mistakenly think of African religions as being exclusively concerned with animism, sorcery, and various tribal rituals. First, one has to consider that Africa is virtually divided in two at the Sahara Desert. (It is cut almost equally in two by the equator, meaning it is bound in the north by the tropic of Cancer and in the south by the tropic of Capricorn.) Islam took hold in the north; Christianity at one time was in the Sudan, and it's still active in Ethiopia, which is the only African kingdom with a Christian state church. Christian missions have spread throughout most of the areas south of the Sahara.

In the dense tropical forests, ancient traditional beliefs are still active, except where missionary zeal has made a presence in a country. In those cases, the majority of people have followed the customs and beliefs of the imported religion. Even so, it is highly probable that there has been an intermingling of the traditional with the new.

Central Beliefs of African Religions

Religion has always played a major part in the different cultures in Africa. Each locale has many varied stories that tie them directly to either a god or the gods they worshiped. However, there is a strong similarity to the stories. First, the god would create the earth, then the animals, and lastly the humans.

Because of the lack of a written language, very little written religious history is available. Most of what is known came in two ways: orally, from parents to children; and the results gathered from the extensive work of archeologists, which revealed a tremendous body of evidence not only of religious practices and ways of life but also how those lives evolved over the years. The traditions were so strong that today's religious practices provide valuable insight into the way they were practiced years ago.

FACT

In the Central African Republic, about two-fifths of the population is Christian, mainly Roman Catholics plus some Protestant denominations. Sunni Muslims are a growing minority. The remainder are either adherents of traditional religions or have no religious affiliations.

Common ground among African religions include a cosmos that is populated by divine beings, the existence of sacred places and spaces (for instance a mountain that a god or sacred spirit inhabits), a notion that males and females are both parts of the cosmic scheme, and the idea that society was organized around the values and traditions from early beginnings. Africans have taken strong steps over the years to stave off the influences of foreigners onto existing traditions and beliefs in an effort to preserve indigenous cultures. These efforts have not always been successful.

Many scholars believe that the African countries that have remained most stable into the twenty-first century are those that retained their traditional ways of life and religions. African religions don't have a dogma consisting of strict religious laws to follow; their entire philosophy is directed to nurturing a proper relationship with the divine and how the divine relates to the earth, life, and community. Their rituals revolve around establishing and maintaining a relationship with the spiritual forces in nature and with the gods. This relationship is accomplished through prayers, offerings, and sacrifices made to shrines and altars.

QUESTION

How many religions are there in Africa?
No one knows for sure. Africa is a veritable hub for missionaries. Thus, in addition to the traditional beliefs and independent churches, the Roman Catholic Church made inroads, as did the Baptists and other Protestant denominations. The Ethiopian church, formed in 1892, had connections with the African Methodist Episcopal Church in the United States.

A sacrifice often means the shedding of blood; the ritual of sacrifice releases the vital force that sustains life. In some parts of Africa, a blood sacrifice must be made to the gods. Nowadays animals are sacrificed, though it wasn't always that way. Typically, a goat or chicken is consecrated, ritually slain, and then either burnt or buried—it's never eaten as a meal by the devotees. The purpose of many sacrifices is to assuage the wrath of the gods, which can be exhibited by drought, pestilence, epidemic, famine, or other dire happenings.

The shrines are unimposing edifices—insubstantial little structures placed wherever it seems appropriate; they don't even have to be permanent. Ancestors play an important part in the beliefs, acting as the go-betweens for spiritual access. People don't automatically become ancestors when they die. First, they need to have lived a good life—a moral life that has contributed to the community. When a person gets seriously ill, the cause is some kind of emotional or social conflict, and it is the ancestor, who has been watching over the person, who delivers the reprimand of illness.

The Rituals of African Religions

There is a common thread in the rituals throughout Africa. This is especially true with those concerned with progress throughout life.

Birth

An expectant mother is an important person. As in the United States a child may grow up to be president, in Africa a male child may grow up to be a chief. The actual birth rarely takes place in the presence of a man. The child is anointed by a priest. Naming the child is very important and usually consists of a given name, followed by the name of the father, then the grandfather's name. After the ceremony, there will be songs, dancing, and a feast.

Puberty

Both circumcisions and clitoridectomies are performed. The justification for what some people call genital mutilation is that it is an important means of establishing gender—that there should be no indication of androgyny. Boys often have their faces painted in preparation for the coming-of-age rite of circumcision.

Marriage

A woman who is to be married is very powerful. For one, she may give birth to a warrior or chief. In some areas, after the wedding has been planned, the groom's family must move to the bride's village. Gifts will be exchanged and in some cultures, an offering is made to the gods. Sometimes a sacrifice will be made, too.

The actual wedding ceremony will include both families, and sometimes the entire village. Not surprisingly, there will be much celebration. For several weeks after the consummation of the marriage, the couple will continue their celebrations.

Death

Death is not seen as the final stage of life, but as going to a place to be with deceased loved ones. The corpse is cleaned and dressed, then placed in the grave with special artifacts to aid in the journey. The corpse will be buried, and afterward there may be an exchange of gifts between family members and an animal sacrifice.

ESSENTIAL

Some tribes initiate girls in what we in the west would call domestic science. This even extends to sexual etiquette and the religious significance of womanhood and female power. Boys may be led by the wise men in the village to a specially secluded place and stay there for up to a year while they learn secret information about becoming a man.

Diversification into Modern Society

African religious beliefs and customs have traveled, particularly to the United States, where elements of the indigenous faiths have frequently remained and/or been absorbed into the local religions. The lasting picture of religion in Africa is one of amazing historical development, as rituals and customs from ancient times have continued into the twenty-first century and commingled with a variety of imported religions.

CHAPTER 17

Pacific Rim Faiths

One of the central components of Pacific Rim religions is their mystical heritage. For instance, the Australian Aborigines have their belief in a world created in dreams. The Maoris of New Zealand and the Polynesians have similar attachments to natural phenomena, particularly the sea and the stars.

Australian/Aboriginal Faiths

Aborigines first traveled to Australia about 40,000 years ago. At that time, there was a land bridge between Asia and Australia. Over the years, the sea levels rose and Australia became an island. The Aborigines numbered about 500,000 in 1788, and some 300 different Australian Aboriginal languages were spoken. Within a hundred years, their population declined to 50,000, mainly as a result of loss of land, adoption of European habits such as drinking alcohol, effects of European diseases, declining birthrates, and violence between the Europeans and Aborigines.

The English colonized the east coast and planned to convert the natives to Christianity from what they considered paganism and superstition. Because the Aborigines did not cultivate crops or domesticate animals apart from the dingo (a kind of wild dog), they were essentially nomadic hunter-gatherers. Then the missionaries arrived and, in 1821, the first Wesleyan Missionary Society established a presence, spreading throughout the land.

There was no cohesive element among the Aborigines, so they never came near an established organized national identity. While there was sporadic resistance against the colonists by various tribes, as the English called them, not much came of the efforts and evangelical Christianity became accepted. Today, more than two-thirds of Australian Aborigines are Christians.

Beliefs of the Aborigines

The colonists concluded that the Aborigines had no actual religion until they discovered something called Dreamtime. The thrust of the Aboriginal existence was their relationship with the environment and handed down oral beliefs. Like all peoples, they asked themselves the universal questions: Who am I? Where did I come from? What am I doing here? Where do I go when I die?

Aborigines believed that when their heroic ancestors died, they went into a spiritual place where they created, through Dreamtime, everything that was: the earth, the land they occupied, every plant, animal, insect, and reptile, and the sky above. It was during Dreamtime that their creators made men and women. Birth was the result of what the creators did; their power was present at every birth, of people and everything else. In addition, some of the tribes believed that spirit children and spirit animals gained life by entering a female's body.

ESSENTIAL

The most important thing to an Aborigine was spiritual heritage. After death, the person's spirit returned to its spirit place. That belief gave rise to burying a corpse facing the direction of its spirit home.

The creators taught men and women how to hunt and gather food, and how to make the tools to carry out those duties. As the generations came and went, the belief in Dreamtime was passed on by living a life known as Dreaming—by living in the same way as their forebears.

Ceremonies

Puberty rituals for a boy generally took place once he had started to grow facial hair. When that happened, he was ready for the initial rituals. Initiation was a symbolic re-enactment of death and rebirth, seen as the way to a new life as an adult. The novice would leave his camp and the women would begin to wail. This symbolism was a prelude to the religious beliefs in which all men participated. Circumcision was an important part of the rites and was a secret sacred ritual. There were other rites, including piercing the nasal septum, pulling teeth, hair removal, scarring, and playing with fire.

The puberty of girls did not have a universal ritual; in some tribes, it was celebrated by either total or partial seclusion or taboos on certain foods. In some areas, defloration and hymen cutting were practiced.

As Christianity became ingrained in the land, the Aborigines adopted the ceremonies of the Christian Church to which they had been converted. What tended to take place, certainly in the early days, was a mixture of Christian ceremonies and indigenous ones. Although the indigenous ones were looked on by the colonists as secular, they were sacred to the Aborigines.

Historically, the marriage ceremony involved the ritual of the man arriving in the camp of his wife-to-be and catching or hunting food, which he presented to his future father-in-law and other members of the family. The prospective wife would often build a new hut for her future husband and herself. She then prepared a meal for him, after which the couple was considered married. However, the ceremony was not a religious occasion.

FACT

There has been much research into whether or not the Aborigines actually had what could be called a true religion. The consensus was that for that to be established there must be evidence of a god. However, there was not even a suggestion of one in the Dreamtime myths. Then again, the definition that says a religion requires a god would also keep Buddhism from being a religion.

In Today's World

In modern times, Aborigines have had problems regarding land rights similar to those of the Native Americans; the Aboriginal people feel dispossessed. Dreamtime is still a part of their heritage, as is their landscape, which was formed by their ancestors and is still alive with their spirits. The Aborigines say that those spirits are as much a part of the land as they themselves are part of its creation.

Steps are being taken to find a just solution. Nevertheless, on Australia Day in January 2000, the words of reconciliation by Governor Sir James Gobbo did nothing to diminish the anger of a group of Aboriginal activists who labeled Australia Day a day of mourning; they burnt the Australian flag in protest.

QUOTE

In the late 1770s, Captain Cook said "... in reality the Aborigines are far happier than we Europeans, being wholly unacquainted with the superfluous conveniences so much sought after in Europe ... they live in a tranquility which is not disturbed by the inequality of Condition."

In 1992 a High Court ruling overturned *terra nullius* (the notion that Australia had been uninhabited when European colonization began), allowing Aborigines a measure of legal entitlement to their ancestral lands.

The Maori Faiths

Since interaction with Christianity, the Maori people, indigenous to New Zealand, have produced some sixty identifiable independent religious movements. The people had no name for themselves until they adopted Maori (which means "normal") to distinguish themselves from the Europeans, who had become more numerous following the discovery of the two islands by the English Captain Cook in the late 1700s.

With the English came a series of diseases, mainly measles and influenza, against which the Maori had no resistance. This led to a decline in the local population. After Great Britain annexed the country in 1840, there was an appreciable increase in the number of Europeans. Today, New Zealand is populated mainly by people of European descent; Maoris comprise a minority.

The British came seeking profit and the Maori chieftains eventually took exception and became involved in the bargaining of their land for sale. Not everyone agreed with that policy and fighting took place within the Maoris. By 1872 the fighting came to an end; the result by then was that the Maori culture had become decimated and the struggle was how to retain the customs and rituals that had existed before the invaders arrived.

Creation

The Maoris have a wonderfully rich mythical origin that began with Ranginui, the sky father, and Papatuanuku, the earth mother. The sky father and earth mother prevented light from reaching the world because they were always in such a close embrace. Their offspring decided to separate them and thus allow light to come into the world. But there was a war about the separation of the parents. Tawhirimatea (god of the winds) won out over Tane (god of forests) and Tangaroa (god of seas). However, Tumatauenga (god of war) came to defeat all of them. Thus, the world developed with wars and violence.

Spiritual Movements of the Maoris

The most spiritual movement in New Zealand, Ringatu, was founded in 1867 by the Maori guerrilla leader Te Kooti (1830–1893). It embraced a benign philosophy including faith healing. Services were held on the twelfth day of each month and on Saturdays. Generally, they were held in meeting houses, and love feasts and communion (without bread or wine but including Bible verses, songs, chants, and prayers) were all part of the services. Te Kooti was elevated to the status of a prophet and martyr. A liturgy produced in the 1960s, The Book of the Eight Covenants of God and Prayers of the Ringatu Church, may have originated orally from Te Kooti.

ESSENTIAL

The Maoris have no official established religion; in fact, many of them have no adherence to any religion, although the Maori version of Christianity is practiced in the Ratana and Ringatu churches.

The Ratana Church

A Methodist farmer, Tahupotiki Wiremu Ratana (1873–1939), founded the Ratana Church. He had established a reputation as a mystical faith healer, which drew the crowds. He preached of moral reform and of one God: the God of the Bible. By a process of political and religious pressure, the Ratana movement disassociated itself from other denominations. The New Zealand Anglican bishops denounced the church; they weren't too taken with their practices of faith healing and the taking of medicines.

By becoming politically involved and gaining some support, in the 1960s the church eventually got back together with the other New Zealand Christian churches. The Ratana church by then was not solely Maori, but had attracted many white members to the congregation.

Polynesian Religions

The world of Polynesia is an exotic but complicated place with its many religions and beliefs. The Polynesian myths include a creation myth describing how the cosmos came into being. The cosmos derives from an original emptiness (kore), primal darkness (po), and gradually gave way to sun, moon, and stars. Gods (Atua), Nature, and humankind emerged, each sharing in the creation drama. The uncreated source (*numu*) is left undescribed or personified as a great creator-god, Tangaroa.

Central Beliefs of the Polynesian Religions

In the nineteenth century, the word *mana* meant "supernatural force or power." It was applied to people, spirits, and even inanimate objects. Polynesian chiefs had such great mana that if another person even touched the chief's shadow, the only way that error could be corrected was by the death of a subject. Everyday life became like a maze through which people had to negotiate to avoid offending mana. It got to the point that almost everything had the mana of a great person or god. When men prepared for battle, they had to go through a ritual of purification that meant eating certain foods, avoiding women, and going away on their own to avoid defilement.

FACT

The belief in gods of varying power, called Tangaroa, Tu, or Lono, gave rise to the necessity of worshiping them. Sometimes this worship required human sacrifice, sexual orgies, and extensive fasting and chanting.

The violation of certain acts such as disturbing the bones of the dead could evoke supernatural punishment. Magic became an important part of society, practiced in order to ward off the vengeance or wrath of mana. This situation gave birth to specialists in magic who were available to offer rituals to protect the people.

Eventually, mana itself was challenged. With the growing belief in Christianity, brought to the islands by missionaries, the meaning of mana was revised to mean the personal attributes of only people in powerful positions, like a clergyman or senior government official. The belief that supernatural aspects of mana were floating around in almost anything was discarded.

While Christianity is the predominant religion in Polynesia, there are smatterings of other religions. In Tonga, for example, about 50 percent belong to the Free Wesleyan Church, 14 percent belong to the Free Church of Tonga, 9 percent are Mormon, and the remainder belong to other denominations.

Polynesians are a family and group-orientated society, with religion making up an important part of their identity. Like the Maoris, the Polynesians are, in the main, Christians and follow the teachings of the Bible.

CHAPTER 18

New Age and Other Beliefs

New Age beliefs share common ground: seeking respect from the traditional religions just as they, in turn, respect the beliefs of those people. This chapter will explore the religions of New Age Spirituality, Prayer and Healing, Spiritism, Spiritualism, and Wicca and Witchcraft.

New Age Spirituality

Unlike most traditional religions, the New Age movement lacks an organized base; rather, it is a network of people owning different spiritual approaches to life. Many New Age followers belong an existing religion, with the New Age philosophy as an adjunct to their central beliefs. Other members have discarded the religion they were born into in favor of a more free-flowing, nondogmatic belief.

New Age spirituality has no holy text, clergy, or creed. While there are no sermons preached, followers and nonfollowers alike attend seminars on various aspects of New Age philosophy. The meeting place might be a New Age bookshop that sells a wide variety of books on the subject. However, the movement did set up communities, often called communes, where members follow the lifestyle.

FACT

There are no reliable demographics on how many people actually practice New Age philosophy. However, the indications are that far more women than men embrace the movement, and that the majority of the followers are Caucasian.

The movement came about in the 1970s and was strongly influenced by Eastern religions and philosophy (particularly Buddhism and Hinduism), Western psychology, Carl Jung's teachings and his concept of the collective unconscious, and Native American beliefs and rituals. With the advances in science, the belief also included a pseudoscientific association with an interpretation of quantum physics.

Adopting beliefs from various sources and integrating them into the New Age movement gives an indication of the motivation of the movement—a search for a new paradigm. While not a registered religion, it is certainly a spiritual movement, a veritable mélange of beliefs borrowed from existing faiths. Its development is linked to the social changes that preceded it—for instance the Beat generation, the Hippie culture of the 1960s, and the anti-Vietnam War groups. Its rise might owe in large part to the general disillusionment of many people within the established churches and governments.

Beliefs

New Age followers were looking for a New World Order that would produce an end to wars, famine, pollution, poverty, and discrimination. The new order would usher in what was termed "the dawning of The Age of Aquarius." The Age of Aquarius was based on the belief that a new sign of the zodiac came along every 2,000 years. The previous sign was Pisces, the fish, which came at the time a new religion called Christianity was emerging. Interestingly, the symbol of the fish indicates Christianity.

The central belief of the movement is that the universe and all that exists within it are one interdependent whole. This means that every existing entity, from atom to galaxy, is rooted in the same universal, life-creating reality. All people, whatever their race, creed, sex, caste, or color, are invited to participate as individuals or within collective environments that share in these basic beliefs and understandings. The movement claims that it imposes no dogmas, but points toward the source of unity beyond all differences—devotion to truth, love for all living things, and commitment to a life without personal judgment of others.

Practices

Attached to the expressed philosophy of the movement are a number of esoteric practices, some of which have strong health applications, including:

- Crystals are believed to have healing energy. Based on the idea that their molecular structure can be shaped to vibrate at a specific frequency, it's believed that crystals can positively affect a person's well-being and good health.
- Astrology is based on the theory that at the exact time of a person's birth the planets were in a unique position. Interpreting those positions in the constellation, which is a highly complicated endeavor, can predict a person's personality and future events.
- The human potential movements, also known as the Emotional Growth Movement, which include Esalen Growth Center, EST, Gestalt Therapy, Primal Scream Therapy, Transactional Analysis, Transcendental Meditation (made famous by the Beatles), and Yoga (an

integral part of many Eastern religions), can thank New Agers for their widespread acceptance and application. Essentially, human potential groups are involved in therapeutic methods designed to help people advance spiritually.

- Aromatherapy, practiced since the beginning of civilization, has been embraced by many New Agers as a therapeutic health adjunct. The oils can be applied directly to the skin, used in baths, or inhaled.

There are countless other therapies and techniques aimed at improving health and/or mental equilibrium. Obviously, many of the practices and ingredients used present a wonderful opportunity for the skeptics. Nevertheless, the placebo effect some people obtain from them can't be discounted.

Books

The New Age movement has no holy writings, but a few books among thousands of New Age books have made a lasting impression on many followers. The first of eight books by the same author came out in the late 1960s—*The Teachings of Don Juan: A Yaqui Way of Knowledge* became a cult book. People who have read it say it transformed them and became their manifesto. The author, Carlos Castaneda, is a former anthropologist who became a sorcerer's apprentice, psychic visionary, and original philosopher.

ESSENTIAL

A nonprofit organization founded in 1978 established a networking center for a Course in Miracles students. They publish a periodical called *The Holy Encounter* and offer free services for students of the course to help them connect with others and understand and integrate the principles into their lives. The entire publication is written to express a nonsectarian, nondenominational spirituality.

The second book, created by Dr. Helen Schucman, is a series of workbooks collectively called *A Course in Miracles*. She claimed the words came through a process of inner dictation directly from Jesus. It is described as a Christian-based interpretation of the Bible. The book states that, "its goal for you is happiness and peace." The book offers a one-year training program; it begins with the process of changing the student's mind and perception. According to the preface, "at the end, the reader is left in the hands of his or her own internal teacher, who will direct all subsequent learning as he sees fit."

The third set of publications is the *Conversations with God* series written by Neale Donald Walsch. The content of all three books is the author's conversations with God. According to the record, Mr. Walsch called out in anguish, "What does it take to make life work? And what have I done to deserve a life of such continuing struggle?" His questions kept coming and he wrote them down on a yellow legal pad; the list ended up looking like an angry letter to God. Then, he heard a reply in his mind coming from a voiceless voice, a voice Mr. Walsch felt very strongly was that of God, who said, "Do you really want an answer to all these questions or are you just venting?" That was the start of it all.

Recently, German-born spiritualist Ulrich Leonard Tolle, commonly known as Eckhart Tolle, has developed a personal growth/self-help philosophy that might be classed New Age. One of Tolle's teachings asserts that before we can become immersed in the present we have to dis-identify ourselves from thoughts of the past; our preoccupation with our own egos keeps us from being in the present. His latest book is *A New Earth: Awakening to Life's Purpose*.

Prayer and Healing

It isn't too often that science, religion, and politics meet, but The National Institutes of Health has funded research into the effectiveness of prayer on the healing of the sick, including patients with cancer and AIDS.

Today, there are many healing centers set up in churches all over the country where people may go for advice about praying for an ill loved one. To the members of any religion or belief, the power of prayer, the laying on of hands, and the recordings of miracles is nothing new.

Reaction of Today's Society

In today's society, a medical scientist would have grave doubts about the recordings of miracles ascribed to Christ in the Bible. The scientist would have to follow a medical protocol in order to establish the process and validity of the disease, its symptoms, possible treatment, and outcome. But these facts are not available for miracles; the scientist would have to put down the whole affair as being apocryphal.

The closest a scientist might come to account for someone whose disease went away without medical treatment would be spontaneous remission—as in some cancer cases—which is often brought into play when there doesn't appear to be a logical answer for why a patient suddenly appears to be cured.

Reliance on the ability to heal through an unknown power as opposed to the medical establishment is exhibited by some members of established religious faiths. For instance, Christian Scientists say that healing comes through scientific prayer or spiritual communion with God. They maintain that prayer recognizes a patient's direct access to God's love and discovers more of the consistent operation of God's law of health and wholeness on her behalf.

FACT

The British medical journal *The Lancet* took a poll. The results indicated that 73 percent of people believe praying for someone else can help cure their illness; 75 percent of patients wanted their physicians to address spiritual issues; 50 percent of hospitalized patients wanted their physicians to pray with them; and 28 percent believed in the ability of faith healers to make people well through their faith and touch.

Spiritual healers believe it is possible to channel a healing energy to a patient by praying to God. Eastern religions believe that the spirit, mind, and body have to be in harmony or balance to sustain good physical and mental health. Disease is said to begin in the spirit and mind; therefore, the healing must begin there.

Experiments and Research

Reliable research into such topics as ethical distant healing is difficult because many factors need to be controlled. Scientific research often uses the double-blind method to control variables. For example, when a pill is given to selected patients in a study group, none of them knows who is getting the real thing and who is getting the sugar pill. At the same time, none of the researchers knows whether they are giving the real thing or a sugar pill to the subjects. (They are both blind to the identification of which is which and to whom it's delivered.)

In 1988 a cardiologist named Randolph Byrd carried out a well-designed, double-blind experiment in an effort to determine if prayers had any effect on patients in the Coronary Care Unit in San Francisco General Hospital. A computer randomly selected which of the 383 newly admitted patients would be prayed for and who would not. The experiment was carried out over a ten-month period. The results were remarkable; those prayed for were five times less likely to require antibiotics, three times less likely to develop complications, and none had the need for an endotracheal intubation (a tube inserted into the patient's throat). Twelve of the patients who weren't prayed for did need the procedure.

The reaction to the experiment from the medical establishment was mixed because it was claimed the experiment was not completely scientific. However, after revising the experimental procedures, Dr. Byrd's findings were replicated; seemingly, prayers work.

Spiritism

Spiritism should not be confused with spiritualism (discussed later in this chapter). Spiritism is a modern and mainly Christian belief centering on the communication with spirits of the dead. The dead retain their personalities and are accessible through a "medium," a person trained to channel communications between the earthly world and a world of spirits. Spiritualism is a doctrine of belief in a spiritual order of beings as real as the material world and a belief that the soul is a spiritual substance.

Judging by scripture, some form of Spiritism goes far back in history. In spite of the assertions of traditionally religious people that the Bible strictly forbade attempts to communicate with the dead through spirit mediums, there is a very clear indication in the Bible that such an attitude was not universal.

For instance, 1 Samuel 28: 7–19 reads, in part: "Then said Saul unto his servants. 'Seek me a woman that hath a familiar spirit, that I may go to her, and inquire of her.' Saul puts on a disguise and goes to the woman. He says to her: 'I pray thee, divine unto me by the familiar spirit, and bring me him up, whom I shall name unto thee.'" (He was seeking out Samuel.)

The woman prevaricates and points out that those with familiars and wizards have been punished. Saul assures her she won't suffer. The woman obeys, and Samuel appears to Saul, whereupon they have a conversation in which Saul asks Samuel's advice.

Many religions indulge in one form or another of Spiritism, including Yoruba, Native North Americans, and sects in Haiti. Other religions, while adhering to their traditional beliefs and practices, also dabble in Spiritism. It is estimated that there are at least 20 million people who are Spiritists.

Modern Spiritism

Modern Spiritism is said to have begun in the home of the Fox family in Hydesville, New York, in 1848. The Fox sisters, quite by accident, discovered their mediumistic powers when they heard strange knocking noises and pieces of furniture moved as if by invisible hands. Eventually, whoever was doing the knocking and moving the furniture about began to answer questions. The story spread and attracted widespread interest, since to some it provided tangible evidence of an afterlife.

Other disturbances of the same kind were reported in the house of a Presbyterian minister, the Rev. Dr. Phelps. None of these happenings could be objectively confirmed, but that did not lessen the public's enthusiasm. The claims of such stories remain controversial, though Spiritism survives as a minor religious movement in many Western countries. In fact, it bears similarities to spirit possession in many non-Christian religions.

Beliefs and Customs

There is no ministry within the belief of Spiritists; neither are there vestments, altars, banners, candles, processions, talismans, amulets, or sacraments. Those who profess to be serious Spiritists believe that God is the supreme intelligence and the primary cause of all things. The universe is God's creation and encompasses all beings. Beyond the physical world is a spiritual world, which is the habitation of incarnate spirits. All the laws of nature are divine moral laws and man is an incarnate spirit in the material body.

Probably the most important and most used Spiritist practice is trying to get in touch with those who have died. Communication with the spirit world manifests itself in various psychical ways: telepathy, clairvoyance, and trance speaking. Physical phenomena include levitation, automatic writing, poltergeists, and the mysterious substance called ectoplasm. There is also the practice of reading auras, a sort of invisible dressing around your body that can be seen only by a person versed in reading auras.

ESSENTIAL

According to Spiritism, the relationship of spirits and man is constant and has always existed. The good spirits lead you toward goodness and aid you in your troubles. While humans have free will, they must take responsibility for their own actions.

So far, no results of Spiritist practices have been scientifically validated. The major traditional religions are quick to cite these results, just as the Spiritists are quick to point out that there is no scientific evidence to validate the spiritual claims of traditional religions.

Spiritualism

There is no point at which spiritualism can be said to have begun. In prehistoric times, people were motivated to seek out unseen and unknown entities that controlled things. This is in keeping with the Spiritualist doctrine, which maintains that a spiritual order of beings—including souls—might be every bit as real as bodies that make up the material world.

Hence, a Spiritualist could attribute sun or rain to a sun god or rain god, which he worshipped because the sun and the rain were essential to well-being. Other gods were instituted to suit the needs of the people, who had no direct control over events. If things went wrong, the people felt they had displeased the gods somehow. One way of dealing with that was to make offerings and sacrifices.

Spiritualism is a philosophy characteristic of any system of thought that affirms the existence of immaterial reality imperceptible to the senses. This leads some to conclude that there is something going on out there. But what?

Spiritualists believe there are other planes of existence. For example, the next higher plane is similar to this earthly one but operates at a higher rate of vibration and luminosity. One method of service in spirit is to communicate and help illuminate those who are living on the earthly plane.

Mediums in the spirit and physical worlds adjust their vibrations to enable communication between the two planes to take place. Life moves in a gradual state of evolution, culminating in the arrival in the spiritual realm. Like Spiritism, Spiritualism believes the understanding gleaned on the earthly plane continues to the next level; what are left behind are the pains, struggles, and frustrations of the material world. Life is about continuous growth, and consciousness never dies because it is part of God and the infinite.

QUESTION

How does a person become a Spiritualist?
You could start with a book: *Teachings and Illustration as They Emanate from the Spirit World* by Mary T. Longley. Or you could write to the National Spiritualist Association of Churches in Lily Dale, New York. The association has been in existence since 1893.

True Spiritualists believe in the core philosophy that each human is a soul clothed in a material body through which mental and spiritual faculties function, and that it is within this material body that the spiritual or etheric body resides.

The Spiritualists Declaration of Principles is published not as a binding creed but as a consensus on the fundamental teachings of Spiritualism by Spiritualists. In part, it says:

We believe in infinite intelligence.

We believe that the phenomena of nature, both physical and spiritual, are the expression of infinite intelligence.

We affirm that communication with the so-called dead is a fact.

We affirm that the precepts of prophecy and healing are divine attributes proven through mediumship.

Practices

A medium is a person whose body is acutely sensitive to vibrations from the spirit world. Because of that sensitivity, the medium is able to participate in prophecy, clairvoyance, clairaudience, laying on of hands, visions, revelations, healing, and a host of other esoteric actions.

Wicca and Witchcraft

Witchcraft has usually referred to a malevolent exercise of preternatural powers—more often than not by women—attributed to a connection with the devil or evil spirits. Accounts of witchcraft go back more than 2,000 years—even ancient Greek and Roman texts include accounts of witchcraft.

America has suffered its own infamous rendezvous with witchcraft. In 1692, an infamous trial was held in Salem, Massachusetts. Nine-year-old Elizabeth Parris the daughter of a Salem Village minister, and her eleven-year-old cousin Abigail Williams, began to exhibit strange behaviors such as blasphemous screaming, convulsive seizures, and so on. Other Salem girls began to demonstrate similar behavior. Physicians concluded that the girls were under the influence of Satan.

Pressured to identify some source of their afflictions, the girls named three women and warrants were issued for their arrest. The women were examined and found guilty of witchcraft. This set hysteria in motion among the populace, resulting in the death of twenty-four people accused of being witches.

FACT

The publication of *Malleus Maleficarum* (Hammer of Witches) in 1487, describing witches' Sabbaths, night flying, intercourse with the devil, transformation into animals, and malicious spells cast on men and cattle, greatly increased superstition and persecution.

The Christian witch hunts in the sixteenth and seventeenth centuries resulted in thousands of alleged witches being persecuted and executed, usually by burning. Before 1700, at least 200,000 people were executed, mainly in continental Europe. Greater scientific knowledge in the seventeenth century led the educated to reject a belief in witchcraft, but popular belief has survived much longer. In fact, it's recorded that between 1994 and 1995, over 200 people in South Africa were burnt to death after being accused of witchcraft.

Witchcraft and sorcery are frequently misunderstood; the two are separate entities. A witch is someone who has innate magical powers. (The term "witch" applies to both men and women; "warlock" is now considered to be derogatory.) A sorcerer is someone who uses potions and spells to get their way.

Central Beliefs

Wicca is said to derive from an ancient Celtic society older than Christianity. Other sources say the religion is a modern one without a long historical connection. Modern Wiccans maintain that present-day Wicca is a merging of some of the ancient Celtic beliefs, deity structure, and seasonal days of celebration with modern material from ceremonial magic.

The general belief is that Wicca arose as an important movement in England during the 1950s. The movement has claimed a fast-track expansion into North America and Europe. Some estimates put the number of adherents at 750,000.

Covens

Some Wiccans worship in a coven. Traditionally, a coven consists of thirteen people who are emotionally connected. The thirteenth member will be the High Priestess or Priest. Typically, covens meet in private homes or meeting rooms, though on some occasions, such as holidays, they meet outdoors. Nights of the full or new moon are times of choice.

Practices

Witchcraft members adhere strictly to an ethical code called Wiccan Rede. They believe that whatever they do comes back to them threefold. Thus, if they did harm they would get harm back to the power of three. Therefore, they have no incentive to curse anyone; the curse would come back to haunt them three times over. Witches may practice some form of ritual magic, which must be considered "good magic." Their ethical code is spelled out in the saying: "An' it harm none, do what thou wilt."

The Council of American Witches write in paragraph eight of their Principles of Belief: "Calling oneself 'Witch' does not make a witch, but neither does heredity itself, or the collecting of titles, degrees, and initiations. A witch seeks to control forces within her/himself that make life possible in order to live wisely and well, without harm to others, and in harmony with nature."

QUESTION

How do Witches cast spells?
Typically, a Witch will start a spell by casting a circle, burning some incense, lighting a special candle, then doing some rhythmic chanting. An analogy has been made between a Witch casting a spell and a person being in a church. The churchgoer hopes his prayers are answered; the Witch hopes that a good spell is cast.

A deep respect for the environment features strongly in Wiccan religious activity. So, too, does the value of femininity. Witches generally worship a god and goddess, seen as different aspects of the same deity. The deity is known as the ultimate omnipotent god force in the universe and is the same God most people worship. However, Witches relate better to both a mother and father figure, which is why the term goddess figures predominately in the craft.

The Handfasting Ritual

One of the most charming Wiccan rituals is called Handfasting. The ceremony was derived from the medieval wedding practices used in Scotland, Wales, and Ireland. Handfasting is basically a Wiccan marriage ceremony. Originally, the ceremony was not considered a wedding, but a declaration of intent to marry. If after a year and a day the couple are still committed to each other, they would be legally married at an official ceremony.

Before the ceremony can begin, the area chosen is swept free of debris and negativity by the Maiden of the Broom. Once that's done, a High Priestess circles the couple three times, incanting:

Three times round,

Once for the Daughter,

Twice for the Crone,

Thrice for the Mother,

who sits on the throne.

Everything proceeds with the giving of the vows, the placing of wedding bands, and thanks to the elements. The ceremony ends with a repeat of the opening stanza.

Wiccan Festivals

Based on the Celtic calendar, the Wiccan calendar recognizes two seasons: winter and summer, each of which begins with a celebration. The eight major holidays are called the Eight Sabbats. Some covens may follow the festivals; others may have alternatives. Minor holidays are called The Lesser Sabbats.

Note that the dates given in the list below may vary:

- **Yule**. The Winter Solstice, late December. The Sun God is born at Yule.
- **Imbolg** (also called Imbolc), February 2. The first signs of waking up from winter (also known as Groundhog Day).
- **Ostara**. The Vernal Equinox, late March. The magical times when day and night are equal.
- **Beltane**, May 1. A great fertility celebration (also known as May Day).
- **Litha**, late June. The Summer Solstice (also known as Midsummer and St. John's Day) is the halfway point of the year.
- **Lughnasadh**, August 1. The beginning of the harvest season.
- **Mabon**, late September. The Autumn Equinox. A time to give thanks for the earth's bounty.
- **Samhain**, October 31. Samhain is the Celtic New Year's Day. It is also known as Halloween.

CHAPTER 19

Evidentialism and the Existence of God

Evidentialism is a position in the philosophy of knowledge that says our beliefs are only justified if they are grounded in evidence. Applied to religions, Evidentialism claims you are not justified in having a *full* religious belief unless there is conclusive evidence for the belief. In short, Evidentialism requires that believers "prove up" before they are entitled to hold strongly to beliefs.

The Demands and Applications of Evidentialism

Among other things, Evidentialism entails that believers apportion their belief to the evidence. How would this affect the specifics of religious belief? To take an example, if the arguments for the existence of God do not "prove" God's existence, believers should not have a full belief in the existence of a supreme being. Put another way, they should at least hold a measure of doubt.

Evidentialism also applies to other religious notions. Some believers claim to have had "religious experiences" in which they report having contacted a transcendent being or felt God's presence in some way. Evidentialism requires, at the very least, that the believer correlate his private experience with his assertion, if any, that God exists.

Other examples are more specialized. Can a believer point to the evidence that bolsters his belief that the Koran is the word of Muhammad or that Jesus was God incarnate? If the balance of evidence does not favor such beliefs, he cannot believe such statements with full confidence. Again, no belief can be held with full confidence unless there is conclusive evidence for it.

Contemporary Evidentialism

According to contemporary Evidentialists, even moderate forms of belief based on faith will not do. Writing in *The Encyclopedia of Philosophy* in 1973, Paul Edwards outlined a conception of an atheist as someone "who rejects a belief in God" for any number of reasons, including a lack of positive belief for this claim.

In his book *Primary Philosophy* (1966), Michael Scriven argues that the theist and the atheist don't share the burden of proof in arguments for the existence of God equally. Interestingly, Scriven does not say that the atheist needs to prove the nonexistence of God in order to say that God does not exist. On the contrary, Scriven maintains that the believer must prove the existence of some god or other, and if he fails to do so, "there is no alternative to atheism."

Put another way, if you can show that a belief in God is unfounded given the evidence, that is enough to tip the scales toward atheism. Scriven makes use of several analogies to make his point. If someone maintains the Loch Ness Monster exists, his claims suffer from a lack of evidence. But since unknown species have been discovered before, one cannot say at the claim is false. In addition, the claim makes no reference to supernaturalism. So you take a skeptical attitude and suspend judgment.

But Scriven thinks the case is different when a claim is unsupported by empirical evidence *and* lacks general support. Such is the case with claims about supernatural entities unprecedented in our experience. Scriven uses the example of Santa Claus. Claiming that Santa exists is to make such a radical statement that "explicit disbelief" is the appropriate response, not mere suspension of judgment. That is, you are justified in saying that Santa Claus does not exist, even though no one has positively disproved his existence. After reaching a certain age, you see that there are no reasons to believe in the existence of this being. You don't take an agnostic attitude toward Santa; rather, you assert that it is foolish to believe in his existence or in the likelihood of his existence. Scriven applies the same reasoning to the existence of God.

Arguments for the Existence of God

Throughout the history of philosophy and theology, there have been various arguments for the existence of God. Philosophers and saints of the medieval period, 400–1400 c.e., were notable for producing arguments for God's existence.

ESSENTIAL

St. Aurelius Augustine espoused the dictum *Credo ut intellegium*—"I believe that I might understand." As a philosopher and a man of faith, Augustine had to pursue the truth and observe Christian wisdom. To Augustine's mind, faith was primary. Of Augustine's thoughts about the conflict between faith and reason, Aquinas wrote ". . . Whatever he found contrary to faith, he amended."

St. Augustine (354–430) offered one of the first arguments for the existence of God. In his book on the will, *De Liberio Arbitrio*, (The Freedom of the Will), Augustine spelled out the argument. It was manifest to Augustine that our minds are capable of knowing eternal truths. If you think of your mind as a container wherein various eternal and necessary truths are stored, these truths are like effects that require a cause. There must be a causal explanation for this, and Augustine's explanation is that God is the immutable and eternal ground of such truths. The "proof" of God's existence, then, is that the mind is able to think about eternal truths and there must be a cause for these thoughts.

Of course, this "proof" of God's existence reveals Augustine's Platonic heritage. For Plato had argued that if the mind apprehends eternal truths such as perfect justice, beauty, and equality, there must be a world of ideas—of "forms"—that causes the ideas of them.

St. Anselm of Canterbury (1033–1109)

St. Augustine was the first thinker in the Age of Belief (another name for the medieval period of philosophy) to propound an argument for the existence of God, but his argument would not enjoy the fame of St. Anselm's Ontological argument.

ESSENTIAL

Anselm was already a teacher of other monks, so his method in arguing was one of "faith seeking understanding." "I do not seek to understand in order that I may believe," he wrote, "but I believe in order that I may understand." He made it particularly clear that his enterprise of proving God's existence could not even begin unless he had already believed in God.

Anselm was an Italian, born in Aosta. After his mother's death, the young Anselm began traveling to avoid constant quarreling with his father. In 1059, he arrived at the Monastery of Bec in central Normandy. In 1093, he became Archbishop of Canterbury in succession to his former teacher, friend, and religious superior Lanfranc. He died serving that post in 1109.

Anselm thought that faith and reason could lead to the same conclusions. Indeed, he thought that natural theology—that is, basing conclusions about God's existence on logical arguments—could provide a rational version of what he already believed. He was also Augustinian in another way, saying he was not trying to discover the truth about God through reason alone, but wanted rather to employ reason in order to understand what he was already believing.

His argument is better known as the ontological argument. In the second chapter of his *Proslogion* he writes:

> . . . *For it is one thing for an object to be in the understanding, and another thing to understand that it exists. When a painter considers beforehand what he is going to paint, he has it in his understanding, but he does not suppose that what he has not yet painted already exists. But when he has painted it, he both has it in his understanding and understands that what he has now produced exists. Even the fool, then, must be convinced that a being than which none greater can be thought exists in his understanding, since when he hears this he understands it, and whatever is understood is in the understanding. But clearly that than which a greater cannot be thought cannot exist in the understanding alone. For if it is actually in the understanding alone, it can be thought of as existing also in reality, and this is greater. Therefore, if that than which a greater cannot be thought exists in the understanding alone, this same thing than which a greater cannot be thought is that than which a greater can be thought. But obviously this is impossible. Without doubt, therefore, there exists, both in the understanding and in reality, something that which a greater cannot be thought.*

St. Anselm employed a conceptual or *a priori* argument. The proof of Anselm's argument does not depend upon sense experience or any other kind of experience, but can be known independently of experiences or *a priori*. In fact, when Anselm defined God as "a being than which none greater can be thought," he thought that the existence of God followed from that concept alone.

Like Plato, Anselm is a rationalist; ideas of perfect things have existence. In this case, a single premise about God's nature functions like the given in a geometric proof, from which God's nature can be deduced. Once the idea of God is in my understanding (just as the idea of the painting is in the painter's mind before he paints it), it must follow that it also exists in "reality."

David Hume: Matters of Fact and Relations of Ideas

Every bit as spirited as the arguments employed to argue for the existence of God were those counterarguments employed by various philosophers against his existence. Typically, philosophers arguing against the traditional arguments for God's existence have pointed out logical flaws in the style of arguments used. Perhaps no philosopher did this with greater persistence than David Hume.

David Hume (1711–1776) was a Scottish philosopher noted for his empiricism and skepticism. According to Hume, all knowledge begins with your experiences and your experiences begin with various "sense impressions" you have of the world around you. Given such a starting point, it is hard to see how you might derive a proof of God's existence. And Hume, a noted agnostic, says exactly this.

Hume allowed that there were just two kinds of reliable human reasoning. He divides all knowledge into "matters of fact" and "relations of ideas." This has been called Hume's Fork. According to Hume, if some object of reason is neither a matter of fact nor a relation of ideas, it cannot count as knowledge at all. In the *Treatise on Human Nature,* he attempts to show that:

All the objects of human reason or enquiry may naturally be divided into two kinds, to wit, Relations of Ideas and Matters of Fact. Of the first kind are the sciences of Geometry, Algebra, and Arithmetic; and in short, every affirmation which is either intuitively or demonstratively certain . . . . Propositions of this kind are discoverable by the mere operation of thought, without dependence on what is anywhere existent in the universe.

Matters of Fact, which are the second object of human reason, are not ascertained in the same manner; nor is our evidence of their truth, however great, of a like nature with the foregoing. The contrary of every mater of fact is still possible; because it can never imply a contradiction . . . . That the sun will not rise tomorrow is no less intelligible a proposition and implies no more contradiction that the affirmation that it will rise.

You are never sure of matters of fact. To follow Hume's example, you can have impressions of the sun rising on seven consecutive days. Further investigation will tell you that it has always risen, since the earth has rotated around it for billions of years. So you may think you are entitled to say, "I know for certain that the sun will rise tomorrow," but you cannot know this. All that you know—and all that anyone knows—is that it has always risen; you cannot know that it will continue to rise. You only have sense impressions to this point in time, not beyond this point.

As Hume proclaims, "The contrary of every mater of fact is still possible; because it can never imply a contradiction." It is unlikely that the sun will not rise tomorrow, but its not rising is still a possibility. As opposed to relations of ideas, which are known *a priori*, you know matters of fact *a posteriori* or after experience.

Now if, as Hume contends, the only objects of human knowledge are matters of fact and relations of ideas, then many "spiritual" entities thought to be real will have been lopped off by Hume's logical scalpel. If you have no impression of metaphysical entities like gods, souls, selves, ghosts, angels, substances, and other nonperceptible entities, these things are not objects of knowledge.

Hume's View of the Arguments

As a consequence of his division of all knowledge into matters of fact and relations of ideas, Hume is a noted skeptic of God's existence. Hume was inclined to deny the traditional arguments philosophers used to demonstrate the existence of God.

Consider St. Thomas Aquinas's "5th Way" or design argument. St. Thomas Aquinas (1225–1274) argues for God's existence in the following way:

The fifth way is taken from the governance of the world. We see that things that lack knowledge, such as natural bodies, act for an end and this is evident from their acting always, or nearly always, in the same way, to obtain the best result. Hence, it is plain that they achieve their end not fortuitously, but designedly. Now whatever lacks knowledge cannot move towards an end, unless it is directed by some being endowed with knowledge and intelligence; as the arrow is directed by the archer. Therefore, some intelligence being exists by whom all natural things are directed to their end, and this being we call God.

Aquinas's design argument—or one of its many variants in the history of philosophy—may be the most popular one among believers, but Hume thinks the argument breaks down. For one, the inference from an orderly universe to a maker of the universe "is uncertain, because the subject lies entirely beyond the reach of human experience." The whole argument from design rests upon the proposition "that the cause or causes of order in the universe probably bear some remote analogy to human intelligence." But how can we assign a cause to the universe when we have never experienced the cause? The existence of the universe is surely an empirical fact, but we cannot infer from it the existence of God, since we have sense impressions of neither God nor of the alleged act of creation.

FACT

Hume's early essay *Of Superstition and Bondage* forms much secular thinking about the history of religion. At the time, philosophers had to be circumspect in their critiques of religion. In fact, less than fifteen years before Hume was born, eighteen-year-old college student Thomas Aikenhead was put on trial for saying openly that he thought that Christianity was nonsense. He was later convicted and hanged for blasphemy.

In sum, such metaphysical substances don't exist on either prong of Hume's fork. At the end of the *Enquiry Concerning Human Understanding*, Hume writes:

If we take in our hand any volume of divinity or school metaphysics, for instance, let us ask, Does it contain any abstract reasoning concerning quantity or number? No. Does it contain any experimental reasoning concerning matter of fact and existence? No. Commit it then to the flames: for it can contain nothing but sophistry and illusion.

As logically and fervently as Hume argues, he cannot be considered an atheist, for atheists say without hesitation that there is no God. Hume has not asserted the nonexistence of God; rather, Hume is an agnostic and so argues that we cannot know of the existence or nonexistence of God since we have no impression of him.

Hume's empiricism strikes down arguments for the existence of God, just as the empiricism of Aquinas supported such arguments. A different consideration for the existence of God—and one that has troubled believers and nonbelievers alike for centuries—is the problem of evil.

The Problem of Evil

The problem of evil is an intractable and pesky philosophical problem for any believer in theism. The problem of evil is posed as a dilemma that is the consequence of a definition of God and a set of facts about the world. The definition of God according to the theist is a being all-good (omnibenevolent), all-powerful (omnipotent), and all knowing (omniscient). Some thinkers add the characteristic of omnipresence, but this attribute is irrelevant to the attempted solution of the problem.

ESSENTIAL

The British philosopher John Stuart Mill (1806–1873) thought God's alleged goodness and omnipotence could not be reconciled with evil in the world. In *Three Essays on Religion,* he wrote, "Not even on the most distorted and contracted theory of good which ever was framed by religious or philosophical fanaticism, can the government of Nature be made to resemble the work of a being at once good and omnipotent."

Following the theist's set of the attributes that belong to God, there is a statement of facts about the world. There are evils in the world that can be better understood divided into two categories. First, the physical world is riddled with calamities. There are earthquakes, mudslides, tidal waves, hurricanes, and other events that lay waste to human and animal habitats. In addition, disease and pestilence are maladies affecting man and nature that must be placed in the physical category.

In addition to these physical maladies, there are "willed evils," i.e., those evils that result from man's free will. These include warfare, murder, treachery, libel, and a collection of other events, actions, and intentions that come not from a breakdown in the workings of nature, but of man's incomprehensible cruelty and general ill-will toward his fellow man.

St. Augustine on Evil

Augustine may be the first philosopher to frame the problem of evil and address it in a formal way. He uses the Platonic division of a sensible realm and a realm of ideas to provide the metaphysical underpinnings for his answer to that problem.

When he was a young man, Augustine's Christian ideas seemed inadequate to him. He was flummoxed by the ever-present problem of moral evil. The Christians said that God is the creator of all things and that God is good. How, then, is it possible for evil to arise out of a world that a perfectly good God had created? Because the young Augustine could not find an answer to this question, he turned away from Christianity.

Breaking it down further, if God is all-knowing, he knows how to stop evil. If he is all-powerful, he can stop evil. Finally, if he's all good, he cares to stop evil. Why then is there evil in the world? In his response to this ponderous problem, Augustine revealed his Platonic influence.

QUOTE

St. Augustine (354–430) thought that human beings were morally responsible for those evils resulting from the misuse of their own wills. In *The Enchiridion on Faith, Hope, and Love,* he wrote ". . . The turning of the will from God is without doubt a sin, we cannot say, can we, that God is the cause of sin?" Augustine's defense of God allowing man free will has been called "the free will defense" of human sin.

On the subject of willed evils, Augustine argued that God does not cause such evils; moral evils can be traced to the absence of goodness. It results from something gone wrong with the will, perhaps a temptation to act on a desire or to do what you know to be wrong. As disease is the absence of health in the body, sin is the absence of health in the will.

There are two parts to Augustine's doctrine on the will. One part is that the universe itself is the result of God's free and sovereign will in making it. With respect to humanity, everything is to be explained on the basis of the will. Augustine was unlike the Greeks in thinking that will and not the faculty of reason is primary. The intellect follows the will, not the other way around. But what determines the will to act as it does? Augustine, a libertarian on the matter, contended that nothing determined the will; the will is completely free. He argued that if one stone is pulled out from under another, the one on top drops to the earth. The stone of course has no will and succumbs to gravity. But people are not stones and their spirits are not forced in one direction or another.

Augustine thought that natural evils—including disasters such as hurricanes and tornadoes and the like that can raze villages and end people's lives—did not result from God's agency either. To explain how natural evils occurred, Augustine returned to Plato's thinking. In this world of changes—what Plato called a world of "becoming"—change gives rise to natural processes. Matter is evil and is subject to change and these changes give rise to famines, diseases, plagues, and so on, which in turn give rise to human suffering. From Plotinus, Augustine acquired the idea that evil is not a positive reality but a privation—that is, the absence of good. The world is imperfect, but this does not reflect on God by implying that He is imperfect or responsible for the imperfections of the world.

CHAPTER 20

Mysticism

The word "mysticism" eludes definition. The word is a Greek derivative, denoting the practices of those who have been "initiated into the mysteries." But the difficulty of a definition is born of the contentions of mystics that their experiences are ineffable, or unable to be captured in language. It is not unusual for such experiences to contain contemplative visions, voices, and ecstatic states of consciousness. Mysticism could be defined as the pursuit of a transcendent, unitive experience with some absolute reality. Each faith has had its mystics who have sought a different kind of knowledge of a supreme being.

Characteristics of Mysticism

Some philosophers flesh out the concept of mysticism by pointing to the characteristics of the experience itself. Those who, like William James, have had a mystical experiences report it as:

- **Transcendent:** If an experience is transcendent, it lacks a discernible geography. Put another way, you don't know where the experience occurs; it lacks space/time coordinates. It thus makes little sense to say "The experience occurred in her mind," or "The experience occurred in a reality beyond the soul." The experience is thus unlike seeing the stop sign on the corner of Main Street, but it may not be inappropriate to claim that the mystical experience is like your reflection on the piece of music you heard yesterday.

- **Ineffable:** Mystics such as St. John of the Cross and St. Teresa of Avila hasten to point out that since the experience is not rationally decipherable, it cannot be captured verbally in a manner that other experiences are. Naturally, this ineffability raises difficult epistemological questions that will be gone over in the chapter on alleged "proofs" of God's existence. These problems of knowing include, but are not limited to, assessing what the experience means, both for the experiencer and the non-experiencer, and what it proves about the reality content of the experience.

- **Noetic:** The mystical experience purports to convey some illumination about the meanings of your life or about reality itself. "Noetic" also implies that some truth has been realized. What does the experience mean measured against the rest of your life? What kind of reality exists beyond the confines of your everyday experience?

- **Ecstatic:** Mystics point out that the experiences are ecstatic, since they fill the soul with bliss or peace. Accounts of mystical experiences include the claim that the experiences of everyday life seem trivial by comparison with this spiritual ecstasy. "Everything else seem as straw," wrote St. Thomas Aquinas after his vision of God.

- **Unitive:** The experiences are claimed to break down ordinary experiences with their walls between subject and object. In ordinary perception it is tempting to view reality in two parts: subject and world. But the religious experience breaks down this duality in favor of an experience that unites the perceiver with God or some other object of perception.

Varieties of Mystical Experiences

In theistic traditions, mysticism is often described as a "unitive" experience of love and communion with God. In non-theistic traditions, such as Buddhism, it is an intuitive or contemplative approach to understanding some ultimate reality and thereby having a renewed understanding of what is really real. In either case, it is understood as an experience beyond ordinary experience and reason. This does not necessarily mean, however, that the experience is antagonistic to logic or reason.

Mystics in the Roman Catholic tradition claim that the soul undergoes a purification (often called the purgative way), which leads to a feeling of illumination and greater love of God (the illuminative way). After a time, the soul may be said to enter into mystical union with God (the unitive way), which begins with consciousness that God is present to the soul. The soul progresses through a time of quiet and an ecstatic state to a final state of perfect union with God, which is sometimes referred to as a spiritual marriage.

ESSENTIAL

It is not unusual that late in the process there is an experience where the contemplative finds himself completely deserted by God and any hope, beyond the power even of prayer. In many ways this experience—called "the dark night of the soul"—is the antithesis of the joy found in mystical experiences.

Examples of such mystical experiences are plentiful throughout the world's religions. People who have had the experiences insist that they are not fully accessible by just reading about them. One can't intellectualize the experience, for the mystical experience is not just a state of knowing. Reading mystical literature—whether those detailing the vivid descriptions of Teresa of Avila or those of the Muslim Al-Ghazzali—is only an indirect approach to the experience. The direct approach must be one where the subject is unified with the object and transcends the subject-object divisions of everyday life.

Some maintain that mysticism is the heart of all religion and even a key to the unity of all religions. As such, religions prescribe techniques of contemplation and meditation.

Actual Experiences across Faiths

For the believer, the encounter with a transcendent, sacred reality is often proof positive of the reality described in the experience. Consider the description of such an experience by the American philosopher William James (1842–1910), writing in his *Varieties of Religious Experience*.

All at once I experienced a feeling of being raised above myself, I felt the presence of God—I tell of the thing just as I was conscious of it—as if his goodness and his power were penetrating me altogether . . . I sat down on a stone, unable to stand any longer, and my eyes overflowed with tears. . . . Then, slowly, the ecstasy left my heart; that is, I felt that God had withdrawn the communion which he had granted, and I was able to walk on. . . . The impression had been so profound that in climbing slowly the slope I asked myself if it were possible that Moses on Sinai could have had a more intimate communication with God.

I think it will to add that in the ecstasy of mine God had neither form, nor color, nor odor, nor taste; moreover, that the feeling of his presence was accompanied with no determinate localization. . . . At bottom the expression most apt to render what I felt is this: God was present, though invisible; he fell under no one of my senses, yet my consciousness perceived him.

James regards arguments for and against the existence of god as inadequate compared to his mystical experience of the presence of god. No wonder, then, that he regards issues in philosophy such as the existence of god, of the soul, and immortality as very much "open" questions—questions that haven't been settled by science—where one can hold a position without fear of ridicule.

St. Teresa of Avila (1515–1582)

A nun of the Carmelite Order, Teresa became disillusioned with the laxity of the order and tried to reform it by founding a convent in Avila, Spain, and by involving it in a more disciplined life of prayer. She was influenced by St. John of the Cross, and authored several books on

Christian spirituality. One was entitled *The Interior Castle*. The castle she referred to was not a material structure but an interior one: the soul. This soul has many wonderful rooms, she explains, alluding to John 14:2. The number of rooms is seven, since in the biblical tradition seven is the perfect number. The ultimate goal is to occupy the central room and experience "spiritual marriage" with the divine reality. In the poetic language of St. Teresa, this occurs "in the interior, in some place very deep within." This place is the soul.

Teresa wrote movingly not only the indescribable mystical union with God, but she also stressed the continual struggle of attaining heightened levels of spiritual existence. In *The Way of Perfection* she instructed nuns and offered a memorable account of how difficult the spiritual journey is:

Do not be frightened, daughters, by the many things you need to consider in order to begin this divine journey which is the royal road to heaven. A great treasure is gained by traveling this road; no wonder we have to pay what seems to us a high price. The time will come when you will understand how trifling everything is next to so precious a reward.

Now returning to those who want to journey on this road and continue until they reach the end, which is to drink from this water of life, I say that how they are to begin is very important—in fact, all-important. They must have a very great and very resolute determination to persevere until reaching the end, come what may, whatever work is involved, whatever criticism arises, whether they die or arrive on the road, or even if they don't have courage for the trials that are met, of if the whole world collapses.

If the *Way of Perfection* explains the preparatory work for the unitive experience with God, her book the *Interior Castle* reveals vividly the experience itself. A poem in this section is entitled "Occasions When God Suspends the Soul in Rapture, Ecstasy, or Trance."

In her poem, St. Teresa captures several characteristics of the mystical experience. She writes of the ecstasy and rapture, which, however brief, occur when "God takes the soul entirely to Himself." She also claims that the experience is all-embracing for the soul and the soul "seems incapable of grasping anything that does not awaken the will to love."

The unity of the soul with God is "not something the soul can speak of afterward." The unity occurs between the soul and God.

Teresa was canonized by the church, and proclaimed a "Doctor of the Church" by Pope Paul VI in 1970. She is recalled today as a great Catholic mystic.

Mysticism in Islam

In his autobiography, the Muslim philosopher Al-Ghazzali (1058–1101) talks about the experiences the Sufis, who are Muslim mystics. He writes:

The Science of the Sufis aims at detaching the heart from all that is not God, and at giving to it the sole occupation the meditation of the divine being. Theory being more easy for me than practice, I read until I understood all that could be learned by study and hearsay. Then I recognized what pertains most exclusively to their method is just what no study can grasp, but only transport, ecstasy and the transformation of the soul.

Then Al-Ghazzali compares reading of mystical experiences and having one, to knowing about health and being healthy. The point is that being healthy far exceeds the importance of merely knowing about health, as being "in" the mystical experience makes knowing about it pale by comparison. He continues,

How great, for example, is the difference between knowing the definitions of health, of satiety, with their causes and conditions, and being really healthy or filled. How different to know in what drunkenness consists—as being a state occasioned by a vapor that rises from the stomach—and being drunk effectively. Without doubt, the drunken man knows neither the definition of drunkenness nor what makes it interesting for science. Being drunk, he knows nothing; whilst the physician, although not drunk, knows well in what drunkenness consists, and what are its predisposing conditions. Similarly, there is a difference between knowing the nature of abstinence, and being abstinent of having one's soul detached from the world. Thus I had learned what words could teach of Sufism, but what was left could be learned neither by study nor through the ears, but solely by giving one's self up to ecstasy and leading a pious life.

At this point Al-Ghazzali reflects on what has kept him from experiencing the mysteries of the Sufis. He didn't have control of his passions, which kept him from having a unitive experience with God.

Reflecting on my own situation, I found myself tied down by a multitude of bonds—temptations on every side. Considering my teaching, I found it was impure before God. I saw myself struggling with all my might to achieve glory and to spread my name.

What follows this personal revelation is an account of his attempt to break away from his life in Baghdad, at the end of which he fell ill with a paralysis of the tongue.

Then, feeling my own weakness, and having entirely given up my own will, I repaired to God like a man in distress who has no more resources. He answered, as he answers the wretch who invokes him. My heart no longer felt any difficulty in renouncing glory, wealth, and my children. So I quitted Baghdad, and reserving from my fortune only what was indispensable for my subsistence, I distributed the rest. I went to Syria, where I remained about two years, with no other occupation than living in retreat and solitude, conquering my desires, combating my passions, training myself to purify my soul, to make my character perfect, to prepare my heart for meditating on God—all according to the methods of the Sufis, as I had read of them.

Yogic Mystical Experience

The word "Yoga" means in English to "yoke," denoting a union between the soul and the divine. Its primary meaning is probably "work" in the sense of spiritual practice. In Sanskrit it means "ascetic discipline," a discipline aimed at liberation (from the cycle of rebirth and suffering), enlightenment, or an ecstatic transcendence of the world.

The Yoga-sutra was a "how-to" book on yoga practice. The true person or self that you encounter in meditation is entirely aloof from the world, not tied up with our bodily, emotional and mental selves. In this sense, the Yogi hankers for transcendence, which is accomplished by breath control and an utterly focused meditation by which one achieves a kind of mental silence, or as in the *Yoga Sutra* (The foundational text of Yoga), a "cessation of the fluctuations of mind and awareness."

Here are some of the passages from the *Yoga Sutra*:

1.1 Now instruction in yoga.

1.2 Yoga is cessation of the fluctuations of mind and awareness.

1.3 Then the seer (the conscious being) rests in the true self.

1.4 At other times, he identifies with the fluctuations.

1.5 The fluctuations are of five types, and are either detrimental or non-detrimental:

These five are:

1.6 (a) veridical awareness, (b) its opposite (illusion), (c) thought and imagination, (d) sleep, and (e) memory . . . .

1.12 The cessation of the fluctuations is accomplished through practice and disinterestedness.

1.13 Practice is effort to hold fast the cessation.

1.14 Practice is firmly grounded only through proper effort uninterrupted and stretching over a long time.

1.15 Disinterestedness is the intention to control on the part of someone who has no desire either for worldly or revealed objects . . . .

1.33 Calming illumination of the mind if furthered through friendship, compassion, happiness, and indifference to objects whether pleasant or painful, virtuous or full of vice.

1.34 Or, this can be brought about by controlled exhalation and retention of the breath.

1.35 Or, this (calming illumination) is brought about by particular activity centered on an object and arresting mentality.

1.36 Or, it is brought about by activity that is free from sorrow and humiliation.

These methods of self-control and hyper-concentration are necessary and are used to attain the larger ethical and spiritual goals of Yoga:

2.27 For a yogin, sevenfold wisdom and insight (prajna) arise as the highest foundation.

2.28 By practice of the "limbs of yoga," impartiality is attenuated. Awareness is illuminated up to discriminative discernment.

2.29 (Ethical) restraints, constraints, asanas, [yogic postures, stretching exercises] breath control, withdrawal of the senses, and concentration, "meditation," and mystic trances are the eight "limbs of yoga."

2.30 Of these the restraints are noninjury (ahimsa), truthfulness, refraining from stealing, celibacy, and lack of avarice.

The ultimate goal of fierce concentration and meditation is *samadhi,* the final state of union with the divine and liberation from the cycle of life and death; it is a state that cannot be adequately described within the constraints of human language.

Buddhist Meditation

Buddhists have their own version of a transcendent experience, which is achieved by meditation or zazen. Buddhists acknowledge that meditation is incredibly difficult, requiring feats of concentration that many people are not used to or unwilling to cultivate.

Samadhi is not dissimilar from the quest for nirvana in *Buddhism*. The prerequisites for *nirvana* can be expressed as three principles: abstention from harmful actions (*shila*, "moral conduct), a disciplined mind (*samadhi*, "mental concentration") and a proper understanding of the self and the world (*prajna*, "wisdom"). In Buddhism these principles are connected to the law of karma, or moral retribution, that impacts the process of death and rebirth. According to Buddhists, the incentive for abstaining from harmful actions is that such actions will lead to punishment in a future life and thereby make it difficult to escape the cycle of death and rebirth. The function of mental concentration is to remove desires and hatreds that lead to harmful actions. And "wisdom" results in an erroneous understanding of self that feeds the whole process of desire, hatred, and harmful action.

CHAPTER 21

Atheism and Agnosticism

Atheism is the philosophical view that there is no divine being or God. But the simple Greek word takes on many different meanings in the current debate. One such meaning is that the opposing sides assume that the existence of God implies the existence of divine providence and of divine intervention in the world. This chapter's discussion of atheism begins with a famed contemporary philosopher, Bertrand Russell.

Bertrand Russell

The importance of Bertrand Russell's (1872–1970) work on twentieth century philosophy can hardly be overestimated. Russell's most lasting contributions have been in mathematical logic and the philosophy of logic, but Russell was a polymath who not only grasped several fields of philosophy but the applications of them. His work ranged into the natural and social sciences, not to mention being a very public figure in debating political issues. He was a leading influence in the Campaign for Nuclear Disarmament and for numerous peace initiatives until his death in 1970.

Concerning arguments for the existence of God, Russell was a notable skeptic. He proclaimed there was no reason to believe in a deity, and in his book titled *Why I am Not a Christian* (1927), he expounded and criticized the arguments for God's existence. Before going into his counterarguments, it is important to see the way that Russell understood the relationship between philosophy and religion.

In his *History of Western Philosophy*, Russell stated:

Philosophy, as I shall understand the word, is something intermediate between theology and science. Like theology, it consists of speculations on matters as to which definite knowledge has, so far, been unascertainable; but like science, it appeals to human reason rather than to authority, whether that of tradition or that of revelation. All definite knowledge—so I should contend—belongs to science; dogma as to what surpasses definite knowledge belongs to theology.

Russell's views, propounded in his book *Why I am Not a Christian*, trace to this profound distinction between philosophy and theology. The book provoked a strong backlash among pious readers, intellectuals included. Appearing as it did at a time of religious revival, it was met with a hostile response. In fact, Russell's book inspired a counter book by H.G. Wood, a member of the Society of Friends and later a professor of Theology at the University of Birmingham. Wood's book *Why Bertrand Russell is Not a Christian, An Essay on Controversy* was published the following year by the London Christian Movement. Not to be outdone, Russell responded in a review entitled "Why Mr. Wood is Not a Freethinker."

Russell asserts that there are two different "items" essential to the belief system of anyone calling himself a Christian: a belief in God and a belief in immortality. Put in this way, the title *Why I Am Not a Christian* is misleading. His subsequent arguments against the existence of God apply not only to Christianity but to Hinduism, Judaism, Islam, and several other smaller religions which accept those same two beliefs.

FACT

A beginning to atheism can be located more than 2,300 years ago. In ancient Athens, the materialists Leucippus, Democritus, and Epicurus concluded that the world was composed of atoms in perpetual motion. In his work *De Rerum Natura* (On the Nature of Things), Lucretius (99–55 B.C.E.) revived the atomist theory during Roman times. Atomism was regarded as heretical during the Christian era and was persecuted.

Russell sets out to attack the first of those beliefs. He notes with curiosity that the Catholic Church has "laid it down as a dogma" that the existence of God can be proven by unaided reason, as well as being accepted by faith. Russell proceeds to take on several of these arguments.

The First-Cause Argument

St. Thomas Aquinas (1225–1274) made use of five "ways" for the existence of God. The second of these five ways—or arguments—was the "first cause" argument. Aquinas wrote: "The second way is from the nature of efficient cause. There is no case known (neither is it, indeed, possible) in which a thing is found to be the efficient cause of itself; for so it would be prior to itself, which is impossible." Imagine that you look outside your window and see a tree branch swaying. That branch is being moved by the wind. That wind has its causes, and so on. But as with motions, you cannot go on to infinity in a series of causes. If there is no first cause, then there will be no intermediate causes, like the wind and the swaying tree branches that result from it. "Therefore it is necessary to admit a first efficient cause, to which everyone gives the name of God," Aquinas concludes.

Russell followed the reasoning through, writing, "If everything must have a cause, then god must have a cause. If there can be anything without a cause, it may just as well be the world as god, so there cannot be any validity in that argument. It is exactly of the same nature as the Hindu's view, that the world rested upon an elephant and the elephant rested upon a tortoise; and when they said, `How about the tortoise?' the Hindu said, 'Suppose we change the subject.' The argument is really no better than that."

The Design and Natural Law Arguments

Next Russell takes on what he calls the "argument from design." This was Aquinas's fifth way. It is at once the most renowned of the five arguments and the one that the proverbial man in the street is most apt to embrace. It appeals to anyone who believes that the universe is too orderly and too good to have occurred without being designed by some supreme being. Design of the universe implies a designer.

The design argument has lost some steam since the nineteenth century, specifically since Darwin, who, says Russell, "understood much better why living creatures are adapted to their environment." It is not that the environment was made suitable for us; rather, it is the other way around. Creatures grew suitable to the environment and that is the basis of adaptation.

ESSENTIAL

Could it really be, Russell wonders, that if a being with omnipotence and omniscience were given a million years to perfect his design he could produce nothing better than the one we have? "Nothing better than the Ku Klux Klan or the Fascisti?" Russell persists. And still believers persist—in calling such a being supreme.

Even a casual acquaintance with the most basic laws of science shows that "human life and life in general on this planet will die out in due course: it is merely a flash in the pan." Life is but a momentary stage in the ultimate decay of the universe. What we now see in the moon, Russell maintains, is the sort of thing to which the earth is tending—something dead, cold, and lifeless.

Agnosticism

Agnosticism can be personal and confessional, as when a person shrugs his shoulders and says, "I have no firm belief about God." But this is unphilosophical, noncommittal agnosticism; it is the kind of agnosticism that makes no argument.

By contrast, philosophical agnosticism makes a stronger, more general claim. This claim is that no one ought to make a positive belief for or against the divine existence. This stronger claim invites a counterargument, whereas the first personal revelation does not.

Scientist W.K. Clifford made a strong case for agnosticism. Clifford's assertion, made vivid in his pungent essay "The Ethics of Belief" (1877), claims that, "The existence of a belief not founded on fair enquiry unfits a man for the performance of his necessary duty." Later he puts the matter more strongly: "It is always wrong for anyone to believe anything upon insufficient evidence. Stated without the negations, agents have a duty to examine all beliefs and strive to accept only true ones."

But is the unjustified belief excused if it provides some comfort to the believer? Not according to Clifford. "Belief is desecrated when given to unproved or unquestioned statements," Clifford asserts. He goes on to claim that we have a universal duty of "questioning all that we believe." Clifford illustrates his meaning with the story of a ship owner who sends his well-worn ship out to sea.

Though he knows the ship could benefit from an inspection, he stifles all doubts and suspicions about the vessel's seaworthiness. He achieves a kind of blissful self-deception about the ship. The ship sinks in mid-ocean, the owner "got his insurance money" and "told no tales," for he had "acquired a sincere and comfortable conviction that his vessel was thoroughly safe and seaworthy." To what degree does the owner's untested belief make him morally culpable? His greed spurred him to circumvent the duty to raise questions. He thereby worked himself into a credulous state of mind that was morally reprehensible.

In no uncertain terms, Clifford maintains that the owner was "verily guilty of the death of those men." It is not just the consequences of lost lives that make his belief immoral, it is that the belief was ill-gotten, "because he had no right to believe on such evidence as was before him." For it is clear that, "He had acquired his belief not by honestly earning it in patient investigation, but by stifling his doubts." And if by chance the ship had reached port safely? This changes nothing: the owner's unearned optimism was still reprehensible.

The New Atheism: Antitheism

Scientific reasoning is offering up new challenges to religion in the present century. Religious views of the world have been challenged strongly since Darwin's publication of *The Origin of Species* in 1859. Now scientific problems like global warming and regimes that mix politics with religion have led many to doubt the global utility of religion. Some of the newer publications are not atheistic but antitheist, since they argue against the view of the Judeo-Christian-Islamic tradition that proclaims that God not only exists, but is a loving God who intervenes in human history by answering prayers and performing miracles.

It is a time of religious ferment in the United States. This may be true of any time period, but it seems especially true now. The battle over whether to teach Charles Darwin's theory of evolution in the schools or whether to teach creationism—now called "Intelligent Design"—continues, even though that battle was fought in Dayton, Tennessee, in "The Scopes Monkey Trial" some eighty years ago. The Ten Commandments have often been removed from public places by court order.

Richard Dawkins and *The God Delusion*

Richard Dawkins is one of the preeminent scientists in the world. An Oxford professor and paleontologist by training, Dawkins is, because of a series of vigorously argued books and numerous speaking appearances, a famous public figure. But his atheism owes not just to his hard scientific evidence; Dawkins believes that religious belief is fundamentally irrational and has ravaged mankind from the Crusades to September 11. Religion continues to lead to war, bigotry, sexism, and child abuse.

Dawkins's books and lectures have drawn letters from people reminding him of the less extreme forms of religion, such as the views expressed in the writings of Paul Tillich and Diedrich Bonhoeffer. But he claims that the decent, understated sort of religion is "numerically negligible." What predominates instead are the likes of Pat Robertson, Jerry Fallwell, Ted Haggart, Osama bin Laden, and Ayatollah Khomeini.

It isn't just fundamentalists and fanatics who rule the roost, either. There are nonviolent but fundamentalist Christians who are so passionately opposed to evolution and any science that threatens their world view that their minds cannot be changed. He quotes Kurt Wise: "If all the evidence in the world turns against creationism, I would be the first to admit it, but I would still be a creationist, since that is what the word of God indicates."

Dawkins provides his own version of the same words: "If all the evidence in the universe turns against creationism, I would be the first to admit it and I would immediately change my mind. As things stand, however, all available evidence—and there is a vast amount of it—favors evolution." He says both the fundamentalist and he have a passion, but his passion is based on evidence; their passion flies in the face of evidence and is truly fundamentalist. Want to contradict evolution, he asks rhetorically? He quotes a fellow scientist as saying, "Find me fossils of rabbits in the pre-Cambrian period."

One of the common ideas that Dawkins hears is that people need religion—humanity has a need for comfort. But he asks: Isn't there something childish about the notion that the universe owes us comfort? In fact, he quotes Isaac Asimov in saying that if we inspect every piece of pseudoscience—from astrology and tarot cards to contacting mediums and palmistry—you will find some kind of comfort, too. Asimov's remark about the infantilism of pseudoscience is just as applicable to religion. Inspect every bit of pseudoscience and you will find a security blanket—a thumb to suck on or a skirt to hold. Moreover, it is astonishing to find how many people fail to understand that X is comforting does not imply that X is true.

A related complaint to the notion about comfort is the idea that life must have a purpose. The human soul requires that X has a purpose, Dawkins's readers tell him. This provides consolation for the believer. But, "the consolation content of the belief does not raise its truth value," Dawkins observes. He adds that if the consolation that religion offers is founded on the neurologically highly implausible premise that we survive the death of our brains, do you really want to defend it? Due to the failure of many people's educations to provide palatable alternatives, nonbelief is not an option.

Dawkins's Treatment of St. Thomas Aquinas's Five "Proofs"

Without hesitating, Richard Dawkins claims that the five "proofs" asserted by St. Thomas Aquinas in the thirteenth century don't prove a thing. In fact, Dawkins attacks Aquinas's first three arguments—the Unmoved Mover, the Uncaused Cause, and the Cosmological Argument— in one fell swoop.

Aquinas's first argument, the Unmoved Mover, says that nothing moves without a prime mover. In Aquinas's mind, however, this leads to a chain of motions going back in time indefinitely and the only escape from the regress is God. In similar fashion, the Uncaused Cause argument says that nothing is caused by itself. Since every effect has a prior cause, this chain of causes will also go on indefinitely, unless God is invoked. Finally, his third argument—the Cosmological Argument—states there must have been a time when no physical things existed, but it is apparent just by looking around that physical things exist now. Therefore, a nonphysical entity must have brought them into existence, and this we call God.

FACT

An outspoken atheist, Dawkins is renowned for his contempt for religious extremism, from Islamist terrorism to Christian fundamentalism. Besides taking on extremists, he has also argued with liberal believers and religious scientists.

Dawkins's terse treatment of the argument says that each makes use of a regress and then brings God into the picture in order to terminate the regress. This move assumes without proof that God himself is immune to the regress. All of this is arbitrary, according to Dawkins. To conjure up a being and give it a name is one thing, but to go further and give that being the qualities normally attributed to God—such as omnipotence, omniscience, goodness, creativity of design, listener to prayers, miracle performer, and listener to innermost thoughts—is quite another matter.

Aquinas's fourth argument is an argument from gradation or degree. We notice in the world degrees of goodness or perfection, but these degrees can only be judged by comparison with a maximum. Since human beings can be good or bad or a mixture of both, the maximum of goodness does not reside with us. So the need for a maximum brings God into the picture, since He sets the standard for perfection. The problem with this argument, according to Dawkins, is that just positing a maximum of goodness doesn't bring existence to that maximum.

CHAPTER 22

Ecumenism

The ecumenical movement aims to promoting worldwide Christian unity. This is fitting, since the term "ecumenism" is derived from the Greek word *oikoumene*, which appears in the New Testament to mean the Roman Empire (e.g., Luke 2:1) or, simply, the entire world (e.g., Matthew 24:14). Gradually, the term meant something close to the entire church, as opposed to what is divisive, or to the whole faith of the church, as opposed to what is partial. The ecumenical movement aims to do good deeds, to lend aid to victims of war, poverty, oppression, and natural disasters.

What Is Ecumenism?

In the nonreligious vernacular, the word "ecumenical" means "general in extent or influence." It's rarely a good idea to be fetishistic over the etymology or even the present meaning of terms, but in this instance the definition lands right on the mark. In short, ecumenism is the antidote to what comes off as narrow, and even dogmatic, sectarianism.

As a priest in the Church of England and later the Archbishop of Canterbury, William Temple (1881–1944) proclaimed, "The ecumenical movement is the great new fact of our era." What was it that excited him so? The promise of the movement was that after centuries of separation and hostility, Christians had begun to capture "the simple biblical truth that the church of the people of God and the body of Christ must exemplify in the world how God gathers people together from the ends of the earth to live as a new humanity." Cooperation, not separation, was the operative concept.

These words were not idle; the ideal of unity bore fruit. In time, churches representing over 1.5 billion members are now engaged with one another in councils of churches, theological dialogues, various forms of collaborative missions, common prayers, and other expressions of ecumenical life.

Beginnings

Ecumenism has its roots in several religious groups that crossed denominational barriers in the mid-nineteenth century. These groups include the Evangelical Alliance, founded in England in 1846. The American branch of the same was formed by Phillip Schaff in 1867. Others that crossed denominational barriers were the Young Men's Christian Association (1844), the Young Women's Christian Association (1884), and the Christian Endeavor Society (1881). Composed of larger Protestant denominations, the Federal Council of the Churches of Christ was organized in 1908 and sought to represent Protestant opinions on religious and social matters. In addition, the movement known as Church Reunion in Great Britain and as Christian Union (1910) in the United States was attempting to achieve a creed behind which all Christians could unite.

Despite these historical precursors, the movement took flight with the 1910 World Missionary Conference in Edinburgh. That movement spawned four seminal ideas, establishing a set of interfaith priorities going forward. These ideas included:

- **Common Service:** The Life and Work Movement, whose inaugural movement occurred in Stockholm in 1925, led to interchurch aid for the victims of war, poverty, oppression, and natural disasters. In addition, the churches were called to oppose economic and social injustice, including racism and sexism.
- **Common Fellowship:** The first world conference for church unity was part of the Faith and Order movement. The conference was in Lausanne in 1927.
- **Common Witness:** Concerns over cooperative mission and evangelism were voiced in the International Missionary Council, first held in Jerusalem in 1928. Here the priority was interfaith relations, a priority still in the forefront today.
- **Common Renewal:** This final element shows that ecumenism is not some feel-good call for democratic tolerance or simple matters of interchurch cooperation. The stress is not merely on Christians getting along, but that churches be renewed and transformed to the point where they are open to the gifts of other religions.

FACT

Christian ecumenism cannot be confused with interfaith pluralism. Pluralism claims that faiths with mutually exclusive doctrines are equally valid. This view emphasizes the elements common to various religions. Ecumenism encourages dialogue between faiths but does not intend to reconcile their adherents into some religious unity. Rather, ecumenism seeks mutual respect across faiths, not to mention toleration for other views.

The World Council of Churches has met periodically since 1948. During that time, the Eastern Orthodox Church, Roman Catholics, and Pentecostalists made the council representative of various forms of Christianity. But the Council did not embrace Fundamentalism. Its embrace of liberation movements, including Liberation Theology, was not without controversy.

Ecumenism and the Second Vatican Council

A turning point in the Catholic Church—and thus a turning point for the ecumenical movement—was reached with the advent of Pope John XXIII (1881–1963). He was responsible for the seismic shift in the church by calling the Second Vatican Council (1962–1965), though he did not live to see its fruition. The upshot of the Council brought about a different approach to a twentieth-century world, part and parcel of which was a stronger emphasis on ecumenism.

QUOTE

According to *A Concise History of the Catholic Church*, "The Second Vatican Council (1962–65) urged Catholics to work and pray for greater unity among the churches. It especially recommended dialogue with other Christians as a way of achieving unity."

Before the Second Vatican Council, the Catholic Church was merely on the periphery of the ecumenical movement. But the Council contained a new vision of the church's role, which would now seek greater unity with all men. One result was a period of self-scrutiny in the church.

Opposition to Ecumenism

While the frequency of ecumenical dialogues has been awe inspiring, major divisions between Protestants, Catholics, and Orthodox continue. The issues of papal primacy, the Marian dialogues (relating to Mary's Immaculate Conception and Assumption), and apostolic succession remain as important doctrinal differences.

One group opposed to the ecumenical movement is the traditional Orthodox Church, which insists there is but one church and that church is orthodox. Leading the antiecumenical movement in the 1980s was the Orthodox Church in America (OCA). Christian ecumenism comprises the three largest divisions of Christianity: Roman Catholic, Eastern Orthodox, and Protestant. While the Roman Catholic Church has always desired full unity with estranged communities of fellow Christians, it also has rejected what it saw as a promiscuous and false union that would mean being unfaithful to or glossing over the teaching of Sacred Scripture and tradition. In 1964, Pope Paul VI stressed that unity cannot be bought at the expense of truth. That is, in matters of faith, "compromise is in contradiction with God who is Truth."

Some Eastern Orthodox churches commonly baptize converts from the Catholic Church, thereby refusing to recognize the previous baptism of the converts. By contrast, the Catholic Church has always accepted the validity of all the sacraments administered by the Eastern Orthodox and Oriental Orthodox Churches.

QUESTION

What is an ecumenical council?
It is a conference of bishops of the entire Christian Church who are brought together to discuss and resolve issues of church doctrine and practice. For many, the Second Vatican Council—the twenty-first such council—is the one that forever changed the Church's relation to the modern world.

Aside from differences in doctrine, another substantial obstacle to union is found in the differences between Protestant and Catholic churches over ethics. There are seemingly unconquerable differences between the churches over abortion, the death penalty and euthanasia, active homosexuality, premarital sex, women's rights, birth control and new reproductive technologies, and economic and peace issues.

North American Protestants regard pluralism, freedom for theological inquiry, and a regard for democratic decision making as important values. Rome, in the view of Protestants, has been authoritative and rigid and threatens to grind the ecumenical movement to a complete halt. James A. Nash, executive director of the Massachusetts Council of Churches, summed up how dim matters now stand: "In the absence of structural changes, what kind of unity, if any, is possible for relatively democratic and pluralistic church with a church that stresses hierarchy and homogeneity?"

Further Developments of Ecumenism: Liberation Theology

Liberation theology has been a significant addition to the landscape of the ecumenical movement. Who needs to be liberated? According to liberation theology, the answer is the poor.

In attending to the fortunes of the dispossessed, this movement has been called "a new way of doing theology." More than just "getting along," liberation theology seeks a kind of theological metamorphosis. It aims at transforming the fortunes of the poor. It echoes Karl Marx's famous dictum that the task of philosophy is not merely to understand the world but to change it.

Liberation theology contends that African Americans suffer from several forms of bondage: social, political, economic, and religious. According to liberation theology, the goals of Christian theology are and must be connected with liberation of oppressed classes of people.

Christ preached a message that favored the poor. Thus, "A rational study of the being of God in the world in light of the existential situation of an oppressed community, relating the forces of liberation to the essence of the gospel, which is Jesus Christ," James Hal Cone writes. Cone, a distinguished professor of Systematic Theology at the Union Theological Seminary in New York City, is grounded in systematic theology and holds no punches in explaining what the ideals of Christianity ought to be. In his book *A Black Theology of Liberation* he wrote,

FACT

Cone's views came to the forefront during the 2008 Presidential campaign, when Barack Obama's pastor, The Reverend Jeremiah Wright, claimed that he had been personally inspired by Cone's theology. Because Reverend Wright was being called a black separatist, Obama was branded with the same label. Wright claimed that his church, which didn't preach black superiority or black inferiority but did espouse self-determination, was singled out because of its presidential candidate association.

The black theologian must reject any conception of God which stifles black self-determination by picturing God as a God of all peoples. Either God is identified with the oppressed to the point that their experience becomes God's experience, or God is a God of racism . . . . Liberation is not an afterthought, but the very essence of divine activity.

Cone has persistently criticized the "white church" for ignoring or failing to address the problem of race. He has been publishing on the matter since 1969 and says, "Theologically, Malcolm X was not far wrong when he called the white man 'the devil.'"

Leonardo Boff and Liberation Versus Traditional Theology

In 1968, a meeting of Latin American bishops in Medellin was a crucial event for the liberation theology movement. At that meeting, documents were delivered under the title *Justice and Peace*. Injustices visited on the people of Latin America by neocolonialism and imperialism were discussed, not to mention the liberation from various forms of servitude and the kingdom of God in this world. Leonardo Boff was the leader representing Brazil.

Boff named five points distinguishing liberation theology from traditional theology:

1. The primacy of the anthropological element over the ecclesiological, since their focus is primarily on the person to be helped and humanized rather than on the church
2. The utopian perspective is placed over the factual—the future over the past, since they see the social process as permanently open to transformation—a possibility opened up by Jesus
3. The critical over the dogmatic, to counteract the tendency of institutions to fossilize
4. The social over the personal, in view of the increasing misery of the masses
5. Orthopraxis over orthodoxy—Christ didn't come to give us a set of intellectual concepts to master but a way of acting and living in the world

The Vatican issued its critique of liberation theology in April 1986 in a document entitled "Instruction of Christian Freedom and Liberation." The document warned against "collectivist solutions to poverty." It also took the stance that sin was individual, not social. The concept of sin refers primarily to the individual who is free to violate the moral law. Only in a secondary sense can it be applied to social structures in the sense of "social sin." It also reminded liberationists that poverty assumes many forms, and that the Church's love and compassion must extend toward all manner of poor—including the infant in danger of being aborted, the elderly, the abandoned, and the lonely. Finally, it made clear that the clergy must steer clear of direct involvement in the political process.

FACT

Boff did not see eye to eye with Joseph Cardinal Ratzinger (later Pope Benedict XVI), who singled out Boff for attempting to apply liberation theology to the Church itself. Boff, who was the cardinal's student, saw the solution to the ills of the church as a decentralized church, but Ratzinger thought the church needed to be more centralized. He once likened the church to a construction site where the blueprint had been lost and each worker was doing his own thing.

One More Ecumenical Perspective: Religious Inclusivism

Swami Vivekananda (1863–1902) was a follower of Sri Ramakrishna, the leading nineteenth-century Indian mystic and spiritual leader. In 1893, Vivekananda traveled to the United States to attend the Parliament of World Religions in Chicago, and then in England and Europe. He made quite an impression there, speaking with wit and great intelligence. Vivekananda espoused the virtues of Hinduism for being "inclusivist" and how it accepted "all religions as true" save for those that make exclusivist claims about other religions.

When he addressed the audience, he said:

Sisters and Brothers of America . . . I am proud to belong to a religion which has taught the world both tolerance and universal acceptance.

We believe not only in universal toleration, but we accept all religions as true. I am proud to belong to a nation that has sheltered the persecuted and the refugees of all religions and all nations of the earth. I am proud to tell you that we have gathered in our bosom the purest remnant of the Israelites, who came to Southern India and took refuge with us in the very year in which their holy temple was shattered to pieces by Roman tyranny. I am proud to belong to a religion which has sheltered and is still fostering the remnant of the grand Zoroastrian nation. I will quote to you, brethren, a few lines from a hymn which I remember to have repeated from my earliest boyhood, which is every day repeated by millions of human beings. "As the different streams having their sources in different places all mingle their water in the sea, so, O Lord, the different paths which men take through different tendencies, various though they appear, crooked or straight, all lead to Thee."

Sectarianism, bigotry, and its horrible descendant, fanaticism, have long possessed this beautiful earth. They have filled the earth with violence, drenched it often and often with human blood, destroyed civilizations and sent whole nations to despair. Had it not been for these horrible demons, human society would be far more advanced than it is now. But their time is come; and I fervently hope that the bell that tolled this morning in honour of this convention may be the death-knell of all fanaticism, of all persecution with the sword or with the pen, and of all uncharitable feelings between persons wending their way to the same goal.

Several days later Vivekananda spoke again:

Why we Disagree

I will tell you a little story. You have just heard the eloquent speaker who has just finished say, "Let us cease from abusing each other," and he was very sorry that there should be always so much variance.

But I think I should tell you a story which would illustrate the cause of this variance. A frog lived in a well. It had lived there for a long time. It was born there and brought up there, and yet was a little, small frog. Of course the evolutionists were not there then to tell us whether the frog lost its eyes or not, but, for our story's sake, we must take it for granted that it had its eyes, and that it every day cleansed the water of all the worms and bacilli that lived in it with an energy that would do credit to our modern bacteriologists. In this way it went on to become a little sleek and fat. Well, one day another frog that lived in the seas came and fell into the well.

"Where are you from?"

"I am from the sea."

"The sea! How big is that? Is it as big as my well?" and he took a leap from one side of the well to another.

"My friend," said the frog of the sea, "how do you compare the sea with your little well?"

Then the frog took another leap and asked, "Is your sea so big?'

"What nonsense you speak to compare the sea with your well!"

"Well, then," said the frog of the well, "nothing can be bigger than my well; there can be nothing bigger than this; this fellow is a liar, so turn him out."

That has been the difficulty all the while.

I am a Hindu. I am sitting on my own little well and thinking that the whole world is my little well. The Christian sits in his little well and thinks the whole world is his well. The Mohammedan sits in his little well and thinks that is the whole world. I have to thank you of America for the great attempt you are making to break down this little world of ours, and hope that, in the future, the Lord will help you to accomplish your purpose.

It cannot be denied that an invaluable achievement of Ecumenism has, at times, been the rapport, cooperation, collegiality, and philosophical and practical discussion that developed between the main Christian churches since the mid-twentieth century. Progress could be counted among the mergers of individual churches, such as the first union between Episcopal and Nonepiscopal churches. In 1960, a proposal was made to bring together the American Methodist, Episcopal, United Presbyterian, and United Church of Christ denominations.

It was Edmund Schlink, a leading German Lutheran theologian in the ecumenical movement, who offered a guiding principle by insisting that Christian ecumenists focus on Christ, not their separate church organizations. There are larger, overarching issues over which there should be no disagreement, despite the petty differences between denominations. "No one's spiritual myopia should come at the cost of the larger truths of the faith," Schlink said wisely. "The idea is to see the risen Christ at work in the lives of various Christians or in diverse churches."

Glossary

Agnosticism
The belief that we don't have knowledge of God and that it is impossible to prove that God exists or does not exist. Also used to refer to the suspension of judgment about some types of knowledge, such as the soul, immortality, heaven, hell, and extraterrestrial life.

Ahimsa (Sanskrit)
Noninjury

Allah
The Arabic word for God, used by Christian Arabs as well as Muslims.

Animism
The belief that all things are alive, for example the belief in the reality of the soul immanent in and pervading all things—including humans, animals, rocks, rivers, trees, the earth, the moon, the stars.

Atheism
The belief that gods do not or God does not exist. Also, the disbelief in any kind of supernatural existence that is supposed to affect the universe.

Atman (Sanskrit)
Self or soul; the Upanishadic term for an individual's true or most basic consciousness.

Avatara (Sanskrit)
God incarnate. According to Indian theism, God takes birth as a divine man or woman whenever world events demand, e.g., Krishna as portrayed in the Bhagavad-Gita.

Bhagavad-Gita
"Song of God," an important Hindu text

Bhakti (Sanskrit)
Love of God.

Bible
Scriptural revelation according to Christianity.

Brahman
The Absolute, the One, God in Hindu thought. Brahman, in distinction to the classical Westerner concept of God, is not thought to create *ex nihilo*, but to be the "ground" of all being.

Brahmanism
The most conservative strand of Hinduism, centering on rituals and liturgies performed by priests called Brahmins, who are the highest of four principal Hindu castes.

Buddha
The awakened; an epithet of Siddhartha Gautama, the founder of Buddhism, after his enlightenment.

Caliph

Successor to Muhammad's temporal, but not spiritual, authority over the Muslim community. The Caliphate no longer exists.

Ch'i (Chinese)

A vital force important in Taoist mysticism.

Classical theism

The mainstream theology of Judaism, Christianity, and Islam, articulated by Philo, Christian Church fathers, Avicenna, and others within western religious traditions.

Conceptual atheism

The view that God could not possibly exist because the concept of God is incoherent (like the concept of a round square).

Cosmological argument

An argument purporting to prove the existence of God from the premise that everything in the universe that exists is contingent (and the universe as a whole) and these contingencies, or the universe as a whole, can only be explained in reference to a necessary being, namely God.

Deism

The belief that God as the first cause created the universe and created the unchangeable laws by which the universe is governed. Also, God is in no way immanent in God's creation, but totally different from it, transcending it as a watchmaker transcends the watch he has made and set in motion.

Dharma

The key ethical concept in Hinduism (Sanskrit) "right practice."

Dualism

The belief that two gods exist, one a force for good, the other a force for evil, both vying for control of the universe.

Empiricism

A view that emphasizes experience and experimental method for all factual knowledge; the view that all knowledge begins in experience.

Existentialism

A philosophical stance stressing individual freedom and choice, the absurdity of the universe or its ultimate incomprehensibility in scientific terms, and each person's making religious or other meaningfulness for himself. Religious existentialists also stress the importance of blind faith.

Factual atheism

The view that God, though possibly existing, does not exist in fact.

First-cause argument

An argument claiming to prove the existence of God from the premises that every worldly existent is caused (or causality is universal) and that this fact can only be explained with reference to a first cause.

Free-will theodicy

The view that all evil in the world is the result of choices by free agents and that God in creating free agents does something good. Accordingly, god would not be responsible for evil.

Hadith

The sayings of the prophet, consulted as a source of doctrine on matters not made clear by the Koran.

Hajj

The pilgrimage to Mecca that all Muslims are obliged to make once in their lives, if they are able.

Imam

The leader of group prayer; in Shia Islam, the divinely inspired successor to the prophet or, in general, the spiritual leader of the community.

Indian theism

Also called Vedanta; Hindu and classical Indian views holding God as the divine reality, and usually purporting to be grounded in the teachings of the Bhagavad-Gita as well as various Upanishads.

Islam
"Surrender"; in Islam, surrender to God's will as revealed to Muhammad.

Jihad
Utmost effort or struggle, not necessarily physical, in support of Islam.

Kaaba
The most sacred shrine of Islam, believed to have been erected by the patriarch Abraham; stands in the courtyard of the Great Mosque at Mecca.

Karma (Sanskrit)
"Action"; psychological disposition to act in a certain manner acquired through previous actions; habit.

Koran (Qur'an)
The holy book of Islam; a transcript of God's word as revealed in Arabic to Muhammad. In Arabic, "recitation."

Mahabharata
Indian epic; a poem containing over 100,000 verses depicting a conflict over royal succession. The Bhagavad-Gita constitutes a small portion of this epic.

Mahayana
Northern Buddhism; the "Great Vehicle."

Mecca
City in Saudi Arabia; Muhammad's birthplace and site of the Kaaba.

Medina
The city where Muhammad and his followers migrated in 622 after the message of Islam was rejected by the people of Mecca.

Minaret
The tower of a mosque from which the call to prayer is issued five times daily.

Mishnah
In Judaism, the collection of traditional laws and precepts made by Judah the prince, forming the basis of the Talmud or authoritative source for Judaic tradition.

Monotheism
The belief that there is only one God or perfect being, usually considered to be the creator of the universe or its ground of being; entails the unity of God, that God is single.

Moral evil
Evil perpetrated freely by human beings out of their own choices.

Mosque
A building or enclosed courtyard where Muslims gather for prayer.

Muezzin
The person who calls the Muslim faithful to prayer.

Muhammad
The last prophet in a line that included Noah, Abraham, Moses, and Jesus.

Mystical experience
The enraptured and ineffable state of union with a higher reality such as the realm of perfect forms or with God.

Mysticism
The belief that the ultimate truth about reality can be obtained neither by ordinary experience nor by the intellect, but only by a mystical experience or nonrational mystical intuition.

Mysticism argument
An argument purporting to prove the existence of a spiritual reality, God, Brahman, "Emptiness" or

nirvana from the occurrence of special experiences said to be like sense experiences in revealing realities but unlike sense experiences in revealing something spiritual rather than physical things.

Natural evil
Evils, such as diseases, pain, death, that are part of the world order and not the result of actions freely undertaken.

Naturalism
The view that the physical universe is a closed system, with no supernatural entities or agencies operative in it.

Necessary truth
A proposition whose falsity cannot be imagined; one true in "all possible worlds."

Negative theology
The belief that nothing positive can be known about God; God is known only by such formulae as "God is not this" and "God is not that"; stresses the transcendence of God; God is thought "wholly other."

Nirvana (Sanskrit)
"Extinction" or "blowing out." In Buddhism, the experience thought to be the personal enlightenment; salvation.

Omnibenevolent
An attribute applied to God; pure moral being, capable only of love, mercy, compassion, and charity and incapable of willing evil.

Omnipotent
An attribute applied to God; all-powerful and/or of infinite power.

Omnipresent
An attribute applied to God; wholly present in all things at all times; there is nowhere God is not.

Omniscient
In attribute applied to God; all-knowing, infinite knowledge.

Ontological argument
It is an *a priori* argument purporting to prove the existence of God from the concept of God together with other premises.

Philosophy
The discipline concerned with claims about what is real (metaphysics), how we know (epistemology), and how we should live (ethics); also includes evaluative efforts concerning the most general of abstract concepts and claims of other disciplines including individual sciences and religious systems.

Problem of evil
The challenge to the existence of God that attempts to demonstrate that two kinds of evil, moral evil and natural evil, are inconsistent with the description of God as an omnipresent, ominbenevlolent, and omnipotent being.

Ramadan
The ninth month of the Islamic lunar calendar; month of fasting: no food or drink may be taken from first light to last light.

Religious experience
The view that there are states of mind in which one directly experiences a divine being.

Revelation
According to some theologies, the source of right belief about God or the supreme reality; commonly identified with scripture (Bible, Koran, Bhagavad-Gita).

Rig Veda
The oldest text in Sanskrit; a collection of poems and hymns to various Indo-European gods and goddesses.

Spiritism
The belief in the existence of spirits affecting the real world and/or humanity and that human beings can, by specific means such as propitiation, ritual, or initiations, come into contact with spirits.

Spiritual
Immaterial; incorporeal; consisting of spirit.

Spritualism
The belief that the underlying ultimate reality (or foundation of reality) is spirit or a world soul that is the universe or pervades the universe at all levels of activity.

Sunni
Majority Muslim group, comprising about 85 percent of all Muslims.

Talmud
The authoritative source for Judaic tradition; comprised of the Mishnah and Gemara. There are two Talmudim, one compiled in Babylon and one in Palestine.

Tao
The "supranational" way of both heaven and Earth, according to the ancient Chinese teaching of Lao Tzu.

Theism
The belief in divine things, gods, or a god. Opposite to atheism, this is usually the belief in one god (monotheism) transcending yet in some way immanent in the universe.

Theodicy
The branch of rational theology that says God exists as omnibenevolent ("all loving") despite the appearance of evil in the world.

Theravada
"The doctrine of the Buddhists elders" and early school of philosophic Buddhism, appearing in the Southern Canon.

Torah
In Hebrew, "law"; Judaic scripture. Sometimes said to refer only to the Pentateuch or first five books of Judaic scripture.

Trinitarianism
In Christianity, the doctrine that god, though one, is also three persons, namely, the Father, the Son or Christ, and the Holy Spirit.

Upanishads
Mystic and speculative treatises regarded as sacred by many Hindus; forming the source texts for the classical Indian philosophic schools of Vedanta.

Vedanta
Originally an epithet for the Upanishads; in the classical period, any of several schools defending Upanishadic views.

Yoga
Self-discipline, mystic discipline; a classical Indian school of philosophy holding that the individual conscious being is utterly distinct from nature and that through yogic practice a blissful and utter aloneness is realized.

Zakat
The alms tax, a mandatory donation to charity, one of the essential duties of all Muslims.

APPENDIX B

Additional Resources

Armstrong, Karen. *Buddha* (New York: Penguin, 2001).

Armstrong, Karen. *Holy War: The Crusades and Their Impact on Today's World* (New York: Anchor, 2008).

Ayer, Alfred Jules. *Language, Truth, and Logic* (New York: Dover Publications, Inc., 1946).

Bokenkotter, Thomas. *A Concise History of the Catholic Church* (United States: Doubleday, 2004).

Breuilly, Elizabeth. *Religions of the World* (New York: Facts on File, Inc., 1997).

Capitan, William H. *Philosophy of Religion: An Introduction* (Indianapolis: Pegasus, 1972).

Coogan, Michael D., general editor. *Eastern Religions* (New York: Oxford University Press, 2005).

Dawkins, Richard. *The God Delusion* (Boston: Houghton Mifflin, 2006).

Dennett, Daniel C. *Breaking the Spell: Religion as a Natural Phenomenon* (New York: Penguin, 2007).

Dougherty, Jude. *The Logic of Religion* (Washington, D.C.: The Catholic University of America Press, 2003).

Edwards, Paul, ed. *Immortality* (Amherst: Prometheus Books, 1997).

Farah, Caesar E. *Islam: Beliefs and Observances* Sixth Edition, (Hauppauge: Barron's, 2000).

Flew, Anthony. *There is a God: How the World's Most Notorious Atheist Changed His Mind* (New York: HarperCollins, 2007).

Gatje, Helmut. *The Quran and Its Exegesis* (Oxford: Oneworld, 2000).

Harris, Sam. *The End of Faith: Religion, Terror and the Future of Reason* (New York: W.W. Norton and Company, 2004).

Harris, Sam. *Letter to a Christian Nation* (New York: Vintage Books, 2006).

Hesse, Hermann. *Siddhartha* (New York: MJF Books, 1951).

Hitchens, Christopher. *God is Not Great: How Religion Poisons Everything* (New York: Twelve, 2007).

Hitchens, Christopher. *The Portable Atheist: Essential Arguments for the Nonbeliever* (Philadelphia: DaCapo Press, 2007).

Kaufmann, Walter. *Critique of Religion and Philosophy* (Garden City: Anchor Books, 1961).

Lippman, Thomas. *Understanding Islam* (New York: Plume, 2002).

Manji, Irshad. *The Trouble with Islam: A Muslim's Call for Reform in Her Faith* (New York: St. Martin's Press, 2003).

Maqsood, Ruqaiyyah Waris. *Teach Yourself: Islam* (Abingdon: Bookpoint Ltd., 2003).

Norwen, Henri J.M. *The Genesee Diary: Report from a Trappist Monastery* (Garden City: Doubleday, 1976).

Paulos, John Allen. *Irreligion: A Mathematician Explains Why the Arguments for God Just Don't Add Up* (New York: Hill and Wang, 2008).

Phillips, Stephen, H. *Philosophy of Religion: A Global Approach* (Fort Worth: Harcourt Brace, 2006).

Shouler, Kenneth A. and Susai Anthony. *The Everything® Hinduism Book* (Avon, MA: F+W Media, Inc., 2009).

Taliaferro, Charles. *Philosophy of Religion: A Beginner's Guide* (Oxford: Oneworld Publications, 2009).

Yogananda, Paramhansa. *Autobiography of a Yogi* (Los Angeles: Self-Realization Fellowship, 2005).

Yoshihito, Tagada. *Talking about Buddhism—Q & A* (Tokyo: Togansha International, Ltd., 1997).

Index

Find out Everything on Anything at **everything.com!**

The new **Everything.com** has answers to your questions on just about everything! Based on the bestselling Everything book series, the **Everything.com** community provides a unique connection between members and experts in a variety of fields. Since 1996, Everything experts have helped millions of readers learn something new in an easy-to-understand, accessible, and fun way. And now Everything advice and know-how is available online.

At **Everything.com** you can explore thousands of articles on hundreds of topics—from starting your own business and personal finance to health-care advice and help with parenting, cooking, learning a new language, and more. And you also can:

- **Share advice**
- **Rate articles**
- **Submit articles**
- **Sign up for our Everything.com newsletters to stay informed of the latest articles, areas of interest, exciting sweepstakes, and more!**

Visit **Everything.com** where you'll find the broadest range and most authoritative content available online!